Planning Development with Women
Making a World of Difference

Kate Young

MACMILLAN

First published 1993
Reprinted 1994

Published by THE MACMILLAN PRESS LTD
London and Basingstoke
Associated companies and representatives in Accra, Auckland, Delhi, Dublin, Gaborone, Hamburg, Harare, Hong Kong, Kuala Lumpur, Lagos, Manzini, Melbourne, Mexico City, Nairobi, New York, Singapore, Tokyo

ISBN 0–333–55928–2

Printed in Hong Kong

A catalogue record for this book is available from the British Library.

Cover photograph courtesy of Ernesto Jimenez

Contents

Introduction

This book is a rather idiosyncratic account of the appearance and growth of concern with women and development over the past three decades. Many of the chapters are based on materials that were prepared for use in the courses on gender and development I ran at the Institute for Development Studies, University of Sussex. As a personal account, certain things have been given emphasis which others working in the field may not feel are as important as other aspects. But this book is in no way intended as a definitive, 'correct' account. Over the next few years it is probable that a great many other books will be written which go over much the same ground but from a number of different perspectives.

The book is intended for use by students in any of the social sciences who are considering working in some aspect of development. It has been assumed that many readers will be students enrolled in universities in countries where libraries may have little of the development literature, either because of foreign exchange constraints or the difficulty of acquiring books and journals. I have therefore tried to refer only to standard texts, and not to refer to a vast number of them. However, I have referred to much of the literature on women and development. This may cause particular difficulties, given that librarians with a small budget may not give this literature priority. In an attempt to overcome the problems this may cause, two lists of books are given in the bibliography. One includes details of books and journals referred to in the text; the other gives details of alternative materials. In this way I hope that readers may get a chance to read some of the relevant literature, however haphazard their university library's collection may be.

The layout

Chapters 1, 2 and 3 give an overview of the terms and evolution of the main debates in development during the three UN Development Decades (1960–69, 1970–79, 1980–89). These were roughly from economic growth and modernisation of the 1950s and 1960s, through (re)distribution and basic needs, to the return to an emphasis on economic growth and the exaltation of the market mechanism of the 1980s. How women fit into these debates is outlined, as are shifts in the perception of the problematic of 'the woman question' and its solution.

In the First UN Development Decade women were viewed largely from the perspective of family welfare and were virtually invisible in development planning. In the Second Development Decade, the Women in Development (WID) movement expanded rapidly: women, not relations between women and men, were the main focus of analysis. The recognition of women's economic contribution, particularly in the poorest sectors of society, and their needs as economic actors came to the forefront in the basic needs approach. The accusation that women are invisible to development planners resulted in much activity designed to generate disaggregated statistical data. The 1980s saw the further consolidation of WID. Funding emphasis shifted from poverty and meeting basic needs to efficiency – to utilising women more effectively, by improving their productive capacity within the framework of the market system. The first three chapters lead to the conclusion that throughout the whole period, perceptions and solutions to the women in development question have, in the main, gone with the grain of mainstream development thinking.

Chapters 4, 5 and 6 look at specific sectors of the economy in which women are engaged: agriculture, industry and the informal sector. Chapter 4 draws on materials about Africa, both because of the preponderance of women farmers in agriculture and the wealth of literature available. In Chapter 5 industrial development is examined in the context of Asian development because of the heavy use of female labour in manufacturing for export. Chapter 6 covers the informal sector; Latin American case material is used because of the wealth of research carried out in the region on the informal sector and casualised labour, and because of the predominance of women in the sector throughout the region.

Two of these chapters review changes in development strategies over the last three development decades, touching on the impact of policies and strategies on women. All three make suggestions as to how development planning could be adapted to support and enhance women's participation and empowerment. The chapters establish the case for a close examination of social and economic relations between men and women.

Chapter 7 turns to the question of statistical data and discusses the problem of the conceptual schema which guide the collection of census data. Two aspects of this complex issue are examined: women's economic activity and the household as a unit of analysis. The need for statisticians, planners and economists to re-examine their theoretical frameworks is argued, and for basic concepts like productive and reproductive work to be re-evaluated.

Chapter 8 contrasts the two main perspectives – Women in Development and Gender and Development – and looks at their strengths and weaknesses from the policy and implementation point of view. Chapter 9 examines some of the issues involved in planning development with women and, as an outcome of this, raises the question of empowerment and political action. Its underlying argument is that sustainable change in women's material conditions will never come about without tackling the underlying structures which produce the imbalance between the genders. But these structures are also deeply embedded in the current models of development; conventional socialist and capitalist development models are productivist in bias and emphasise rapid economic growth rather than sustainable growth. For the latter, far greater attention needs to be paid to the conditions which will allow growth over generations. One condition is the dismantling of the pervasive structures of inequality between men and women. Another, and which follows from the first, is the questioning of the relationship between humanity and nature itself, and of the ability of the planet earth to sustain and maintain humankind as well as its other living beings.

'We do not own the earth, we hold it in guardianship for our children.'

Acknowledgements

This book is based on many of the materials used in the series of short study courses on Women, Men and Development at the Institute of Development Studies, University of Sussex. It also makes use of materials produced for the MA in Gender and Development and for the EEC/IDS 'Training for Trainers' project (published as *Gender and Third World Development*) – in particular the modules on agriculture, and on statistics, written by Ann Whitehead and Alison Evans respectively.

I am greatly endebted to Buzz Harrison, who worked extremely hard on the original manuscript, providing illustrations, tables and references, and improving chapters. Without her efforts the book would never have been finished. Thanks too to Helen Dalton from Kenya who tried hard to find some positive case materials, and to Nina Bowen from the United States, who tidied up the final manuscript.

The book also owes much to all those who collaborated on the Women, Men and Development study course and contributed to its success. For each study course an international team of people with different specialisms was put together. The members of the course team usually came to the Institute several weeks before the start of the course. We then worked through the course content, each person making suggestions as to how they could contribute to its improvement. Particular thanks are due to Pat Mohammed, the first co-director of the course. Her input into the original format was invaluable, and her Trinidadian warmness, humour and good counsel were key factors in its success, as was the hard work that Alison Evans put into the preparations for this and two further courses. Many warm thanks are due too to Shireen Huq (Bangladesh), Marge Hinawaeola (Papua New Guinea), Neera Desai (India), Agnes Morell (France), Faustina Ward Osborne (Guyana), Emelina Quintillan (Philippines), Helen Dalton (Kenya), Jean Stubbs (Cuba and UK), Theresa Kaijage (Tanzania), Jacinthe Kumarswamy (India), and Liliana Cetrangulo (Argentina). I am also endebted to colleagues, past and present at IDS for their support, in particular Gordon White, Christine White, Mick Moore, Mike Faber, Robin Murray, Emmanuel de Kadt, Manfred Bienefeld, Reg Green, and Robert Chambers. To Jill McCabe, Alison Tesfachew and Ann Watson warm thanks are also due.

The Ford Foundation provided the grant (No. 865–0319) which enabled me to take all too brief but much appreciated periods of time off from planning and running courses, and trying to keep up a research and conceptualising capacity, to write the book. Without the grant I would also not have been able to call upon the services of Buzz, Helen and Nina.

Thanks too to Adah for giving me a bolt hole for writing when I needed it, to Charlie for his loving support, and to Justin for urging me on when depression struck. I am equally grateful to Liz Paren whose patience has been almost inexhaustible.

My last great debt of gratitude is to those people around the world who were incredibly supportive of, and enthusiastic about the work we were doing at IDS, from the early days of the Subordination of Women Workshop, right through to the Short Courses and the first MA in Gender and Development in the UK. From them I learned a very great deal, both in terms of theory and practice, and of taking a principled stand on what can broadly be called feminist issues in very hostile environments.

This book is dedicated to them and to all those who are struggling for the creation of a more equitable and just future society in which men and women will be true partners and helpmeets, and in which the enormous disparities of wealth and power between the industrialised countries and those of the south will have disappeared, and in which all people can live lives unshadowed by want and deprivation.

London, June 1991

The present moment, then, is not a culmination but a point of choice. The purpose of analysis is to understand better the structure of the choice and the collective projects that are feasible responses to it.

R. W. Connell, *Gender and Power*

1 From growth to basic needs and back to growth

Between 1945 and 1965 over 50 countries in Africa, Asia and the Caribbean became independent nations. Many of them were deeply impoverished; their colonial inheritance left them with distorted or fragmented economies, poor or virtually non-existent systems of education, health, land and water management, communication and transport. Levels of literacy and education were low – in most parts of Africa and many Asian countries 80 per cent illiteracy was normal and 50 per cent primary school enrolment figures were considered an achievement. Provision of health care was lacking in all but the largest urban centres and even these services were often rudimentary. Many of these newly-independent ex-colonies also had very fragile political institutions and social integration was impeded by sharp ethnic and cultural divisions. Arbitrary or disputed boundaries imposed by the colonial powers were a source of potential and actual conflict.

Most of these new nations aimed to become economically as well as politically independent, yet the times were not particularly propitious. Tension between two opposed economic and political systems, capitalism and socialism, meant pressures to become aligned. Many nationalist leaders who had hopes of taking their countries along a 'third way' and to avoid being drawn into the hemispheric contest, found these hopes to be unfulfillable. The absence of alternative models to a market or a planned economy presented politicians and planners with serious difficulties.

Even those who were relatively convinced of the adequacy of the market economy had little actual experience of how to bring about economic growth, nor the social, political and other changes needed to ensure the majority of the population would benefit. William Rostow in 1960 brought together much of the thinking on how the ex-colonies were to 'modernise' in his *The Stages of Economic Growth* (Rostow, 1960). Today the approach seems rather naive. It assumes that all countries will go through a number of definable stages, similar to those already experienced by the 'advanced' countries, but each at their own pace. The various stages involve the move from traditional subsistence economy to the spread of money-based exchange, take off into market relations, the move into international trade and eventually the development of a mass consumption economy. The development of the market plays a key role in the process.[1] This economic stages theory mirrored a sociological theory of modernisation which posits that people would move from a traditional way of life based on ascribed positions and an acceptance of collective values, to a modern way of life based on positions gained by merit, and an open and questioning attitude with a more individualistic set of values. Modern education was to play a key role in the transition.

As economists, politicians and policymakers tried to tackle the problems of mass poverty of the ex-colonies and other developing countries, a specific brand of economic theory began to be developed. Informed by many of the ideas of the British economist, John Maynard Keynes, development economics largely held sway until the mid to late-1970s. Not all developing countries had the same problems – in fact they were very heterogeneous, nor of course did all development economists hold identical views, but most did focus on the structure of the economy, promoted macro-economic planning and a considerable degree of government intervention in the economy.

Going for growth

Initially common obstacles to rapid economic growth were identified, the most crucial of which were the lack of capital and/or means of capital formation (i.e. people with money to invest or enterprises which created profits which could be invested in expanded capacity); lack of skilled labour and management expertise; lack of infrastructure and technology; and lastly lack of foreign exchange. Given these constraints, the proposed solutions were: the stimulation of the rate of savings and investment (capital accumulation); the pulling of surplus labour away from the low return, low productivity 'traditional' rural sector into a new 'modern' urban, manufacturing sector (i.e. to pull labour from agriculture into industry and from unskilled manual work to skilled non-manual work); the hiring of non-national 'experts' until local ones could be trained; and the importation of modern technology (Roxborough, 1979; Colman and Nixson, 1986).

Manufacturing

Developing manufacturing capacity was given particular emphasis. The idea was that LDCs (Less Developed Countries) would first shift from producing agricultural and primary products for export to manufacturing mass consumer goods for the domestic market (and later the international market) using largely unskilled labour. With the knowledge acquired from this stage they would be able to move to production of more sophisticated intermediate

2

and luxury consumption goods, and then, in a third stage, to producing capital goods themselves. By this time new entrants to the labour force would be better educated and skilled. Planners worked with a very simplified two-sector model of the economy: a modern, industrial and urban sector pulling the economy into the twentieth century, and a traditional, agricultural sector providing the labour and the consumption needs of those in the modern sector.

One aim of developing industrial capacity was to enable developing countries to sell goods on the world market and thereby gain scarce foreign exchange. Ricardo's theory of comparative advantage was adduced to suggest that developing countries would benefit from specialising in the production of certain goods (including raw materials) for trade.[2]

Many development advisers believed that direct investment and bilateral and multilateral aid would both help a country to acquire needed capital goods and technology and to become rapidly integrated into the global economic system. Foreign companies were therefore encouraged to set up branches or new enterprises; large sums were borrowed from international or bilateral donors to create new enterprises and invest in crucial infrastructure (roads, railways, hospitals, schools, etc.).

Investment alone was not sufficient to facilitate, dynamise and direct the economy. Development economists therefore, following Keynes, argued for state intervention to create the conditions for economic take-off. The intervention would involve firstly, fiscal and monetary measures to encourage foreign investment – preferential tariffs, tax exemptions, repatriation of profits, etc.; secondly, measures to control labour militancy; and thirdly, playing the role of entrepreneur itself (managing enterprises such as mines, factories and trading/ marketing boards).

By the late-1960s in fact a number of countries had built up quite a large production capacity, but this was often achieved by allowing what became known as world market factories to be based in their countries. Free Trade Zones were set up where foreign manufacturers enjoyed special conditions (tax exemption, repatriation of profits, prohibition on labour militancy, etc.), and could produce goods for their home markets at much lower costs and higher profits. Typical world market factories produced clothing, pharmaceuticals, textiles and electrical and electronic goods.

Agriculture

At first, little thought was given to the need to modernise domestic agriculture (i.e. the production of food crops rather than cash crops) in developing countries but by the mid-1960s it had become clear that for many countries, particularly those in Asia, inability to produce sufficient food for the growing urban masses was a major constraint to the development process (Myrdal, 1968).

In many countries (for example in much of Latin America) land reform was an urgent need if land was to be more productively used. Land reform is, however, politically difficult to implement. As a result, the development of high yielding varieties (HYVs) of grains (mainly maize, wheat and rice) and their associated technical packages (the Green Revolution) were welcomed as a means to increase aggregate food output without political difficulties. Introduced into areas (for example Mexico, India, Pakistan, Indonesia, Philippines) where farmers had the means to adopt the new but more costly (capital intensive) production processes, the Green Revolution brought a shift from production for subsistence or own use to production for the (domestic) market, and certainly allowed many Asian countries to produce enough for domestic consumption and even export as well.

In other areas, for example in Africa, although HYVs were introduced (particularly maize), considerable efforts were made to encourage smallholding peasant producers to shift from subsistence to cash crop production largely for the export market, so as to bring in foreign exchange much needed by the state. The farmers themselves, it was assumed, could procure their own subsistence needs through the market. But little attention was paid to ensuring the development and integration of local and regional marketing networks. Crops all too often were chanelled directly to the nearest urban areas to meet the needs of the rapidly expanding cities, leaving the rural areas poorly supplied. To meet the town dwellers ever growing demand for food, major infrastructural projects, notably in West Africa, involving the introduction of irrigation or control of river basin water flows, were put in place to increase production of marketable foods, particularly rice.

Impact of going for growth strategies

The strategies based on these ideas were initially apparently highly successful. Many countries returned growth rates of 5 per cent and above per year. For example, on average, during the First UN Development Decade (1960 – 69), the growth rate of Kenya was 7.1 per cent, of Brazil 8 per cent, of South Korea 8.5 per cent (World Bank, 1978). The low-income countries as a whole (as defined by the World Bank) had growth rates of 3.6 per cent during this period, while the middle-income countries averaged out at 5.7 per cent. Many of these countries were growing and industrialising faster than the IMEs (Industrial Market Economies) had in the nineteenth century.

What these growth rates also reflected was an overall boom in the world economy, which came to an end with the two oil price rises of 1973 and 1979. And, as critics have since pointed out, the focus on LDC growth rates disguised the growing disparity between the already industrialised north and the industrialising south. During the 1960s the global gross international product increased by one trillion dollars. But this was very unevenly distributed, with

80 per cent going to rich industrialised nations and only 6 per cent to the poorest (those with per capita annual incomes of less than $200).

The growth figures for the 1960s also indicate the beginnings of a trend which was consolidated in the 1970s: certain 'developing' countries were moving ahead swiftly, while others stagnated. This foreshadowed the emergence of the Newly Industrialised Countries (NICs) of Latin America and South-East Asia and the falling behind of many of the countries of sub-Saharan Africa now categorised as Least Developed Countries (LLDCs).[3]

National growth rates measured as changes in GDP/GNP (Gross Domestic Product/Gross National Product) year-on-year also concealed the pattern of growth. Scholars who looked at the quality of life of the bulk of the population found much less reason for optimism. Gunnar Myrdal, for example, found that the assumed benefits of development were not reaching the majority of ordinary people, particularly the poorest (Mydral 1968). In his study Myrdal uses various indicators of standard of living such as food, clothing and energy consumption, and levels of literacy. While the theory predicted that through the trickle-down effect all social strata would benefit from economic growth fostered by modernisation and industrialisation, in reality the development-as-growth paradigm was accompanied by the economic and social marginalisation of large sectors of the population. Increasing income disparities, underemployment – both urban and rural – chronic food shortages and the impoverishment of a large proportion of the rural population, indicated that all was not well. The trickle-down effect, which should have spread the benefits of increasing wealth to the mass of the population through job creation, increased demand for local products and increased demand for a wide range of services, had not materialised.

Assessing the impact of the Green Revolution in Asia Keith Griffin notes: 'The Green Revolution represents an attempt to substitute technical change for institutional change, to use scientific progress as an alternative to social progress' (1989, p. 144). Despite the enormous increases in production that these technical solutions to food shortage brought, they involved a limited number of crops. Most were durable and marketable staples (maize, rice, wheat) rather than the basic staples of the bulk of the rural poor – pulses, root crops such as cassava and yams, and grains such as millet or quinoa. In many areas these subsistence crops already were or became the province of women; but they were offered few of the incentives to increase production that their male counterparts were given. Studies, such as that by Kathleen Staudt (1985), showed that agricultural extension workers rarely gave women subsistence crop farmers the same degree of attention and care as male cash crop farmers. In addition to producing food for their families, the women also had to accommodate their husbands' need for more labour on their cash crop fields. Women producers became overburdened rather than more productive, and looked to ways to lessen their work burden. In some cases this led to substitution of lower nutritional value crops for higher value but higher labour intensity crops.

Food crop production was also affected by the fact that land with better soils was taken for cash crop production. Rural poverty worsened because the increased cost of production of the HYVs and cash and export crops led to many small farmers and tenants having to sell land or losing rights in land; cash crop producers were also beggared by the instability of commodity prices.

Not only were these negative economic and social indicators worrying but the political situation in many countries had also deteriorated. Both Nigeria and Pakistan suffered civil wars – in the latter case ending with the secession of East Pakistan (now Bangladesh), Malaysia experienced violent race riots and Iran the overthrow of the Shah bent on modernising the economy at the cost of considerable repression. In Latin America and Africa authoritarian and often military governments became common in the 1970s, and almost everywhere there were growing levels of militarisation. The worrying question was to what extent economic growth was being promoted at the cost of popular discontent and subsequent repression.

Growth in question

The paradox of apparent growing wealth and greater poverty led both to the questioning of the dominant model of economic development and a search for explanations of its failure. Some observers argued that the model failed to address squarely issues of distribution; others that the model had too benevolent a notion of the benefits of trade. Many development economists responded by arguing that the main reason for failure was unanticipated population growth rates. With the success of their health programmes, infant and child mortality had decreased rapidly, but this was not matched by declining birth rates. We will briefly look at the critiques of the model and then at the population issue.

Insufficient attention to distribution

Growing evidence of gross poverty and new forms of poverty led to criticism of the conventional philosophy of grow first and distribute later and to questioning of the trickle-down assumption. An influential study published in 1974, entitled *Redistribution With Growth*, by Hollis Chenery and others, encapsulated the new thinking. It stressed the benefits to be gained from the inclusion of distributional factors in development planning, and showed that the mass of the population did not benefit from growth of the industrial and modern sectors and the increasing wealth of the urban entrepreneurial class through the trickle-down effect because the majority of the population – both rural and urban – were only minimally incorporated into the market. Research showed that the majority of the poor do not derive their livelihood from regular employment but rather from casual labouring and sale of goods and services, and other forms of what is called informal sector activity.

Given this, the authors of *Redistribution With Growth* (RWG) advocated a poverty-oriented approach; that is targeting the poor (the lowest 40 per cent of the population), and giving them assets or access to productive resources so they can have a permanent source of income. By raising the purchasing power of the bulk of the population, a demand for basic goods (manufactures and agricultural products) and services would be created, and in turn this would lead to more employment. Logically, the authors note that agriculture and manufacturing must be reoriented toward production of labour-intensive, mass consumption goods, and that price distortions which favour urban goods over rural ones must be eliminated. The authors do not discuss how governments will be able to reorient distribution towards the poor and away from the literate and articulate urban beneficiaries of growth without redistribution.

The redistribution approach made several valid points: the need to recognise the heterogeneity of social groups and the particular constraints that specific categories of the population face in their attempts to wrest a livelihood in a rather hostile economic environment. It also alerted development planners to the fact that, for reasons which the book does not explore, women formed a large proportion of the poorest: an observation which became the basis for much subsequent research and policy demands.

Employment issues had also been the concern of the ILO (International Labour Organisation) researchers in the 1960s. Focusing on the incapacity of industrial and modern sectors to absorb labour, ILO studies showed that large sectors of LDC populations were impoverished, not because they did not work, but because the types of economic activities they engaged in were low productivity, low return and unstable. They used the term 'informal sector' to describe the myriad activities of the working poor.

They noted that most governments are hostile to informal sector workers in part because they usually work on the streets, live in self-built shacks and huts in the interstices of the urban environment, and represent in many areas a real health hazard. As a result, city or municipal authorities frequently tried to rid themselves of the living evidence of the economy's failure by attacking the street workers and dwellers, burning down their houses and destroying their minimalist means of production. The ILO researchers, in contrast, argued that the survival strategies of the poor should be built upon and supported, and that this would help the economy in general.

To meet the needs of the 40 to 60 per cent of the population living on the margins of survival, the ILO proposed a new development strategy: the basic needs approach (BNA) (ILO, 1976). The BNA focused more sharply than RWG on the problem of how most people actually take part in development processes. Its main objective was to create the conditions which would, by the year 2000, give gainful employment to those who needed it, and meet most people's essential needs. These needs were identified as being of two types: those which could be met through individual effort – food, shelter, clothing – and those which should be met through public provision – health, sanitation, potable water, transport, education.

The focus on basic needs initiated a gradual reconsideration of women's contribution to development. The question of who provides most of the family's basic needs (food, water, clothing, health, heat) in most societies elicited the answer: women. Yet the conditions under which women were expected to provide for their families were appalling; little development concern had been directed to ameliorating these conditions. The implications of the fact that these time-consuming, arduous but essential tasks are given little or no value either by families or development planners was not addressed.

The strategies for achieving the BNA objectives were both economic and political, and included investment in labour-intensive production of basic goods and services, the use wherever possible of indigenous rather than external resources and of appropriate technologies. A crucial component of the strategy (like that of RWG) was the easing of poor people's means of access to socially valued resources, such as land, capital, education, employment opportunities, public services. Planning and other political institutions had to be reformed so as to encourage the greater participation of the poor in decision-making processes. The international monetary system and system of trade also needed reform so that national action on basic needs provision would not be blocked.

The BNA, like the RWG approach, relies heavily on the state to reorientate the economy. The state must play a prescriptive role in devising policies to meet society's basic needs. In guiding the course of development it must ensure that the inadequacies of a poorly-developed market system are compensated for or eliminated. In fact, a government's ability to pursue such strategies is dependent not only on the political will of those in power, but on its political capacity in terms of institutional structures. Yet in many countries both will and capacity were lacking. Strangely, despite all the recommendations for state action, analysis of the different forms of the state in developing countries was neglected, as was the study of the extent and composition of civil society.

The harsher economic climate of the late-1970s and early-1980s made BNA a deadletter almost as soon as it was put forward, at least as far as macroeconomic planning was concerned. Criticised for being overly idealistic and welfarist, for ignoring economic realities, the BNA did, none the less, add another dimension to development thinking. By raising the issues of autonomy and decision-making, cultural hegemony and indigenous knowledge, a much more overtly political dimension to the debate was opened up.

Although never implemented as a development policy, BNA was incorporated quite successfully into development practice: it has proved effective in individual project planning and drawing up local and regional plans, in getting planners to identify the basic needs of (and with) their target groups. Those who advocate the needs of particular groups – women, the poorest, the landless – have used it to get the concerns of their constituents integrated into the planning process. The problem, of course, is that such plans have to be implemented within the parameters set by macro-economic plans and national development strategies. And it is here that the needs of those without voice or political power get aggregated into invisibility.

Inequalities of trade

As we have noted, many policymakers considered production for the international market a prime means for development. This view was attacked by economists working with the UN Economic Commission for Latin America (ECLA) (see e.g. Celso Furtado, 1964; Osvaldo Sunkel, 1969). They were particularly critical of the benevolent role assigned to foreign capital and aid, and to international trade in the development process. Believing the classical theory of comparative advantage to be seriously flawed, they argued that on the contrary, the world economic system is characterised by the unequal distribution of gains from trade. The industrialised Western nations (the 'core'), because of their economic power, benefit at the expense of the less developed and largely agricultural or primary product producing countries (the 'periphery'). Trade and specialisation in the periphery does not equalise disparities in levels of development nor stimulate balanced growth as the theory of comparative advantage predicts. Rather, developing countries are merely exposed to the vagaries of levels of demand from the centre and fluctuations in commodity prices, and become ever more dependent on imports and exports rather than increasingly self-sufficient.

The ECLA economists identified restructuring the terms of trade between centre and periphery as a precondition for LDC development. This was taken up by the group of 77 developing countries who, in 1973, launched a campaign for a New International Economic Order (NIEO), with the support of UNCTAD (UN Conference on Trade and Development). Among the requirements of NIEO were the stabilisation of commodity prices, ending of tariff barriers against LDC manufactures in developed country markets, reform of the international monetary system and the system of trade and tariffs (GATT), regulation of multinational corporations (MNC) activities, and the promotion of south-south trade.

In some ways NIEO was a direct challenge to BNA. Many LDC economists and politicians feared that concentration on meeting the basic needs of the poorest would divert attention (and resources) away from industrial development and that their countries would remain forever dependent on northern manufactures. They suggested that BNA was little more than a ploy to divert attention away from structural imbalances in the world economy. However, many distributionists argued that, while NIEO would undoubtedly benefit entrepreneurs, politicians and bureaucrats, given the LDCs' polarised distribution patterns and the organisational weakness of labour (or the actual prohibition on labour organisations), the vast majority of people in the LDCs would not materially benefit.

Others argued that exclusive focus on the effects of international trade blocked understanding of the role that class and other internal factors play in impeding progressive social and economic change. Two Brazilians, Fernando Cardoso and Enrique Faletto, argued that the effect of both trade and direct foreign investment in peripheral countries is to produce narrowly based economic growth, highly unequal income distribution, and a *comprador bourgeoisie* (Cardoso and Faletto, 1979). The latter, rather than promoting national economic interest and growth, is self-interested and parasitic, and opts for conspicuous consumption (imports of luxury goods) rather than (re)investment of profits in enterprises which build up the industrial base of the country. Their work fell within what became known as the dependency critique of development. In policy terms, dependency theorists' recommendations ranged from radical restructuring of the world economy, to specific measures designed to reduce dependence on the core countries.

Others were also sceptical of the benefits to be gained from NIEO but on different grounds. They suggested that, since developing countries were not homogeneous, the supposed benefits of international restructuring and national self-reliance would not be experienced by all of them. By the end of the 1970s in fact three different trajectories of developing countries were becoming clear. Among the 100 or so countries, a sub group of 31 was identified as being least developed (LLDCs). This group all had an average income of less than $100 per capita, an adult literacy rate of less than 20 per cent and a manufacturing sector providing less than 10 per cent of GDP. Twenty-seven of the LLDCs were in sub-Saharan Africa, most of the rest were in Latin America. At the other end of the scale were the 12 or so newly-industrialised countries – the NICs. This group of relatively prosperous and politically powerful countries, such as South Korea, Taiwan, Brazil and India, stood to benefit most from NIEO. Since they had already consolidated their trading positions within the world economy, they had the necessary bargaining power to face confrontations with the economies of the north. The remaining countries were likely to benefit little from NIEO since they produced few manufactured exports, and were dependent on the north for manufactured and intermediate capital goods.

Population growth

Rather than questioning the adequacy of their models, many economists and planners, as we noted, blamed population growth. They argued that good policies had been blown off course by an explosion in population growth, itself partially a result of welfare policy successes, notably the decline in mortality, both adult and child. In fact, between 1955 and 1970, the rate of population growth in the LDCs did rise from 1.99 per cent per year to 2.6 per cent. Although the birth rate fell by 23.1 per cent between 1950-55 to 1975-80, the death rate fell even faster – by 47.8 per cent (from UN Statistical Tables, cited in Colman and Nixson, 1986, pp. 104-5). The increasing rate of population growth, the economists claimed, underlay the continuing poverty of the Indian subcontinent, sub-Saharan Africa and Latin America.

At the time, there was little agreement as to the relationship between economic growth and population growth. Some theorists suggested a positive relationship: a growing population contributed to economic growth by stimulating demand and investment, providing an ever growing labour force, expanding domestic markets and encouraging technological innovation. Simon Kuznets (1966), for example, defined modern economic growth as 'a sustained increase in population obtained without any lowering of per capita output'. Other studies showed strong direct (negative) effects of rapid population growth on the rate of labour absorption, and the cost of public provision of education, health, housing and sanitation (UN, 1965), and weaker direct effects on income distribution, food availability, resource endowment and the environment.

An alternative explanation for population growth came from developing countries: poor economic performance and the restructuring of the economy had led to greater poverty among the mass of the population, particularly rural people – and poverty stimulates birth rates. The by now classical argument was made that poor families have many children to enhance their likelihood of survival, given that children provide their parents with free labour when young and security in their old age (Mamdani, 1972). The best form of contraception according to this argument is a rapid rise in well-being of the poor.

Demographers sought to identify the level of economic development at which the demographic transition occurs (i.e. when fertility stabilises at just above mortality). Many concluded that the turning point occurs at levels of urbanisation, per capita income, and literacy greater than those then found in sub-Saharan Africa and south Asia (but found in Latin America and South-East Asia). It was suggested that the former countries appeared to be caught in a fertility trap in which infant and child mortality had fallen somewhat but not sufficiently for fertility to fall as well (Farooq and Simmons, 1984; Ridker, 1976).

Despite these findings, national governments as well as international donors became convinced that population control policies were needed to reduce birth rates (UN, 1975). Although it was argued that raising women's status in society, giving them education and employment, had positive fertility effects, few governments or aid advisers focused on this. Instead, a technical solution was preferred: promotion of contraceptives would bring down high birth rates faster and more cost-effectively than providing schooling or employment or raising women's status.

The neo-liberal counter revolution

Another response to the failure of many developing countries to grow was an ever more vociferous attack on the basic premises of development economics itself. During the 1970s a number of orthodox economists had criticised a range of development practices and the theories behind them. By the 1980s their criticisms and their own preferred economic theories held sway. This 'counter revolution' as John Toye calls it (Toye, 1987) should not be seen as a coherent theory, but broadly speaking its exponents have rejected interventionist approaches in favour of free market forces. At different extremes are writers such as Bauer (1984) who argues that aid in itself is damaging, and the economists of the World Bank and the IMF who advocate both structural adjustment and the liberalisation of market forces. One of the most influential and certainly most widely quoted of the 'counter revolutionaries' or neo-liberals has been Deepak Lal. In *The Poverty of Development Economics* (Lal, 1983), he criticises what he calls 'the dirigiste dogma' – essentially reliance on planning and intervention in the economy – backed up by 'theoretical curiosities' – or the tendency to theorise at macro level with insufficient attention to micro-economic detail.

The neo-liberals put a large measure of the responsibility for the failure of many LDCs to grow at the door of the development economists, primarily because of their belief that the price mechanism could be supplanted by Keynesian interventionism – government intervention in markets through pervasive planning – and that the establishment of an industrial sector was crucial enough to be supported by tariff barriers and other forms of protection backed up by government control of wages, prices and imports. They also criticised the basic needs advocacy of distributing productive assets to relieve poverty. According to the new thinking, the main problem in the LDCs (as elsewhere) is that of resource allocation and since the most rational allocator of resources is the market, it should be promoted; this will stimulate faster and more balanced economic growth than macro-economic policies.

The main onslaught of the counter-revolutionaries then centres on the perverse effects of much state intervention as well as the incapacity of bureaucrats to run businesses efficiently and without corruption. They maintain that the desire to industrialise leads to wasteful duplication rather than the benefits of comparative advantage; that it is inefficient to adopt protectionist measures which prevent domestic consumers from getting cheaper/better foreign products. At the most extreme, they also criticise welfare measures, such as provision of subsidised foods, free health care and schooling, as a waste of scarce resources on non-wealth creating activity.

Behind such arguments lies the assumption that the state is by definition more inefficient than the private entrepreneur, that there are no circumstances in which collective management of resources is better than private, and that there are few circumstances in which the government has the duty to regulate the activities of private entrepreneurs. However, governments operate within a specific configuration of political forces. In some cases the social and political situation may be such that governments are able to funnel benefits to rather narrow sectors of the population (i.e. those who underpin its power). In others, political and social institutions within society are strong and widespread enough to ensure that benefit is more evenly spread. But this cannot be taken for granted.

In reality the workings of the economy and the political system cannot be separated as simply as some neo-liberal thinkers would seem to imply. Single-minded concentration on economic policy leads to ignoring the way in which social and political factors influence both the workings of specific policy prescriptions and how the effects of those prescriptions are felt by the population. This narrowness of focus is as much a shortcoming of those structuralists who call for widespread state intervention, as it is of the neo-liberals. Both fail to take into account the way the state and the market are inextricably linked. The 'state' is not an amorphous entity controlled by 'dirigiste dogmatists'. It is a complex arrangement of institutional structures and political interest groups, the workings of which are dependent on many different historical and cultural factors. The effectiveness of economists' prescriptions will always be mediated by such institutions (Toye, 1987), so it is important to take them into account. The choice of policy prescriptions will depend to a large extent on the structuring of and interests behind the political process.

Despite the short-comings and over-simplifications of their theories, neo-liberals won the day and by the 1980s their development prescriptions had become the new orthodoxy. Economic growth was once again the central issue, the withdrawal of the state and allowing the free play of market forces the major motor of development. Alternative readings of what was needed for the developing countries were largely silenced. Only after the terrible decade of the 1980s, now known as the lost decade for development, are voices once again being heard which question the orthodoxy, and castigate it as doctrinaire ideology (South Commission Report, 1990).

Defining development

Throughout the period we are concerned with, the meaning of development has been widely debated; in many respects this debate echoes an earlier one last century on the nature and meaning of 'progress'.

In the 1950s and 1960s development was largely understood as rapid economic growth measured in terms of GNP. And, as the writers of the 1990 UNDP Human Development Report note, with the goal of development reduced to increasing GNP, the question of promoting individual well-being receded from its earlier prominence.[4] 'Growth in the capital stock was seen as the means of achieving development, and the growth rate of per capita GDP became the sole measure of development.... Income at the national level ... became a measure of activity of the total mass of quantity of goods and services produced, ... rather than a measure of individual well-being.' (UNDP, 1990, p.104). It was assumed that well-being would follow automatically from economic growth. 'A tenuous link between income and well-being was made through the notion of income per capita, which compounded the shift of emphasis from welfare to production by its insensitivity to distribution. In time, distribution was altogether forgotten, and the argument of "trickle-down" was made to defend such neglect. Thus, income moved from an admittedly partial monetary measure of well-being to centre stage as a measure of production and as the sole measure of welfare in its per capita form' (UNDP, 1990, p.104).

Unlike the experts, most lay people have a less technical or abstract conception of 'development'. For us it implies a change for the better: the ordering of society and social and economic processes in such a way as to lead to the eradication of gross poverty, ill health and illiteracy and to rising standards of living and increased material comforts for all. Many would argue that development must be about people not merely about production or productive capacity; that it is a process of enlarging people's choices; enabling them to take part in reaching a consensus about the goals and processes of change.[5] Many also feel it should include enhancing the capacity of human beings to realise their potential for creativity and spirituality.

Over the years, studies have documented the ugly 'unacceptable' face of economic growth – exploitative conditions of work and starvation wages, health hazards, environmental degradation, restriction of political rights of the majority, severe inequalities of wealth and access to socially desired rewards. Since few consider these things as desirable, a distinction is now often made between development and economic growth.

While this seems eminently sensible, an economy does need to be capable of providing the investment needed to build the schools, hospitals, theatres; the transport, electricity, water, drainage and sewage systems which are necessary for enhanced living standards. Without a vital economy, talk of the eradication of poverty is meaningless. Since economic growth and a healthy economy (using the restricted meaning of the term) are not a sufficient condition to ensure social health, development strategies and economic policy must work together; and this is of course where political dispositions become crucial.

As we have seen, development experts stressed the benefits of industrialisation as against dependence on agriculture, of production which is oriented to the world market, i.e. to exporting rather than to the domestic market. There was little questioning of the capacity of states, or the world system itself to support rapid growth; of whether the world market could absorb the massively increased production, and no concern until the late-1970s about the capacity of the natural world to sustain such a high level of extraction as well as dumping of noxious or unusable by-products of industrialisation.

In the 1990s definitions emphasise self-reliance and the well-being of the majority of people. The South Commission, for example, defined development thus: 'Our vision is for the South to achieve a people-centred development: a form of development that is self-reliant, equitable, participatory and sustained. We envisage a process of development achieved through the active participation of the people, in their own interests as they see them, relying primarily on their own resources, and carried out under their own control' (South Commission, Overview and Summary, 1990, p.8).

Statistical measures of development

Whichever definition of development is used, practitioners need some relatively simple means of measuring progress. The indicators chosen will obviously reflect the particular understanding of the concept of development. However, each possible set of indicators, whether tied to health, mortality, education, welfare, equality, political freedom, or economic prosperity, will have its attendant problems, and no one indicator on its own will make up what it means to be 'developed'. For example, a country with excellent education and health provision but without political freedom is unlikely to be considered developed by many.

As we saw above, the indicator of economic performance thought to be most accurate, universally usable and understood as well as easy to apply was the level of the Gross Domestic Product (GDP) or Gross National Product (GNP). The former refers to production actually within a country, the latter to the total final output of goods and services produced by an economy, whether within its boundaries or without. This measure is used in Western national accounting procedures and tends to reflect definitions of productive activity as these are understood in an industrialised market economy.

In recent years GNP has been extensively criticised as a measure for several reasons (see e.g. Seers, 1972). Firstly, the term is less objective than it appears because the decisions about what should be included and what excluded are not value-free. For example, much non-market production is excluded; this may not distort understanding of the economy in many IMEs but when the measure is used in countries with large non-market sectors, serious distortions are bound to occur. Equally, production of harmful goods that pollute the atmosphere or injure health, or military wares that kill are included. Secondly, data collection techniques have been found to be inconsistent and faulty. Lastly, concentration on changes in GNP as an indicator of economic growth gives no indication of how wealth or income are distributed or of 'quality of living' factors. GDP per capita figures can provide a highly distorted picture of reality, for example, in countries where sharp inequalities in distribution of wealth may well mean the top 20 per cent of the population enjoys a very disproportionate proportion of total wealth.

To get round this difficulty a number of alternative indices or measures have been proposed. For example, researchers at the UN Research Institute for Social Development (UNRISD) looked at a range of indicators, some relating to mortality and morbidity, others to social factors such as urbanisation, as well as economic indicators. By relating each indicator to per capita GPD in a series of regressions they were able to identify a threshold level of development (McGranahan and Pizarro, 1985). On the other hand, Morris D. Morris (1979), wanting to focus on development as achieved well-being rather than as activity, proposed a Physical Quality of Life Index using three indicators – infant mortality, life expectancy at age one, and literacy, combining them in a simple unweighted index.

The United Nations Development Programme (UNDP) more recently has claimed that development really is about people and has devised the Human Development Index to give a much more accurate picture of human well-being in developing countries than per capita GNP or GDP (UNDP, 1990). They suggest that to obtain as comprehensive a picture as possible, any system for measuring and monitoring human development should include many variables, but that this is not feasible given the current lack of relevant comparable statistics. Too many indicators could also produce too complex a picture. So they suggest that for the time being the measure of human development should focus on the three essential elements of human life: longevity, knowledge and decent living standards. Women might well point to the fact that freedom from violence or physical assault is an equally essential measure; without such freedom women cannot fully enjoy the other three elements.

Summary conclusions

By the end of the 1970s, the trends emerging at the onset of the decade were consolidated as far as the three different trajectories of 'Third World' countries were concerned. At one extreme were the NICs which, along with oil producing countries, continued to show rapid rates of growth. Standard of living indicators showed improvements in key areas such as life expectancy, maternal and infant mortality. The LDCs also maintained growth, but at a considerably lower level, often without much increase in industrial and especially manufacturing capacity. But at the other end of the spectrum, growth rates in the LLDCs had stagnated and indicators of poverty worsened. Indeed during the 1970s, Africa's gains in per capita income were less than half of the average of all developing countries.

Development strategies to some extent reflected these trends. The concern with poverty issues reached a peak during the 1970s, with calls for redistribution of wealth, with growth and demands to ascertain and meet people's basic needs. But equally, the concern over the dynamics of the international system voiced by those within the south (and some in the north) also reached a peak during this period – hence the demands for a New International Economic Order. In the 1980s the plurality of views has diminished and at least in the early part of the decade the free-market view held the foreground, at least in the multilateral agencies. By the 1990s this view is again being modified and undermined.

Notes

1 The theory has been extensively criticised for being tautological – the richer countries have by definition achieved higher stages of growth. Also, the international context in which the colonies were trying to 'modernise' was very different to that facing the Western countries when they were moving out of feudalism.

2 The classical nineteenth-century economist Riccardo suggested that a country should specialise in producing what it produces well and cheaply and exchange these goods in the market for the other goods it needs, produced in turn by countries specialising in them. This is known as comparative advantage. He used the example of Portugal exchanging its wine for English wheat.

3 Making any distinction between more and less developed countries has also been criticised because of the value judgements involved. It presupposes that some countries have reached a way of life to be emulated by all others. But many people argue that the 'developed' countries make a reckless and ultimately destructive use of natural resources, have a lifestyle which dehumanises, and that their economic growth continues to be at the expense of those countries considered 'under-developed' or 'developing'. To avoid such loaded terminology, the World Bank now uses the terms low, middle and high-income countries. However while this avoids value judgements, level of income tells us little about the actual level of development of the health, education or welfare system.

   We have followed conventional definitions, using the terms Least Developed Countries (LLDCs), Less Developed Countries (LDCs), Newly Industrialised Countries (NICs), and Industrial Market Economies (IME).

4 'While the pioneers of measurement of national output and income stressed the importance of social concerns, economic growth became the main focus after the Second World War.' (UNDP, 1990, p.104).

5 UNDP suggest that human development is a process of enlarging people's choices. 'The most critical ones are to lead a long and healthy life, to be educated and to enjoy a decent standard of living. Additional choices include political freedom, guaranteed human rights and self-respect ...' (UNDP, 1990, p.10).

2 The appearance of the invisible woman

Women are noticeably absent from the discussions of development theory and practice during the First UN Development Decade (1960-70). While cleavages of class were considered, differentiation between groups of people within a given class, or the likelihood of them having different interests and priorities, were given scant importance. In the early literature, for example, peasants are considered as a homogeneous group. Equally, with little research available and impact analysis unknown, development planners and theoreticians worked with models which made certain assumptions as to the likely effects of economic change. In fact it is hard to find indicators of the health, welfare, and political equality of people in developing countries up to about the mid-1960s. The UN Statistical Yearbooks for the mid-1950s and early-1960s, for instance, give no 'standard of living' data for many countries. The data gap is particularly noticeable for the countries of sub-Saharan Africa – except for statistics on the European population.

Mothers and housewives 1960-70

People involved in development practice faced different problems. For example, rural community development schemes did make explicit attempts to get local people to identify types of projects which would encourage self-sustaining rural development, but their emphasis on 'the community' smoothed over any distinctions between the interests and concerns of richer and poorer, women and men. Despite the fact that their success often largely depended upon women's commitment, no particular efforts were made to identify women's needs. At the time most development practitioners considered that women's needs were taken care of by 'the family', conceived of as a corporate unit headed by a (male) household head, who exercised benevolent authority and control over its members and resources. From this point of view, any benefit directed at the family head automatically benefits all its members (through a modified trickle-down effect). As a result, project managers and designers saw little wrong with meeting local organisations or groups which were male-only (or male-dominated) to disseminate information, inputs, and equipment.

The question of whether women undertook economic activities which could usefully be supported never appears to have been addressed. When women were explicitly considered, it was virtually always as mothers and childbearers. It was further assumed that everyone's interest would be best served by helping women improve the way in which they cared for their children and catered for the family's needs. As a result family welfare programmes were devised which gave women instruction in home economics, in improved nutrition, health, and hygiene.

Development thinking drew heavily on a notion of the specialisation of functions (the sexual division of labour) within the family – men taking care of the economic livelihood of the family (possibly 'helped' from time to time by his wife/ves), women being engaged in those tasks proper to the mother and housewife. Since men's needs were considered to focus around their economic activities, and given the developers' desire to augment productivity, it was to men that development planners' attention turned. Women's concerns as cultivators, processors of food, traders, wage workers and unpaid labourers did not enter into the planners' model. That women might be an integral and essential element in development planning and implementation was also never contemplated.

Producers and providers 1970-80

During the Second UN Development Decade (1970-79), women's issues and development came to be conceptually linked for the first time. A combination of factors brought this about. Early confidence that economic growth could be achieved by judicious manipulation of macro-economic levers was shattered. Development planners shifted from looking only at economic growth to issues of the equity of distributional patterns, targeting the poor, building on local capacity and cultural autonomy. With the more 'people-centred' approach of the 1970s, women's contribution to the family economy as much as to family welfare came to be appreciated.

Worries about population growth rates put women squarely in the picture; more attention to agriculture and food crop production led to greater appreciation of women's work within it; greater concern with distribution issues led to research into the conditions of the poor and poorest and the finding that women constituted a large proportion of the poorest; the concern with basic needs led to the realisation that it is women, particularly in the poorer strata, who provide almost all their families' basic needs. Lastly, the growing strength of the women's movement in all parts of the world led to women within the United Nations system and within national aid agencies beginning to make specific demands for women's voices to be heard in development decision making.

In fact there were two rather different perceptions of what was happening to women. One was that women were being excluded from the development process because planners and policymakers ignored women's important economic activities. Given this, the need was to integrate women into development; some even argued that women should be asked about their needs and concerns. This perspective led to the (later) argument that women were a neglected resource for development.

The other viewpoint was that women were already integrated into the development process, but assumptions about their specific activities led planners both to neglect women's real needs and to over-exploit their labour. As a result, women were losing out relative to men in the development process, both in terms of access to new resources and loss of old and valued statuses. According to this perspective, women were not a neglected resource but overburdened and undervalued. What was needed was a re-evaluation of women's already considerable contribution to the development process and a redistribution of the benefits and burdens of development between men and women.

A growing body of empirical research pointed to the fact that the concentration on women's mothering role had allowed planners to miss their essential productive contributions – especially in agriculture. The publication of Esther Boserup's *Women's Role in Economic Development* in 1970, is often seen as the point from which the Women and Development lobby grew. Her contribution was to draw attention to the fact that women were doing much more than producing and rearing children: they played an essential part in economic production as farmers, workers in the informal sector and employees in many industries.

In particular, by summarising a good deal of earlier research and claiming that women were responsible for producing most of the food crops in sub-Saharan Africa, her book disturbed many of the previous assumptions of official aid agencies and government planners. Boserup indicated that by not giving women, particularly farmers, access to modern tools and training, they were not only being displaced from their traditional productive functions, but also their ability to provide for themselves and their children was being weakened, and their social status diminished.

Women's major role in providing their families' basic needs – food, water, fuel, health and education – was the finding of the Basic Needs promoters. The empirical research they carried out also showed that women (particularly rural women) were not underemployed but rather overworked. ILO's *Employment, Growth and Basic Needs: A One World Problem* (1976), made the point that women needed support to ease their work burden; and they also needed to be recognised as independent economic actors – in other words the family does not necessarily constitute a joint economic enterprise. Lastly, attention should also be given to their more equitable integration into the community, beyond the narrow circle of the family.

The recognition of women's enormous work burden, especially that of poor rural women, and the need to improve their social standing in the wider community was a significant step forward. None the less the report does not develop these insights. Instead it states that whatever strategy is adopted to enable women to contribute more effectively to the satisfaction of their families' basic needs, it must ensure that this is 'within the framework of their traditional responsibilities' (1976, p.61). In other words, the ILO researchers did not envisage the restructuring of the sexual division of labour, nor question whether the nature of traditional household (production) relations might be part of the problem of women's overwork and low social standing.

At the time, little data was available on the social and economic status of women or their contributions to non-market or market production. Equally, apart from some anthropological studies, little was known about family systems – different forms of relations between men and women, husbands and wives – or how these are set within wider social structures of kinship and community, or even how different forms of household manage resource allocation (see Roberts, 1979 for a discussion of the difficulties experienced in 'integrating women into development' because of this). In large measure it was women, in both north and south, who took up the challenge to fill these lacunae in knowledge and the 1970s and 1980s saw a dramatic expansion in research and publications.

The poverty-oriented approach of the BNA and the shift in development concern to bettering the lot of the poor did not, therefore, produce a radical change in development policy toward women. Emphasis remained on women's role as procreators, nutritionists and childcarers, only secondary importance being given to their role as producers – and here interest largely focused on production for the market and women's involvement in monetised relations.

Although research showed that a substantial proportion of the poorest households were headed by women; that in many countries female-headed households were the norm among poorer strata and had been so for many years (e.g. in the Caribbean); that in many others the increasing impoverishment of the majority of the population was leading to greater marital instability and greater incidence of female-headed households, little positive policy response was evident at the national level. International donors, however, began to provide support for small-scale income-generating activities so as to help poor women provide more effectively for their families. Most donors eschewed any direct confrontation with issues to do with gender relations – the socially ascribed relations between men and women – and how these were being affected by socio-economic change.

The concentration on income generation for women, was in part because it was felt that self-employment suited many women's skills, aptitudes and their time availability better than formal paid employment, and in part because inability to provide such employment for most of those seeking wage work was precisely what characterised most LDCs. It was recognised that many women were engaged in informal sector activities, often as own account workers, but also often as unpaid family labour. Large numbers of these working women were the chief, if not the only, economic providers for poor families, and recognition of this fact led to a focus on upgrading what skills they had, giving them access to small amounts of credit to set up or to improve the viability of their enterprises. These women-only projects tended to be small in scale and the amounts of aid chanelled to them very minor. Larger projects designed to improve the conditions for development take-off in rural areas began to add on a women's component which usually provided women some means of earning an income, usually through small-scale production for the market.

Ironically enough while the more conventional welfare projects continued to emphasise womens' mothering and childcare roles, income-generating projects often neglected women's childcare responsibilities. That this did pose a problem – particularly in urban areas – was recognised by some innovative projects which allowed poor working women to leave their children in the care of other women, who, in return for agreeing to adopt better childcare practices, were given easier access to health clinics or to supplementary feeding programmes for the children in their care (and their own). The existence of a potential conflict of interest between mothers and their children, particularly daughters, also came to the forefront. Women's enterprises often either depended on their children's labour or daughters substituting for them in household tasks. Children who would otherwise have gone to school were kept back, or allowed to go very intermittently, and eventually dropped out. Problems such as these were rarely tackled at the policy level but solutions sought piecemeal.

Although much development concern in the 1970s focused on poor rural women, women's employment in industry was expanding very rapidly in many South-East Asian and Caribbean countries as transnational corporations (TNCs) opened branches, often in Free Trade Zones (FTZs) specially designed to attract foreign manufacturers. This gave rise to a heated debate as to the benefits or otherwise for women of incorporation in the modern sector (see e.g. Elson and Pearson, 1980). Many who were concerned with equity issues – providing women with the education, training and opportunity (as well as the right) to take their place alongside men in a wide range of fora including that of decision-making – argued that modern employment was a prerequisite for women to challenge their inferior social position. Others argued that the types of jobs on offer to women in the modern sector merely replicated their subordinate position within the family. Furthermore the fact that most of the jobs were of short duration, injurious to health, provided few or no skills which could be used in future employment (or self-employment) showed that women were merely seen as a short-term 'throw away' labour force. Writers on both sides of the debate agreed that women were considered socially inferior but disagreed on how this was to be changed. At the time there was little discussion of the role policymakers could play in changing or ameliorating negative aspects of women's employment.

International concern over rapidly expanding populations, led to funding of research into the determinants of fertility, thus women came clearly into focus. The question of why women chose (if they do choose) to have so many children and how they could be dissuaded from doing so became issues of burning concern. A few variables were pinpointed as being crucial to fertility decline: two focused on women – the improvement of education and employment opportunities for women; and increasing women's participation in public life and decision-making.

Research findings suggested that the more years of schooling a woman enjoys, the fewer children she tends to have. In most poor countries in the 1960s, overall education and literacy levels were low, but the disparity between men and women was even more significant. The lack of local education facilities and the high cost of providing them was one constraint; parental resistance to sending daughters to school another – girls' education was felt to be a waste of scarce resources and likely to make them less marriageable. Daughters were better kept at home, where they could help with younger siblings and learn the household tasks they would be performing as married women.

Women's labour force participation was less clearly correlated with lowered fertility rates (Penniment, 1965). Only among women in high prestige, modern sector employment does fertility consistently decline; however, it is unclear whether the significant factor is the women's class position, the employment itself, or the type of employment. Since high rates of labour force participation in typical female jobs can be correlated to high rates of fertility, the type of employment is probably the relevant factor. Yet high quality employment in the modern sector is precisely what most countries find it difficult to provide.

As was noted in the previous chapter, policymakers chose a technical solution to the problem of rapid population growth: the adoption of population control policies and the vigorous promotion of family planning. However family planning (or birth control) and population control should not be conflated. Population control involves the determination by policymakers of a desirable level of population growth and the design of incentives (or disincentives) to achieve this. Family planning in its broadest sense is about providing individuals – both men and women – with the means to determine the number and spacing of their children. It is perfectly compatible with high levels of fertility. Contraception in turn is a vital element in women's right to greater control over their lives. However, women need to be able to choose between a range of methods and be informed of their differing health implications, if they are to gain greater control and sense of autonomy.

In fact, women's own desire for knowledge and greater control over their own fertility was largely ignored when family planning programmes were introduced. Instead they were viewed instrumentally, as the means to bring down the birth rate. Initially, programmes were quite authoritarian in their implementation, did not supply adequate information about potentially damaging side effects of methods, and did not adequately consider the social context – for example resistance from husbands, from men and women of the older generation, and wives' social isolation and powerlessness. By directing programmes only at women, the dynamics of male-female relations were ignored. Although male attitudes about their right to exercise authority and control over their wives sexuality and fertility are critical to the acceptance of family planning methods, little attempt was made to understand or to change them.

Population control programmes focused on women as the most appropriate family planning agents, not merely because they have to bear the consequences of frequent pregnancies and unsuccessful birthing, but also because it was assumed they would be less resistant to using contraceptives.[1] However, the methods promoted and insensitivity to cultural difference, led to many such programmes being brought into disrepute. Women in developing countries felt they were used to try out new methods (including the contraceptive pill, trials being held in Mexico and Puerto Rico) without sufficient information; pharmaceutical companies were accused of dumping contraceptive products banned in the West in the LDCs.

The birth and growth of institutionalised WID

In the previous section we noted that the resurgence of the women's movement in northern countries during the 1970s had its impact on the development industry. One focus of women's anger was their marginalisation from positions of power. The United Nations system came under increasing attack because of its appalling employment ratios – in 1977 women occupied 4.8 per cent of the top two levels of geographic posts (i.e. 1 woman) (see Pietila and Vickers, 1990).

In the United States pressure was exerted on the government to do something for women in developing countries.[2] In 1973 the US Senate adopted the Percy Amendment which added a provision to the Foreign Assistance Act to 'encourage and promote the integration of women' into all aspects of development planning and into policymaking bodies themselves. The US Agency for International Development (USAID) set up a women in development office; its brief being to promote these objectives.[3] Feminists and women involved in some way with the Carter government, who worked in and around Washington

DC or in the UN Agencies (many from Northern Europe) began to network together. The WID (Women in Development) lobby was born. As time went by they were supported by a number of women in universities and other academic institutions who undertook research into a range of issues: women's productive work, their access to resources, the division of labour between men and women, the impact of development policies and processes whether planned or not.

Pressure on the United Nations, particularly led by Scandinavian Non-Governmental Organisations (NGOs), resulted in the decision to hold a world conference on women and development in 1975 and the designation of that year by the UN as the International Year of Women. Despite the lack of the usual two to three-year lead time (the decision was only taken in 1974), most countries strove to produce up-to-date information on the situation of women in their countries for the conference. This immediately showed up the dearth of knowledge about and accurate data on women's lives and activities. In many cases countries had to make informed guesses, in others original research was commissioned, and in still others researchers were asked to cull their raw data to see what they had on women's activities. Some of the country reports, such as the Government of India's *Status of Women* Commission Report, gave deeply troubling accounts of the deterioration in women's position. The UN itself produced a report 'Current trends and changes in the status and role of women and men' (UN, 1975a). It is significant that at this point the 'question of women' was seen in relational terms – i.e. in terms of changes affecting both women and men.

The 1975 UN Women's Conference (held in Mexico City) had as its themes Equality, Development and Peace which neatly encapsulated the major preoccupations of the three world groupings, northern IMEs, southern LDCs and the socialist block countries. The UN meeting was attended by official government delegates and NGOs with consultative status – some 1200 delegates from 133 countries, 73 per cent of whom were women. With too little time for discussion, the meeting adopted most of the World Plan of Action (WPA) presented to the delegates. The Plan had been drawn together by the UN Secretariat as a compendium of recommendations and resolutions adopted on women's issues in the various UN bodies over the preceding 30 years. As such, the WPA was rather a grab bag of desirable changes; it lacked an agreed set of strategies and a timeframe within which its objectives should be achieved. Worse still it lacked any commitment of resources. The responsibility for bringing about change was left to national governments and, as one commentator noted, an army of bureaucrats would be hard pressed to follow through on all the recommendations made.

The WPA listed 14 minimum objectives relating to improved educational opportunities for women, better employment prospects, equality in political and social participation, and increased welfare services. More daringly it asked for recognition of women's unpaid work and a re-evaluation of the roles traditionally assigned to men and women. It recommended that governments should establish national machinery to promote women's interests and that women's units in other organisations should also be set up. A second world conference should be held in 1980 to review and appraise implementation of the WPA. In December 1975 the General Assembly approved the recommendations of the conference and declared 1976-85 the UN Decade for Women.

The UN system committed itself to furthering the Women's Decade in several ways. A voluntary fund, supported by pledges from member governments, was established in 1976 to finance Decade projects. Later renamed UNIFEM, the fund provides direct financial and technical assistance to women's organisations through national governments. A commitment was also made to set up an International Research and Training Institute for the Advancement of Women (INSTRAW), if voluntary funding from government and other sources was made available for its first three years of operation. INSTRAW eventually did open in 1983 in Santo Domingo. The Branch for the Advancement of Women (moved from New York to Vienna) was charged with promoting the UN *Convention on the Elimination of All Forms of Discrimination Against Women*, and other international legal instruments. In the meantime the UN agencies set about collecting data on women worldwide to fill in some of the obvious gaps.

Non-Governmental Organisations concerned with women's issues organised a meeting to coincide with the UN conference. The NGO Tribune attracted a much larger number of participants – more than 4000 – to its 32 formally convened sessions and a further 192 informal ones. Not surprisingly, there were confrontations and repudiations of 'Western bourgeoise feminism' (widely published by a sceptical, if not outrightly hostile press), reflecting different assessments of women's needs between women of the IMEs and the LDCs, and different priorities arising from them. None the less, it was the first time that women from a wide range of countries north and south, socialist and capitalist, could meet and discuss issues of concern to women, from the perspective of women (the official UN meeting still approached the issues from a rather paternalistic perspective).

All in all, the Mexico meetings were a considerable success, attracting far greater participation than was ever imagined, and despite differences of approach, laying firm bases for future work. Perhaps most importantly it gave women a rare moment of encouragement and the opportunity to sense the potential strength of an international movement committed to change and the advancement of women.

Over the next few years a large number of women's NGOs, support groups and international networks began to spring up. For the first time some financial support for women's own organisational initiatives became available from foundations and the more liberal governments' aid agencies. By 1981 the Yearbook of International Organisations listed some 60 international women's

NGOs. Regional groups were also formed to promote the needs and interests of women.[4] At the national level, governments accelerated the process of setting up machinery to promote women's interests (women's bureaux, units, ministries).

The form and nature of the different national machineries inevitably varied according to the political and social system in each country, but they were broadly of three types: those within the formal apparatus of the legislature or executive – such as women's ministries; those with largely advisory status, either within or outside the formal government structure; and those connected with or within a national political party. By the end of the 1970s, six countries had fully-fledged ministries; the majority of others had units without ministerial status attached to the government bureaucracy – bureaux, departments, divisions and so on. Their degree of autonomy ranged from considerable to extremely limited. The third type, women's organisations affiliated to a political party, were mainly found in socialist countries.

The main activities of the national machineries centred on data collection, research and publishing, and sometimes managing specific programmes and projects for women. Some were active in promoting legislation to raise the status of women, and to advance the cause of equality. Most faced multiple constraints, the most important of which was the lack of adequate financial resources.[5]

The Third UN Development Decade (1980-89) opened with the second UN Women's Conference, held in Copenhagen. Its overall themes were somewhat conventionally employment, health and education. The official conference was attended by 1500 delegates, from 145 countries, as well as intergovernmental and non-governmental organisations. Their task was to review progress made and obstacles encountered at the national level in implementing the 1975 World Plan of Action.

In reviewing progress the Conference findings were not particularly heartening. Despite some progress in certain areas and particularly in the increased attention to women in economic, social and political life, there was little cause for rejoicing: 'stagnation and deterioration describe women's condition in national life in most countries since 1975' (UN, 1980a, p.3).

Despite increases in overall labour force participation rates, women were working primarily in the lowest paid and most sex differentiated occupations, particularly in the service sector. Furthermore, the treatment and definitions of economic activity in planning were still in terms of the market, thus ignoring much of women's non-market and home-based productive activity. While there was some improvement in the ratio of girls to boys enrolled in school, sex-stereotyping in educational materials and courses and continuing high female illiteracy rates were worrying. With respect to health, the Conference concluded that 'the situation has not improved much since 1975' (UN, 1980, p.6). The same could be said for political participation, the rates for which did not reflect apparent institutional and legislative gains. Furthermore a substantial gap still remained between these gains and socio-economic and political equality.

The Conference was unanimous about the need for improvement in the lives of women, particularly in the south. Issues such as equality of wages, redefinition of the term 'worker', the need for improved health, education and employment opportunities were all agreed on; links between certain development issues, e.g. the decline in agricultural production, women's labour input and the inadequacy of their economic and social rewards were made for the first time. On a more positive note, it was found that women themselves were becoming better organised and beginning to mobilise internationally around issues affecting their lives.

Conference delegates also reviewed the draft World Programme of Action which had been drawn up at prior preparatory regional meetings. When approved, the Programme would serve as a guide for international, regional and national activities till the end of the Women's Decade in 1985. Sharp ideological splits between north and south, socialist and capitalist countries made it seem unlikely that agreement could be reached. Special attention was paid to three groups of women: refugees and displaced women, women in southern Africa, and Palestinian women living within and outside the occupied territories. A significant point of confrontation was the issue of Palestine which delayed approval of the final draft of the WPA as Israel, USA, and Canada strongly objected to the inclusion of Zionism as one of the 'isms' that was a continuing barrier to development. After much debate and many attempts at compromise, all three countries voted against the Programme.

Another divisive issue was that of cultural imperialism. Delegates from the former Soviet Union, Byelorussia and several developing countries argued that since their languages did not have a word for 'sexism', to include the term in the Programme was to impose a Western concept. Eventually, the relevant paragraph had a footnote explaining 'sexism' as a term used in Western countries. References to violence against women were again objectionable to the former Soviet Union which claimed wife battering was unknown in the country. UNICEF's call to end female circumcision provoked North African and Middle Eastern delegates to argue that only African and Middle Eastern women had the right to speak out on the issue. Finally, the insistence by Eastern European delegates that peace and disarmament should be discussed was interpreted by many Western delegates as political manouvering. Despite these disagreements, the WPA was finally adopted with four countries voting against and seven abstentions.

The WPA's 218 paragraphs include a call for all UN members to create the conditions that will improve the economic, social and political status of women; to set up government machinery to promote women's interests, and to support women's own organisational initiatives: '(a)t the grassroots level, such organisations of women will serve as forums for women to gain self-reliance and will eventually enable women to obtain real access to resources and power' (UN, 1980b, p.105). It also calls for even greater efforts to be made to collect and record sex disaggregated economic and social statistics so as to make women's contributions to development visible.

By the end of the Copenhagen Conference over 70 countries had signed the UN *Convention on the Elimination of All Forms Of Discrimination Against Women*, thereby bringing the 30 article document into force. The Convention sets out in legally binding form internationally accepted principles and measures to achieve equal rights for women everywhere.

The UN Conference was again shadowed by an NGO meeting – the Forum, for which over 8000 NGOs and individuals had registered. Debate at the Forum was also heated, but there was less political stalemate than at the Conference. Issues discussed included abortion, anti-nuclear activity, progress in Iran and Nicaragua, wages for housework, the traffic in women, and sexual violence. There was also growing consensus that the basic problem for women was not their integration into development but the very nature of development itself, its goals and the processes involved in reaching them. And recognition too of the very tenacious resistance to women's demands for a redistribution of resources and values from men to women.

Summary conclusions

Within the development field, the focus on poverty and meeting basic needs helped to get women seen as both critical agents and neglected beneficiaries of the development process. Accordingly, policies were oriented around poverty relief, with emphasis on women's importance in basic needs provision. Although some feminist groups and individuals were also arguing that the whole issue of women's role in development has implications for men and for existing structures of power and the sexual division of labour, much of mainstream WID did not stretch to this analysis (this point will be discussed in Chapter 8 at greater length).[6]

Concern for women did not bring about significant changes in the way the development industry worked, but the UN's promotion of the issue gave a considerable filip to the women involved. The UN's endorsement of national machinery to deal with women's issues, and to give women a greater voice in government policy was welcomed, and by the end of the Decade an increasing number of governments had set up women's bureaux or women's ministries. The endorsement of the *Convention on the Elimination of All Forms of Discrimination Against Women* and even the adoption of the WPA gave women's organisations in many countries a framework and a justification for their activities and demands.

Notes

1 During the 1960s the pill became widely available in Western countries usually on prescription, and always with prior medical examination. In LDCs the pill was also rapidly disseminated, often by highly questionable methods. For example in Indonesia, inundation techniques were favoured which meant that many women began to use the pill without adequate preliminary medical examination. Intra-uterine devices (IUDs) were also widely promoted even though no aftercare service was offered, despite evidence that their use should be carefully monitored (particularly their long-term use given the possibility of ectopic pregnancy).

2 Some ten years earlier the Swedish parliament approved a budget allocation to support women in developing countries as a result of a report from Ambassador Inga Thorsson that development was leaving women behind. Nine years later the Swedish aid agency (SIDA) made an analysis of the situation in developing countries which pointed to a lack of knowledge concerning women's opportunities to participate in social and economic development. However, the agency rejected providing support for women because the situation of women 'could apparently be improved only if the situation of all neglected groups in society were to improve – groups in which women often were the majority.' A further seven years passed before SIDA agreed to appoint a women and development officer (see Himmelstrand in Staudt, 1990).

3 The paternalistic tone of the Percy Amendment gives perhaps an indication of the difficult time the WID office was going to have. Kate Staudt writes that: 'WID office advocates pursued internal bureaucratic politics to encourage the agency to include men and women equitably in development but could document little concrete progress: no more than 4 per cent of development funding went to women and development; one-tenth or less of the agricultural projects ... specified a women's component; fewer than one-fifth of all international trainees were female' (see Staudt in Staudt, 1990).

4 Examples include the Association of African Women for Research and Development (AAWORD) based in Senegal; *Communicacion, Intercambio y Desarrollo Humano en America Latina* (CIDHAL) in Mexico; and the Women and Development Unit (WAND) in Barbados.

5 Such problems are not confined to national machinery. Lack of resources and unpredictability of income also bedevil both INSTRAW and UNIFEM which rely on voluntary contributions from UN member governments.

6 Feminist groups did meet under the aegis of the Asian and Pacific Centre for Women and Development in 1979 to discuss the specific ways in which women's subordination is embedded in different cultures and the strategies required to revive it (UNAPCWD, 1979).

3 The lost decade of the 1980s

The decade opened in the context of global recession and a deteriorating economic situation in the Industrialised Market Economies (IMEs) and increasing indebtedness in the developing world. Of the IMEs, all but Japan showed rates of growth of about half or less than that recorded at the end of the 1970s (Cornia *et al.*, 1987).

The global economy in disarray

The causes of the recession were varied and complex, but certain factors played a key role. Firstly, sharp oil price rises in 1973 and 1979 caused serious balance of payments problems for oil-importing countries, while oil-exporters accumulated large financial reserves and anxiously sought suitable investment opportunities. Secondly, in their attempts to industrialise and modernise, developing countries had always had to borrow money from governments, aid agencies and private banks. With their coffers swollen by petro-dollars, banks were keen to lend in the 1970s, even to countries which were already quite highly committed. While the global economy was buoyant this did not pose a significant problem, but, with escalating interest rates, by the 1980s many of these countries were experiencing serious repayment difficulties. At the same time, and thirdly, falling commodity prices and increased protectionism in the Western industrialised countries led to a sharp drop in many developing countries' income.

Growing trade imbalances and in particular the large trade deficit in the United States led to increasing financial insecurity in world markets. Between 1983 and 1985 the United States accumulated a debt of US$250 billion, almost half the outstanding commercial debt of all developing countries (UNCTAD, 1987). By 1989 this had risen to a staggering $500 billion (almost equal to the LDCs total commercial debt (UNICEF, 1989). Lastly, the monetarist policies adopted in several industrialised countries to counter inflation had the result of restricting the money supply and causing sharp increases in real interest rates which had particularly devastating effects on debtor developing countries (Cornia *et al.*, 1987).

The scourge of debt in developing countries

To fund their programmes of industrialisation and provision of infrastructure, rural development and agricultural modernisation, most of the LDCs had borrowed money freely in the 1970s (particularly when petro-dollars were being recycled through the world system) both from multilateral sources and commercial banks. Interest rates were quite low initially, but when the US, as a means of coping with its own massive balance of payments deficit and deteriorating export competitiveness, raised interest rates sharply to attract foreign investment, the LDCs' burden of debt began to cause problems. Most countries were facing real rates of interest of more than 15 per cent (UNCTAD, 1987) and many were experiencing severe difficulties in repaying their debts. By the early-1980s many of them were having to arrange for their debts to be rescheduled by negotiating new loans to repay existing ones, but often at shorter maturity dates. The worst affected regions were Latin America (commercial [bank] debt) and sub-Saharan Africa (bilateral [government-to-government] debt). The World Bank estimated the total level of developing country debt at US$ 562 billion in 1982.

Banks were relatively content to roll over debts as long as they received interest (and with such high interest rates, the cumulative interest often outstripped the original debt). But after the 1981 moratorium on repayment of the Mexican debt and with fears that other heavily endebted South American countries might also suspend payment, attitudes hardened and capital flows dropped off sharply. Commercial bank lending to the LDCs declined from $38 billion in 1980 to $15 billion in 1985 (World Bank figures cited in Cornia *et al.*, 1987, p.14).

Since the mid-1980s both commercial banks and donor governments have been preparing themselves to write-off or write-down much of the debt. Unilateral action by debtor nations in the late-1980s (e.g. the Brazilian suspension in 1987) was less of a threat to solvency than in the early-1980s: loan-loss provisions have been increased, capital bases strengthened, and non-LDC business expanded. Many development practitioners and NGOs in the UK now argue that the creditor banks should forgive the debt and wipe the slate clean or allow debtor governments to repay the debt in the form of loans or grants to national development programmes (see Payer, 1991).

At the end of 1988 it was estimated by the World Bank that the total debt of developing countries was around $1,020 billion, or around 50 per cent of their combined GNP. On average, debt repayment claimed about 25 per cent of the developing world's export revenues. Even more grotesque is the fact that capital flows have reversed. While in 1979 roughly $40 billion flowed to the developing countries from the industrial north, by the mid-1980s the flow was the other way: '(t)aking everything into account – loans, aid, repayment of interest and capital – the southern world is now transferring at least $20 billion a year to the northern hemisphere' (UNICEF, 1989, p.15). Between 1984 and 1985 the developing countries transferred a net amount of $163 billion to the industrialised north (South Commission, 1990).

The LDCs were also having to cope with much reduced prices for many of their basic export commodities. Though primary commodity prices kept pace with inflation during the 1970s, they declined at a rate of 15 per cent per year between 1980 and 1982. By the end of 1986, prices had fallen to one-third of their 1980 level. In real terms, that is in terms of the prices of manufactures exported by the IMEs, they had fallen by 37 per cent (UNCTAD, 1987). In 1986 alone, for example, falling prices for raw materials wiped $19 billion from sub-Saharan Africa's export revenues – about four times the amount the region received in emergency aid (UNICEF, 1989). Taking the much reduced price of LDC raw materials supplied to the IMEs into account, it can be said that the effective transfer of resources from the LDCs to the IMEs may in fact be as much as $60 billion per annum (UNICEF, 1989).

The low rates of demand for LDC products and lowered prices, high debt repayment and lack of investment capital have led to low rates of growth and even absolute declines in many of the key indicators of economic well-being. On average, the fall in GDP growth rates of the developing countries was sharper than that in IMEs, for example, in Africa, per capita income growth rates have been negative in the 1980s, reaching a staggering –5.2 per cent in 1987. In Latin America, the situation at first glance does not appear so severe: it shows stagnation rather than collapse, with GDP around 2 per cent and per capita income growth fluctuating between low negatives and positives. However, such figures disguise great inequalities within the continent. While the per capita income of the average Latin American in 1988 was 9 per cent lower than in 1980, Enrique Iglesias, President of the Inter-American Development Bank, noted that in some countries the standard of living had slipped back to what it was 20 years before (cited in UNICEF, 1989, p.16). South and East Asia have been less badly affected because of their greater self-reliance and lower levels of indebtedness relative to GNP.

The neo-liberal response

For the crisis-ridden LDCs, the recommended solutions have been stabilisation and structural adjustment policies designed to bring their sick economies back to health. Stabilisation policy packages are designed to induce relatively rapid adjustment through controlling demand. Although they are negotiated between the IMF and individual governments, packages usually involve devaluation, and fiscal and monetary restraint to reduce real income and thus domestic demand both for imports and exports. With a reduction in imports and an expansion of exports, balance of payments should be achieved fairly rapidly (stabilisation packages are generally intended to achieve their aim within a couple of years). Structural adjustment policy packages (SAP), in contrast, emphasise supply: they seek to cure balance of payments problems by expanding and diversifying production of exports. They have a longer time frame – three to five years – and attempt to increase both productivity and efficiency (Elson, 1987, 1990).

Both policy interventions emphasise the need to decrease the role of the state and to increase the role of the market in allocating resources. LDCs' poor economic performance and inability to cope with the deteriorating international economic environment are considered to be due to an over-extended public sector and widespread use of controls and subsidies to encourage or hamper entrepreneurial performance. The solution is thus to cut back state activity which involves cuts in public expenditure (e.g. on social services, government employment), to loosen controls over imports and foreign exchange, and to eliminate subsidies (providing cheap food for the poor and low-cost agricultural inputs for farmers). Private investment and entrepreneurship are encouraged by improved incentives (particularly for exports), lower taxes, higher prices, and the privatisation of government enterprises such as marketing boards, factories and hospitals.

How have LDCs been persuaded to accept structural adjustment or stabilisation policies? Once again, generalisations may promote a distorted picture because the peculiarities of economic problems vary greatly between countries. Nevertheless, in those parts of sub-Saharan Africa and Latin America where these policies have been extensively adopted, the need for additional funds to meet mounting debts has been critical. Since the commercial banks are no longer willing to lend, and much bilateral (government to government) aid is also contingent upon the adoption of structural adjustment packages, LDCs have been forced to turn to the lenders of last resort, the International Monetary Fund (IMF) or the World Bank (IBRD) whose loans are conditional upon acceptance of these packages. Between 1980 and 1985, 65 countries accepted IMF adjustment programmes: 21 in Latin America, 31 in Africa and 13 in Asia. In 1989, 70 developing countries were implementing some form of structural adjustment programme.

Effects of the policies

The success – or otherwise – of the policies dominating the 1980s is already the subject of considerable debate. In purely economic terms some countries, such as Ghana, are apparently undergoing a degree of recovery. Ghana adopted an Economic Recovery Programme (ERP) in April 1983 with IMF support. In 1984, GDP rose by 7.6 per cent, in part because of increased food production. It rose again in 1985 by 5.3 per cent and in 1986 by 5.6 per cent. The extent to which this is the direct effect of an increased injection of funds rather than a reflection of long-term stability is of course open to question. But recovery at what cost to the mass of the population? In terms of human welfare – the standard of living of the majority of the population, their access to adequate food, health services, education and income – assessment is partial, but the signs are not reassuring.

Few studies have as yet been published on the impact of SAP but there are clear indications that they have had negative effects on distribution, incomes and provision of basic services in many adjusting countries (see, for example, Cornia et al., 1987). In some countries government spending on critical social infrastructure has been reduced, while that on defence has usually gone up. In the 37 poorest nations of the world, per capita expenditure on health has been reduced by 50 per cent, and that on education by 25 per cent over the last ten years (UNICEF, 1989). The rationale for such cuts is phrased in terms of 'efficiency', increased private and self-provision of services being emphasised. That this will almost invariably be a semi-invisible cost to most women is a fact which has been by-passed; we will return to this below.

Although impressive gains have been made in certain aspects of health during the decade, increased malnutrition and falling educational standards are evident. Between 1980 and 1987 the rate of decline of the under-five mortality rate has clearly slowed down in 16 countries – ten in Africa and six in Latin America (UNICEF, 1989). Cornia et al.'s (1987) study for UNICEF, *Adjustment With A Human Face*, reports increased malnutrition in almost all the ten countries studied. The deterioration has been particularly pronounced in Ghana and Peru: in Ghana the study noted an increase between 1980 and 1983 from 34 to 52 per cent of children whose weight for age was below the third percentile.

Decline in nutritional status obviously has much to do with reduced food subsidies, increased real prices and lack of employment opportunities. In sub-Saharan Africa these problems have been compounded by adverse climatic conditions. However, Cornia concludes that '... the main forces behind the observed increase in malnutrition were of an economic nature' (Cornia et al., 1987, p.31). Failure to feed a population adequately can have as much to do with inequalities in distribution as with inadequacies in production: in Latin America around 25 million children do not receive enough food, despite the fact that the region has become, after the United States, the world's second major food exporter (UNICEF, 1989). With respect to education, primary school enrolment rates have declined and drop-outs increased. There have also been substantial losses of qualified teachers. The implications for future literacy levels are understandably disturbing.

Overall, Cornia et al. argue that both the proportion and the absolute number of people living below a given poverty line has increased in six of the ten countries studied. Of the rest, only one (South Korea) shows a clear decline in poverty; for the other three the evidence is unclear.

Recently, the argument that radical adjustment would in the short run be painful but in the longer term lead to increased wealth and benefits for all has been modified. The idea that adjustment must be with a 'human face' has gained currency in international development circles. What is meant is the targeting of interventions to the most vulnerable groups, and raising productivity in low-income employment such as small-scale farming and informal sector activity (a return to basic needs).

On balance the neo-liberals' monetarist policies have not been shown to work particularly well. Keith Griffin argues that 'because the strategy tends to neglect macro-economic policy, monetarist approaches to development policy are likely to lead to high unemployment of labour and low utilisation of installed capacity. ... The ideal circumstances required for a monetarist strategy to work properly are in practice unreal.' (Griffin, 1989, p.229). The South Commission has even sharper words of criticism:

> The policy package the IMF has made its standard recipe has been based on a doctrinaire belief in the efficacy of market forces. Financial liberalisation in conditions of inflation has aggravated inflation. Import liberalisation when foreign exchange was extremely scarce has enlarged payments deficits, leading to steeper devaluations than would otherwise have been necessary. Pressure to expand exports – exerted simultaneously on a number of developing countries exporting the same commodity – has led to oversupply, causing prices and earnings to sag for all of them. While lip-service has been paid to the need for adjustment to lead to growth, adjustment has invariably stifled growth and, by causing investment to contract, jeopardised future growth. The drive to secure financial balance in the short run has been at the cost of output and employment as well as of consumption. The poorest people have borne the greatest hardship. (The South Commission, 1990, Overview and Summary, p.11)

The effects on women

The recession and the accompanying adjustment process have been examined in terms both of their impact on women and of the critical role of women in relieving their negative effects. Less attention has been paid to how the dynamics of gender – the socially structured and economically conditioned relations between men and women – affect these processes. Because women and women-headed households predominate among the poor, women (and children) inevitably emerge as those suffering most from reduced food availability, social infrastructure and so on. What little research there is on women and structural adjustment predominantly catalogues the directly negative effects on women as mothers: increases in anaemia among pregnant women; maternal mortality and so on (see Vickers, 1991 on case studies). Statistics on, for example, maternal mortality, are indeed appalling. In sub-Saharan Africa there are currently 700 maternal deaths for very 100,000 live births and in Asia, 500. The figure for IMEs is less than 10 (UNICEF, 1989). However, there are multiple other ramifications to be considered.

Structural adjustment affects women in a number of ways: through the impact of changes in income and prices, in the level and composition of public expenditure, or through changes in working conditions (Elson, 1987). The most damaging may well be the latter two.

Income will change because of the requirement to freeze (state) wages, to curtail employment in the state sector and because the level of demand for the products of the self-employed declines. Prices of the most basic purchases such as food, kerosene and clothing are likely to be the first affected when subsidies are removed. Cornia *et al.* (1987) note that women play a critical part in strategies to offset the effects of adjustment policies, especially those concerned with containing the impact of the fall in income within acceptable limits.[1] These strategies centre on both changed household consumption and increased labour force participation. Women have been crucial in increasing production for household use, particularly of food, and increasing provision of services such as childcare. For example, in Latin America, Mother Clubs have been set up to share childcare responsibilities; communal kitchens (*comedores populares*) enable groups of women to lower the cost of feeding their families by sharing food buying and cooking. Women's strategies for improving their use of existing resources have not only included changing food preparation habits and consumption patterns but, critically, they have not been able to change intra-household food distribution patterns. The evidence on this is not conclusive, but there are indications that where there is already sex bias in the allocation of food, the decline in availability is also distributed in an inegalitarian way (Hassan *et al.*, 1989; Chen *et al.*, 1981).

Women have also increased their labour force participation in many areas, though this is usually in unstable informal sector employment. The importance of small-scale business and entrepreneurship is currently receiving a great deal of attention in both academic and policymaking circles. In many ways, the expansion of unregulated market activity is seen as a vindication of the free market strategy and female 'entrepreneurs' are targeted as a vital element in this. However, as we shall see in Chapter 6, there is inadequate examination of the ways the genders are incorporated into the 'informal sector' and acknow-ledgement of the extent to which women are more likely to end up as marginalised casual workers than as successful entrepreneurs.

Increased labour force participation places certain constraints on the time women can spend on childcare and nutrition-related activities, and unless some of these are taken on by others in the family, levels of care will probably decline. There is no evidence that the intra-household division of labour has moved in the direction of men taking on more domestic tasks, so one must assume that children, and probably daughters, are most likely to be required to take them on. Analyses of structural adjustment and of women's critical role within it have yet to confront socially structured gender relations which are themselves crucial determinants of who bears the brunt of the impact of adjustment. Until they do, the dangerous assumption is perpetuated that the increase in women's unpaid labour input is not a significant cost: 'Women's unpaid labour is implicitly regarded as elastic – able to stretch so as to make up any short fall in other resources available for reproduction and maintenance of human resources' (Elson, 1987, p.4).

Reducing state expenditures on welfare and opening the economy to competitive market forces affects women directly and in ways different from men. Given their involvement in childcare and domestic work (the reproduction and maintenance of human resources), women are more dependent than men on public-sector services (water supplies, electricity, waste disposal and other sanitation measures, education and health facilities, public transport). Public expenditure changes lead to user charges and the closing of facilities. As we have noted, the trimming down of state expenditure on social provision is advocated on the assumption that this will create opportunities for private entrepreneurship. There is another, but unspoken assumption, that much of the extra work created will be taken up by 'the family'; in other words, women. The adaptive strategies at household level to changes in the availability of food, employment, health services and so on (such as seeking out different and cheaper foods, nursing sick children instead of attending a clinic, spending more time in diverse income-generating activities) include time costs which it is implicitly assumed women will bear.

Most research into women's position indicates considerable complementarity between state provision of services and women's ability to undertake economic activities. Given women's weaker social position and their double burden of unpaid reproductive work and paid work in producing goods and services, they cannot compete on equal terms with men in the market. So diminished workplace regulation (of conditions of work, levels of pay, access to training, etc.) is likely to operate against their interests. Changes in working conditions may include the expectation that employees will put in longer hours of paid work and/or increase their number of unsocial hours; for women this will have to be added to the longer hours of unpaid work they have to do as they adapt to reduced public expenditure (Elson, 1987, 1990).

Changes brought about by market liberalisation will have different and contradictory impacts on women of different social groups; some women may benefit from higher prices for agricultural products (if they are own account farmers) although removal of subsidies on fertilisers etc. may wipe out that benefit. The restriction on imports may stimulate domestic production of alternatives, and also benefit traders in these goods. Although the major emphasis is on production for export, where small-scale producers (farmers in particular) are able to expand their production for the domestic market, they will no doubt benefit. Expansion in processing of local products may give rise

38

to a small-scale domestic manufacturing sector, which may, though not necessarily, increase women's income and self-reliance.

Most observers now agree that the neo-liberal solution to debt and other LDC economic problems – structural adjustment – puts enormous pressure on most sectors of the population, but especially on the poorest. As we saw, the South Commission noted that it is the poorest who suffer the most hardship; but among the poor, women are suffering disproportionately. As one observer has put it '...within the poorer groups, the main burden has passed yet again from the men to the women' (Clark, 1986, p.68). Grave as present suffering is, the long-term outcome is also bleak. 'Equally serious and just as important has been the erosion of investment in the region's people – its "human capital" – as expenditures in health, education and nutrition have been severely cut in this decade. Unfortunately this means that the costs of this economic crisis will continue to be paid by new generations of Latin Americans' (Enrique Iglesias cited in Vickers, 1991, p.17).

The consolidation of WID

During the 1980s, the WID lobby grew both in size and assurance. Its institutional base expanded and its influence became more marked. It is now accepted that the 'women's dimension' of any development project deserves consideration, although in practice this may only lead to trivial adjustments. With the retrenchment of the anti-poverty policies of the 1970s and the concentration on economic growth, restructuring and the benefits of market forces and international trade, efficiency has become the catchword in development circles. Promoting the efficiency of women in their production activities has therefore become critical.

Throughout the 1980s institutional WID activists continued to insist that women's invisibility to planners and development practitioners alike was the result of poor data bases and thus their claim to lack of knowledge of women's lives and family systems was genuine. The WID strategy was to argue for, and in the case of several major donor agencies including USAID, to fund, efforts to collect relevant data. The UN itself began to look at census categories, modifying some to become more 'women sensitive', adding a number of questions to standard census questionnaires, disaggregating many of the basic indicators. Many agencies also funded specific pieces of research. As a result, by the end of the 1980s a very large body of data had been assembled (although its quality is still variable) on a range of women's activities and concerns.[2]

Much of the data focuses on women's roles as producers, reflecting the concern that women are a neglected resource for development. Especially during the early part of the 1980s, it became commonplace to hear the argument that perpetuating such neglect is inefficient. Funding emphasis shifted from poverty and the meeting of basic needs towards utilising women more efficiently. As a result, women's entrepreneurial and income-generating activities were encouraged, often to the neglect of their implications for women's time and existing burden of work. Towards the end of the 1980s increasing poverty in most developing countries has again brought the issue of women's welfare to the fore. However, this time round greater weight is being given to the structural causes of their impoverishment.

Academics contributed by producing books and articles on a very wide range of issues – on the whole from a perspective which is much more critical of development practice and impact than the institutional WID literature. Some of this literature addressed the question of gender relations and how changes in social and economic processes affect them. Increasingly too, activists began to contribute to this literature, bringing up a number of issues which, although central to women's lives, had been largely avoided by institutional WID. These concerned violence within individual relationships (a point of contention at the 1980 Copenhagen Conference) as well as in society as a whole; deeply coercive male-female relations which take the form of quasi-slavery, the traffic in women (enforced prostitution) and the international sex tourism industry.

It is a tribute to the persistence of activists and academics alike, that by the 1985 UN Conference to assess the achievements of the Women's Decade (held in Nairobi), such issues were not only accepted aspects of the international women's movement but were given support by institutionalised WID. The *Forward Looking Strategies* (FLS), the major document to come out of the Nairobi Conference, cites violence against women as an important obstacle to progress, and it is the explicit focus of seven of its 372 paragraphs. The document makes clear that economic development does not automatically benefit women and highlights both unequal economic relations between countries and between the sexes. Although adopted by consensus, certain sections of the FLS document caused controversy. The issues of Zionism and the situation of Palestinian women and children were again debated at great length, though this time an acceptable compromise was reached; the term Zionism being replaced by 'all forms of racism', these being agreed to be major obstacles to women's advancement. Paragraphs placing the blame for the economic crisis (and its consequent adverse effects on women in many LDCs) on the coercive measures adopted by some industrialised countries (including trade restrictions), were also forced to a vote, rather than being adopted by consensus.

Hilkka Pietila and Jeanne Vickers in *Making Women Matter* (1990) suggest that the main strategy of the FLS to advance the situation for women is to ensure women get access to education at all levels. They go on to note that '(i)n order to redirect development to correspond with women's views and aspirations, it is necessary that women have access to power and to participation in designing, planning and decision-making on development in all walks of life and at all levels of society, on an equal footing with men.' (1990, pp.67-8).

The sheer size of the Nairobi Conference and the achievement of greater consensus than at Copenhagen, indicate both the strength and consolidation of the WID movement and also its growing political sophistication. Over 2000 government delegates attended the World Conference (representing 157 states plus Namibia), three-quarters of whom were women. Some 700 NGO representatives also participated as observers. The attendance at the NGO meeting – Forum 85 – outstripped all estimates (and almost the capacity of the organisers to cope), and was unofficially put at 20,000.

The Nairobi Conference also served as a forum to discuss national and international machinery designed to further women's interests. By 1985 most countries had some form of national machinery: 16 per cent were ministries (22 per cent attached to the Ministry of Social Affairs or Social Welfare), 17 per cent were located in the office of the Prime Minister, and 20 per cent were NGOs. Of the units within government, more than half had been set up since 1980. However, in spite of their proliferation, many of these units were not very effective. They were still inadequately funded, lacked trained personnel and had little or no political clout. All too often they were predominantly concerned with welfare issues.

The situation in many of the aid agencies was found to be equally disheartening. A good example is that of the United States Agency for International Development (USAID): the WID office was founded in 1974 but its continuing existence was always under threat since many mainstream USAID officials felt that a separate office was unnecessary, and that women's issues should be integrated into the agency's overall·work (but without any mechanism to ensure this occurs). Its budget has fluctuated from an initial $0.3 million to over $2 million in 1982/3, down to $0.75 million by 1985. Consistent attempts to confront bureaucratic resistance and to move from a paternalistic concern with integrating and encouraging women to an emphasis on women's empowerment, has meant that, as the WID office personnel have become more vocal, USAID has accordingly chipped away at its resources and staff (Staudt and Jacquette, 1988; Staudt, 1990).[3]

In many of the aid agencies some provision is made for the monitoring and evaluation of the effects of their activities on women. However, this is often more rhetorical than real, especially in those agencies which have neither a women's section, nor a policy for women. But in some the realisation that women do not have the same needs and interests as men and that accommodation has to be made to both if development efforts are to be successful (quite apart from issues of social justice), has resulted in mechanisms being set up to ensure practitioners take women's needs into account and attempt to include them in decision-making. A good example here is the Canandian aid agency CIDA, which puts all its officers through a brief training course to raise their awareness of the false assumptions held about men's and women's activities and needs. It also has a WID office which gives advice on the ways in which women's needs can be included in project practice. None the less resistance is widespread, and the argument for integration of women's concerns in all policymaking is often a mask for allowing the issue to be marginalised.

More significantly, the Decade has also witnessed the growth and increasing strength of women's own organisations, from the village to the international level. Some of these NGOs have been established to mobilise women around specific issues, aiming to meet clearly identified and often shorter term objectives. Others are more involved in research, 'networking' and raising the profile of women's issues internationally. Examples of the latter include DAWN (Development Alternatives for Women in a New Era) which is 'explicitly reinforcing the development of international feminist alternatives based on Third World perceptions and interests' (Staudt and Jacquette, 1988, p.274), and the Women Living Under Islamic Laws network.

One of the greatest benefits of the UN Women's Decade and its three international conferences has been that women from almost every country in the world have been able to meet, share experiences, debate needs, priorities and strategies. The embryonic international women's movement has the potential of bridging the divisions between women in different areas of the world and also of providing a force which will impell and support those within institutional WID to be more bold in challenging the structures of inequality, as well as supporting multifarious local women's groups. The organisation of women themselves is perhaps the greatest hope women have that the world can be changed.

Summary conclusions

The third UN Development Decade (1980-9) had mixed effects for women. On the one hand, the world recession, the problems of debt and economic crisis, and the policies of structural adjustment have greatly worsened the lives of a vast number of women. More positively, the decade has also witnessed mounting evidence of women's wish and capacity to take their problems into their own hands through organisation and action.

Newly-established women's bureaux and ministries were anxious to 'visibilise' women by, for example, improving data collection techniques and national accounting procedures. But their capacity to change the situation which the mass of data collected revealed, was limited. The majority of women's bureaux were located in government ministries concerned with welfare and social questions, such as social security, health, welfare or youth; they therefore had little power or influence. Not only was the association of women with their traditional caring role institutionalised, but bureaux were thereby denied leverage over critical planning areas and excluded from crucial decision-making processes. Furthermore, in times of competing claims for scarce resources, particularly in economic crises, welfare is usually the first to face cutbacks. Women's bureaux, ministries, etc. faced other grave problems – lack of skilled staff and – critically – social and cultural attitudes which reinforce prejudices and stereotypes about appropriate roles for women in society. As became evident by the end of the Women's Decade, much of the support for integrating women into development was more rhetorical than real; women's bureaux were never backed by adequate financial or political commitment. Although they performed a useful role in sensitising government bureaucracies to women's needs, by the end of the Decade it was clear that the existence of national machineries cannot be taken as evidence of a substantive commitment to the eradication of structural inequalities between men and women. Furthermore, as these units become more institutionalised, there is a danger they will be seen as the only legitimate links between the government and the majority of women, thus marginalising the work of autonomous women's organisations.

Autonomous women's organisations have served three very important functions: mobilising low-income women; monitoring and evaluating government programmes and policies; providing a space within which awareness and empowerment can develop. Their ability to influence government policies has been variable, but they have had some marked successes in terms of providing special services for women (credit, banking, insurance, refuge from violence, sexual education and family planning). When it comes to the broader question of transforming the status of women and raising general levels of consciousness the picture is less clear. Grass roots organisations can be rather parochial, they may be more concerned with welfare issues than issues of structural inequalities between men and women. Some women's organisations set up by upper and middle-class women, lack sensitivity to the needs of poorer women despite their desire to work for them. Organisations based on membership of political parties or movements have their own internal constraints to adopting women's expressed concerns. And of course it has to be recognised that many more women are not within any organisation at all. How are these women's needs and concerns to be articulated and brought to public and policymaking awareness?

Over the three decades we have examined, the analysis of women's role in development has shown a number of shifts in the perception of the nature of the problem and its solutions. In the main these changing perceptions have gone with the grain of mainstream development thinking rather than against it. To a large extent they have addressed issues to do with what we call women's material condition rather than their position in society relative to men (Young, 1988).

Initially concerns were phrased largely in terms of welfare: what could be done to ensure that women had the conditions which enabled them to meet the needs of their children and their families. They were seen largely as mothers and carers rather than as economic actors. With the entry of the WID lobby into the debate, the focus shifted briefly to equity (helping women gain access to the public arena on an equal footing to men). The shortcomings of the whole development process becoming all too evident by the mid-1970s, attention then turned to poverty alleviation and meeting the needs of the poorest of the poor. Women as economic actors were seen as critical resources for the poor. In the 1980s' economic crisis the focus shifted to efficiency, on improving women's productive contribution within the framework of the market system. Thanks to the growing band of women from developing countries who are adding their voices to conventional WID demands, and to those, north and south, questioning the meaning of development for women, the demand now is for empowerment, for enabling women to take control over their own lives. Whether this demand, like the earlier one for equity, will be subverted by bureaucratic and other forms of resistance remains to be seen.

Notes

1 Jeanne Vickers notes that UNICEF estimates a 2-3 per cent decline in national income results in at least a 10-15 per cent decline in income of the poorest classes (Vickers, 1991). She also cites Enrique Iglesias, President of the Inter-American Development Bank who, in a speech in 1988, stated that the per capita income of the average Latin American is 9 per cent lower today than it was in 1980. 'This is the average. It does not take much imagination to realise that behind this statistic are plummeting real wage levels, soaring unemployment (some open, some hidden), increased levels of marginality and acute poverty – in short, an erosion of every measure of social well-being. Today, one-third of Latin America's population – 130 million people – live in dire poverty.' (Vickers, 1991 p.17).
2 The Government of India in 1990 asked women's organisations to propose changes in census categories, and also questions they would like to see asked in the upcoming census. Most of the new questions focused on the unpaid labour of women in the household and women's work in the informal sector.
3 For an analysis of the difficulties of getting WID issues accepted within bureaucracies see Staudt, 1990. The case of a country like Sweden, seen by many as liberal and progressive and in the vanguard of WID promotion is particularly instructive. From the decision of parliament to pay special attention to women in 1964 it took almost 15 years for the Swedish Aid Agency (SIDA) to allow one officer to be in charge of WID matters. Her resource base was tiny. In 1980 it was announced that the WID unit was a temporary arrangement, since women's concerns were to be integrated into all SIDA's programmes. Steady pressure and strategic thinking has led to the employment of local WID officers in the main field offices, and a person on the SIDA Executive having responsibility for WID issues within the organisation (Himmelstrand in Staudt, 1990).

4 Women and agriculture: The case of sub-Saharan Africa

Development strategies in the 1950s and 1960s, as we saw from Chapter 1, aimed to facilitate LDCs' take-off into economic growth and modernisation. They envisaged greater specialisation in the division of labour, urbanisation and industrialisation, and the decline of the agricultural sector in terms both of the population involved in it and the proportion of GDP produced by it. None the less agriculture had an important role to play: it was to provide both the resources – physical, human and financial – to fuel modern-sector growth, and use its goods and services. The agricultural sector was to provide: food and other wage goods to meet the needs of the (expanding) urban population; raw materials for domestic industry; young people (almost entirely conceived of as male) to provide the labour force for the new industrial enterprises; capital from rural savings and taxes to finance both private and state investment in industry and basic infrastructure (transport, communication and utilities); and lastly, foreign exchange from the export of primary commodities to finance both investment in industrial capacity and also the imports (foreign goods, services and technology) needed to support the growth of the industrial and modern sector. The rural population was also seen as a potential consumer of urban sector products.

As we saw in Chapter 1, the strategies used to achieve this varied, both over time and in different parts of the world. In this chapter we will largely concentrate on sub-Saharan Africa.

Agricultural development strategies

Since colonial times sub-Saharan Africa (SSA) had produced a variety of export crops and development planners continued to give them high importance as earners of much needed foreign exchange. Little heed was paid to production of food for immediate consumption. Some of the largest investments in rural SSA were in capital intensive projects designed to bring new land into production or to harness natural resources more efficiently, for example, river basin development. Other projects aimed at increasing the production of export crops, either on large commercial farms or plantations. In some areas peasant smallholders were provided with services, inputs, access to credit, marketing facilities, and agricultural extension so as to produce export crops. They were also placed under the administrative direction of project management teams or parastatal organisations.

By the mid-1960s widespread concern over the slow growth in agricultural production, whether of cash crops or export crops, relative to rapid population growth, persuaded many development experts that a more interventionist strategy for agricultural modernisation was needed. A combination of technically sophisticated measures was developed which became known as the 'Green Revolution'. This involved innovations based on biochemical advances, such as high yielding varieties (HYVs) of various grains, backed up by extensive chemical inputs (fertilisers, herbicides, pesticides), and mechanisation and modernisation of production processes – use of tractors, post-harvest technology and large-scale irrigation schemes. The most extensive use of the HYVs was in Asia; in SSA the introduction of hybrid maize and rice took second place to irrigation schemes and the introduction of tractors and other mechanical aids.

By the 1970s rural sector investments in many countries were doing much less well than anticipated; not only were returns on investment low but there were wide discrepancies in performance. Many of the centralised, top down programmes had also marginalised substantial sections of the rural population from the development process. The environmental impacts of large-scale schemes were causing great concern, as was growing rural poverty.

The search for alternatives led to reformist experiments in rural development and an explosion in micro-economic and sociological research on agricultural production, rural markets, inter-sectoral linkages, migration, and rural off-farm activities, as well as levels of nutrition, health and poverty. The results forced rural development theorists and planners to re-evaluate their conventional two-sector model of the economy. They realised that the model led them to ignore the complexities of agricultural systems, the interaction of ecological, environmental and human factors in shaping different forms of production, patterns of sectoral interdependence, and the precise nature of the connections between improved agricultural production, employment generation and demand for both rural and urban goods.

In response to this, and in keeping with the new redistribution with growth (RWG) approach (see Chapter 2), the World Bank argued that planners and their advisers had to be concerned with income distribution, employment generation, nutritional levels and basic welfare. Development meant improving the economic and social life of the rural poor: small-scale farmers, tenants and the landless. Thus the Integrated Rural Development (IRD) approach was born.

The basic objective of IRD was still to increase the amount of marketed agricultural produce. But this was to be combined with improving rural well-being by increasing the productivity and resilience of agriculture and by supporting non-agricultural productive activities, and by improving basic welfare – health, education, sanitation. In other words, rural development was no longer to be concerned solely with cash cropping, cultivation techniques and technologies, but with all aspects of rural social and economic life. Because of the highly related nature of the subsectors of the rural system and the wider economic system, rural development policy and plans had to be integrated with national development planning. At the same time, the panoply of IRD services was to be targeted at specific population groups: the poor, the landless, women and children. They were also to participate in the design of the services.

The new awareness of the complexities of rural production systems as well as concern over the inadequacies of the transfer of technology strategy, led to a revised form of rural development research: farming systems research and extension approach (FSR/E). This was an attempt to construct and implement a holistic, farmer-oriented approach to agricultural research and extension by looking at specific farming environments as systems of interacting ecological, economic, technological and societal factors. In other words it used an inter-disciplinary approach. Its aims were to identify the specific problems and needs of farming households within the context of their immediate agricul-tural/economic environment, to reduce the degree of error in technological solutions to farm-based problems, and to increase the level of contact between development practitioners and farmers themselves. Its ultimate goal was both food self-sufficiency and improvement in the quality of life of individuals. As phrases such as 'farmer back to farmer' and 'farmer first and last' imply, farmer participation was considered a vital component of the method. By getting farmers to diagnose their own problems, it was felt that resource-poor could be involved in all stages of the research, extension and delivery process.

By the mid-1980s initial enthusiasm for FSR/E had largely died; many felt it had not lived up to its promise of developing effective methods for involving rural people in the design and testing of farm technologies and techniques. Nor had rapid increases in food production in LDCs occurred (except in scattered 'progressive' regions). But some of its preoccupations have been taken up by the rapid appraisal or participatory learning methods proponents – particularly that of getting rural people to talk about how to meet their own needs by means of their own knowledge.

As rural development specialists were seeking to find ways 'to put the last first' (Chambers, 1983), the structural adjustment policies of the 1980s shifted attention back to cash crops. Adjustment policy packages emphasise the im-provement of agricultural performance, especially in export crops so as to ease balance of payments difficulties. Given the need to cut expenditure on imported foodstuffs, increasing food production is also highlighted but for the market rather than subsistence. This continues and intensifies the processes of agricultural commercialisation which have been taking place in sub-Saharan Africa since colonial times.

The overt policy rationale for promoting commercialisation is that it not only raises the income and purchasing power of the small farm household but also facilitates the propagation of improved techniques, equipment, extension and inputs. This new knowledge will then 'trickle-across' to subsistence producers.

As we have seen (in Chapters 1 and 2) most LDCs, and those in SSA are no exception, urgently require foreign exchange for modernisation, industrial development and, more recently, servicing the debt burden. The main emphasis in development policies in SSA since the 1950s has been on providing rural areas with the necessary conditions for cash cropping: building feeder roads, irrigation systems and dams, providing wells, marketing organisations and credit institutions, and using pricing policies to boost incentives. As a result the economies of many African nations were firmly tied to cash crops by the mid-1970s. In 1988 nine African countries were dependent on just one crop for over 70 per cent of their income.

The stress on producing crops for the market has contributed to the neglect of discussion on water and energy issues in rural areas. Intensive mono-cropping programmes and the bringing of ever more land – often previously wooded land – under continuous cultivation has had major ecological and environmental consequences for rural producers. The fertility of the soil has declined through over-cultivation, access to and availability of fuelwood as well as of trees to protect the land from severe erosion has been reduced, and water availability has diminished as water table levels drop under the pressure of intensive water use. Declining supplies of fuelwood and water also have serious consequences for rural women – they have to walk ever further to find water and fuel, and may even have to start cutting into wood stocks to get enough fuel for a hot meal once a day.

Problems with the strategies

An evaluation of the technical solution phase in SSA provides a rather negative picture for a variety of reasons. Numerous large-scale irrigation systems, dams and wells started or built during the 1960s and 1970s, have since deteriorated, often because of lack of qualified engineering and technical maintenance staff or inadequate training of staff. Often, after an initial investment by a donor agency, the government was expected to finance high recurring costs.

Despite a history of failure this type of project still retains its appeal. One observer noted: 'Dams are beloved of politicians, national plan makers, financiers and aid donors alike. They are potent symbols of economic virility and political prestige; they are clearly visible, concrete and finite projects, demonstrably a basis for future economic and social development' (I.Griffiths cited in Timberlake, 1985, p.82). For the people who were resettled to make way for these large-scale schemes, the reality is somewhat different: the rural community is dismembered, productive land is drowned, dams silt up, water pumps break down, agricultural production does not increase and the local area gets no wealthier.

Technical solutions fall foul of social and political ineptitude, but they also fail to work because of the assumptions built into them by (male) planners and development experts who all too often seem dazzled by the promise of the quick technological fix.

The concentration of planners on export crops and indeed cash crops, is blamed both for the decline in availability of food crops and environmental degradation. It is also often argued that cash cropping has squeezed the production of subsistence food crops – with correspondingly negative effects on women. Despite ever increasing areas of land under grain and staple food production, most output is channelled to urban and export markets because of government priorities and farmers' need for cash. Rural producers are then forced to produce their food crops on increasingly marginal and depleted land or to purchase them. The relegation of food crops to poorer quality land or the overcultivation of the small areas reserved for food crops, the tendency to cultivate them poorly or even to neglect them because of the exigencies of cash crop cultivation, all reduce the availability and variety of food crops (and often also their nutritional value). The demands made by cash crop production on both land and labour and the priority given to cash crops by governments, aid agencies and banks, make subsistence farming difficult and unattractive.

While these claims have some truth, especially those concerning land pressure, alternative analyses suggest that there is often a degree of complementarity between cash and food crops (see for example Whitehead, 1988; von Braun and Kennedy, 1986). The critical factor is the policy framework within which both are produced. Many regions are still very poorly integrated into the market. Government marketing institutions make heroic efforts to transport basic staples to the urban areas, but make little effort to stimulate the flow of goods between urban and rural areas, or indeed between different rural areas themselves. Rural producers have to face low producer prices for staples (fixed by governments to please urban consumers) and high prices for non-grain foods (because of the poor development of rural markets). Were markets better organised rural producers would be able to sell a wider range of products and at higher prices as well. As it is, many rural households barely have the means to purchase their basic necessities.

The extent to which the blame for environmental problems can be placed on cash cropping alone is unclear. The expansion of commercial farming has often involved land adjudications which lead to subsistence farmers being pushed onto more and more marginal land, thus intensifying already existing problems. But as Maxwell and Fernando note, cash cropping is not always large-scale and capital intensive: there is 'no necessary reason why the composition of output should determine the mode of production' (Maxwell and Fernando, 1987, p.21). However, there is ample evidence of links between, for example, intensive tobacco production, deforestation and soil degradation.

Impact on women

The ways in which commercialisation has caused changes in the gendered nature of SSA economies is the subject of considerable debate but the consensus is that women farmers have lost out. One reason given is the lack of recognition of women as economic actors. Although community participation in project design was encouraged in the IRD and farming systems phase, project officials largely looked for 'progressive farmers'. A complex web of class, gender, and age differentiations, meant that the poorest and most disadvantaged groups – amongst them a large proportion of rural women – were generally excluded from such meetings. As a result they had little contact with mainstream project officials and few opportunities to make their views and needs known. Women of the better-off groups were hardly consulted either – reports often note that although the women were present, it was the men who engaged with the community development officials. It is difficult to say whether traditional relations between men which included prohibition on 'outside males' talking to wives were mainly responsible for this, or whether project officials assumed that women's needs would be taken care of by the men they worked with. The philosophy behind IRD still drew heavily on a model of rural social organisation in which women figure solely in terms of their domestic responsibilities, and as a result, they were considered peripheral to mainstream economic activity. Project implementers clung to the belief that women's most immediate needs and interests do not stem from their activities as cultivators, food processors or traders, but from those of housewife and mother. True to their philosophy, they directed project benefits to the head of the household in the assumption that all other household members would benefit from his economic advancement. Below we give a few examples of how women's activities and needs were neglected because agricultural projects were assumed not to be of direct relevance to them.

The Mwea irrigated rice project in Kenya is particularly well documented (Hanger and Moris, 1973; Palmer, 1985; Agarwal, 1985). It involved resettling smallholders in a newly-irrigated area to produce rice both for cash and for their own consumption. Plots for rice production were allocated to men, while women were given use rights in smaller plots on which to grow maize and other food crops. Although these plots were too small for family food self-sufficiency, it was assumed that diets would be supplemented by rice. But rice was not liked by the farming families, partly because they were used to the softer consistency of maize. As a result, women had to try to grow enough food on their tiny plots for family consumption, or to produce something which could be exchanged for maize. The settlement was also quite distant from suitable sources of firewood, which increased women's already heavy workload. The project designers also assumed that wives would help on their husbands rice fields, but made no provision for them to receive a share of the resulting income. Given that only men were designated as members of the tenants' associations, one can assume that the planners thought the men would use their income for family rather than personal needs.

Hanger and Moris say that the women found Mwea 'an intolerable place to live' (1973, p.244). Rice yields failed to meet anticipated levels by a large margin – a result of wives' unwillingness to work on a crop which was not in their own perceived interest. Ingrid Palmer (1985) notes that the consultation process at Mwea was very male dominated, consisting of tenants' associations presided over by leading male farmers appointed by the project officials. As such it was an inappropriate forum for women to express their views and needs. Despite the evidence of this experience, planners made many of the same mistakes in a series of irrigated rice projects in the Gambia, involving irrigation and technical inputs (Dey, 1981). Planners presumed that men were the main rice growers and therefore, in their scheme for the cultivation of irrigated rice for national consumption, it was to the men that they gave inputs such as credit, fertilisers and an assured market; the women it was assumed would be ready to help out as part of the household when required. The land to be irrigated was thought to be household (i.e. male) owned and not used productively. When questioned the men did not disabuse the project officials. In fact, the area concerned was land to which women had use rights and on which they cultivated rainfed rice both for family consumption and exchange. As the men, backed by project officials, took over their plots, the women were forced to grow their rice on poorer soils which gave them much lower yields. Household food supplies declined greatly.

The irrigated rice plots also failed to meet projected levels of production. Women's labour in weeding and transplanting was crucial to the success of the project, and assumed by the planners to be unproblematic. However, under customary practice, women were not obliged to work for their husbands. Since they refused to 'help' and the men refused to pay them a wage for their work, production levels dropped. As Jennie Dey points out, if women's existing expertise in growing rainfed rice had been built on, benefits would have accrued all round. Instead the low return on investment in expensive capital-intensive schemes represented a tremendous cost to the government and the local people. The projects produced lower yields than anticipated, weakened women's capacity to feed their families, and, by reducing their access to land, increased their dependence on their husbands (Dey, 1981; Jones, 1983).

The Tiv farm development project in Nigeria was more elaborate and involved schemes of land reform, extension, social forestry, crop improvement and irrigation. Burfisher and Horenstein's evaluation points to a markedly different impact on men than on women; with women suffering a disproportionately high share of the labour increase without any corresponding increase in income (Burfisher and Horenstein, 1985). Female labour requirements rose by 17 per cent, while those of men rose by only 6 per cent. Since men had greater overall responsibility for cash crops, their income showed a greater cash component than women's. This income differential was further exacerbated by the fact that women's wages were set considerably lower than men's. Planners clearly had assumed households were income and labour pooling units, but in reality they did not form corporate units: men and women traditionally had separate sources of income and financial responsibilities. As a result of the planners' ignorance (or prejudice), although production did increase it was at the cost of almost all the economic benefit of the project going to the men and the loss of status and independence for women.

Kathleen Staudt's study in the Kakamega district of Kenya shows how the objective of providing agricultural assistance to all farmers can go astray (Staudt, 1985). By comparing the access of female-managed farms to agricultural services with that of jointly managed farms, she found a clear preferential delivery of services to farms with a man present. Female-managed farms always received less help than those that were jointly managed. With respect to training, jointly managed farms were four times as likely to have a member trained than female-managed farms, and information about training opportunities tended to pass through male communication networks. One possible reason for this could be that extension workers (predominantly male) were inhibited by cultural factors from visiting women farmers. However, it is hard not to suspect that male extension workers themselves gave little importance to women farmers. Credit was an integral part of the programme but access depended on holding title deeds to land. During land reform, men generally acquired title deeds. As a result, they were the major recipients of loans. Despite the acute need of female farmers for credit, only 1 per cent of those in the study even knew the application procedure.

The more sophisticated FSR/E approach did little better. A critical weakness of FSR/E is its inability to integrate all members of the farm-household into its analysis, or to consider male-female relations at the inter- and intra-household level. As a result it is blind to crucial gender and relational differences that affect productive and reproductive behaviour. The emphasis on farmer participation has, in the main, been translated into enlisting the co-operation of male household heads on behalf of their households and dependants. Households are assumed to follow the pattern of the husband as major decision-maker and distributor of household resources. The fact that women are agriculturalists, care for livestock, process food and market produce, and maintain the domestic economy, and as such have technological and extension needs, is no more a central feature of mainstream FSR/E than it was of the earlier technocratic paradigms of the 1960s.

The situation in sub-Saharan Africa today

At the end of 1986, 27 of the 37 countries designated as Least Developed by the UN were to be found in SSA; many were heavily indebted and most had to import food. Yet, '(d)uring the 1950s and until about the early-1960s (sub-Saharan) Africa was a good surplus producing area and most of the countries had surpluses in their trade balances. The value of African exports grew at an average of 5 per cent annually . . . The growth in agricultural production, including food, kept ahead of population growth and on the whole, Africa maintained a healthy growth perspective' (Mutharika, 1987, p.28). Since 1980 the countries of sub-Saharan Africa have suffered severe losses of export earnings as a result of depressed international commodity markets: '(t)he prices of African raw materials today are about what they were in 1930 and some countries have had a 50 per cent cut in their resources because of the cut in commodity prices' (Cassam, 1987, p.12). Many of these commodities are agricultural products. In many countries trade earnings fell by 20 per cent between 1980 and 1986, and as a result many LDCs suffered large external payments deficits and grave economic difficulties (Williams, 1987).

Per capita incomes dropped by as much as 25 per cent in LLDCs; the average income in sub-Saharan Africa today is the same as it was in 1970 if not lower. Taking Zambia as an example, annual per capita income dropped from $600 in 1981 to $200 in 1986.

The situation is even worse when food production is considered. In 1938 the region exported cereals; in 1950 it was self-sufficient in food (Aidoo, 1988, p.57). Food self-sufficiency ratios dropped from 98 per cent in 1972-4 to 86 per cent in 1980 and are expected to fall still further (to 71 per cent by the year 2008) (Aidoo, 1988, p.56). Put another way, food production per head has declined from an index of 100 for 1974/6 to 91 for 1981/3, declining by roughly 0.8 per cent per annum. To bridge the food supply gap African countries have had to import food or become dependent on food aid. Both have risen from an average of 7 kg per head in 1978 to about 10 kg in 1982 (a 43 per cent increase over four years). By 1984 around 20 per cent of export earnings were being used to import food. As Jeanne Henn (1983) points out, there is an implicit conclusion in much of the recent literature, 'that if African food production and distribution systems do not change soon in a fundamental way, Africa may never be able to feed itself' (Henn 1983, p.1043).

There is little agreement as to the precise causes of this catastrophic decline in food sufficiency, but almost all observers point to the neglect of the smallholder (or peasant) farming sector. The mean share of agriculture in total government expenditure was only 9.6 per cent in 1967 (for 29 SSA countries) and 10.2 per cent in 1973 (for 27) (Jazairy, 1987, p.52). This neglect in many countries has encouraged migration to the urban areas. As a consequence urban populations have grown at more than double the average rate of population increase, and the proportion of food growers in the population has declined from 94 to 67 per cent between 1960 and 1985 (Mureithi, 1987).

Another result of the decline in food production has been a decline in nutritional standards; for the region as a whole calorie supply as a percentage of minimum nutritional requirements fell 12 per cent between 1969-71 and 1979-81 from 89 per cent of daily requirement to 77 per cent on average. Over the same period the number of severely hungry and malnourished rose from an estimated 80 million to as many as 100 million and more at the height of the drought (in Ethiopia and the Sudan in the late-1970s). However, 'the point of such figures lies less in the steady worsening they reveal, bad as that may be, than in the continuing, long-term prevalence of food inadequacy. The human suffering so glaringly apparent in the report of drought-related famine has tended to mask the chronic state of malnourishment existing in much of the region for some time. This means that hunger cannot be expected to go away even though the rains have returned' (Jazairy, 1987, p.51).

The situation is made more complex still by the twofold problem of high population growth rates, and declining land fertility and loss of forest cover and water resources. Africa as a whole has some of the highest fertility rates in the world, with a total fertility rate per woman of 6.4 compared with 3.8 for the world as a whole, 4.4 for all developing countries, and 2.0 in developed countries (UNICEF, 1989, p.13). Looked at another way, although population is relatively thinly spread, the rate of population growth is coming into conflict with environmental capabilities. Overall population growth rates of 2.4 per cent a year in the 1960s increased to 2.8 per cent in the 1970s and are likely to be found to have exceeded 3 per cent in the 1980s.

In the rural areas (where more than 72 per cent of the population still lives), this has led both to the shortening of fallow periods and consequent rapid exhaustion (and often erosion) of soil, more use of marginal land, and depletion of forest cover. It is estimated that 5 per cent of forest cover (or 4 million hectares of forest) is being lost every year, while soil losses have reached ten times the rate of soil formation (Jazairy, 1987, p.51). 'With fewer trees less rain is "attracted" and less moisture is retained in the soil; soil erosion and falling water table lead to desertification ... annual erosion of 50 to 100 tons per acre is common; the Sahara – to say nothing of other deserts – is advancing at more than 10 kilometres per year (Mureithi 1987, p.46).

The causes of environmental problems are, however, much more complex than this brief account can do justice to. While rapid population expansion is a factor, the full picture would have to include a discussion of changing climatic patterns, commercial use of land, forms of land tenure, the ability of farmers to upgrade their production techniques given unfavourable terms of trade, and other factors. But even the more detailed examination leaves the impression that the situation is dramatic.

Conceptual issues in women and agriculture

Understanding the complexity of the intra-household distribution of work and its rewards is crucial in any analysis of agricultural development planning, as many of our examples have shown. This involves both the nature of the gendered division of labour and of household forms and their operation. In the past, as now, misconceptions about the different dimensions and determinants of women's productive activity have resulted in gross under-estimations of that activity and to policy failures. Closely connected with production, but not in any unilinear or clearcut way, is the distribution of the products of labour – of income and consumption goods such as food. This will also be briefly addressed at the end of this section.

The gendered division of labour and of sectors of production

Much of the accepted wisdom about the sexual division of labour in SSA derives from Esther Boserup's *Woman's Role In Economic Development* (Boserup, 1970), which was based on a wide range of earlier research. Boserup highlighted differences between male and female farming systems, defining the two in terms of who is responsible for the bulk of food production. Her generalisations stretch to the association of women with backward technology (hoes) and of men with more modern techniques (ploughs). She argues that SSA is the region of female farming par excellence given that in most parts of the continent most of the tasks to do with food production are women's concern; and that this is directly due to colonial policies of agricultural modernisation which drew young men away from subsistence farming to paid labour on modern, commercial farms and plantations, or into the mines.

A number of simplifications have been drawn from Boserup's work which more recent research has questioned. The commonest is that between non-market, subsistence (food) production by women and cash crop (food or export) production by men. A corollary of this is the view that women stick to 'traditional' technology, i.e. the hoe, whereas men adopt modern methods such as the plough, tractor, HYVs, fertiliser, etc. The implication is that women are innately conservative. Empirically, there are many cases where men do take up

55

cash crops and modern production methods and tools. However, this reflects the preconceptions of extension workers and policymakers rather than the instinct of the genes, or an immutable division of labour (cf. Staudt, 1985 *inter alia*). Male farmers are given access to modern tools and other inputs, the credit to acquire them, and the training to make best use of them. Women farmers are rarely targeted for such inputs or training.

The major drawback of this dualist view, however, is that it disguises the degree to which the two 'sectors' are closely interrelated. In reality, most self-provisioning farmers also sell food crops – the ultimate destination of a crop may not be determined until a whole variety of factors are taken into account – and many smallholders, including women, also produce for export (Whitehead, 1984).

Production relations and the rural household

In reality, the sexual division of labour varies widely and is rarely immutable; intra-household production relations are equally varied and complex. To make development interventions more effective, what needs to be established is how the work done by men and by women, young and old, fits together. For example, the difference between sex sequential and sex segregated forms of labour organisation may be critical (see Edholm, Harris and Young, 1975). In sex sequential production, different inputs from each sex are required at different stages in the production process to produce a common product. In sex segregated production, either women or men are wholly responsible for the entire production process, for example men producing maize or millet and women beans or cassava.[1]

In sex sequential forms of organisation, women's control over their work input is typically regulated by prior decisions taken by men in earlier stages of the production process. As Ahmed (1985) points out, this may affect the impact of technological change. He cites the example of palm oil processing, where women are responsible for processing palm fruit which is grown by men. Clearly, the introduction of technology to increase production of fruit (such as tractors to increase acreage) without any corresponding improvement in processing technology, may result in an intolerable increase in women's work burden, or their displacement entirely. Processing of many foods and market crops is typically women's work.

For a realistic estimate of time availability of men or women, an analysis of the distribution of the work tasks of cultivation, animal care and processing between the genders has to be coupled with a similar analysis of the distribution of household tasks and of the time such activities take.[2] For example, a national sample survey of rural Côte d'Ivoire showed that women undertake 67 per cent of all the work done by the combined male and female population over the age of 10. A girl of 10-14 works as much as a man of 20-25, and a woman of 25-30 works a third longer than a man the same age (Jazairy, 1987, p.51).

Jeanne Henn's research in north-western Tanzania and Cameroon provides additional illustrative examples (Henn, 1983). Her studies show great similarities in the work of women farmers as well as the number of work hours put in relative to those of men. The Haya men (Tanzania) put in about 7.8 labour hours per day on average, while the women put in 10.4. For the Beti (Cameroon), the corresponding figures were 7.3 and 10.6. In both cases, women spent considerably more time than men in producing food, while men were more involved in wage and income-generating work. Recent attention to access to productive resources and seasonal changes in workloads also indicates that women tend to be disproportionately adversely affected during the most difficult times of the year (see for example Chambers, Longhurst and Pacey,1981).

The amount of time women spend on 'domestic' tasks as compared to men, is substantial. In Burkina Faso a time allocation study covering the first 14 waking hours of the day showed that women performed 97 per cent of household tasks, 23 per cent of community obligations and 64 per cent of production/distribution and supply tasks. In those hours only 1.3 hours was 'free time' used for resting (McSweeney, 1979). There are signs too that the burden of domestic labour is increasing, particularly as a result of environmental degradation and attendant soil erosion, desertification and deforestation. For example, women, as the main collectors of firewood, have been forced to walk increasing distances in search of fuel. Grainger (1982) estimated that women in (former) Upper Volta were having to walk 4-6 hours a day three times a week to gather wood. As Dankelman and Davidson (1988) point out, loads carried are also enormous: women often carry up to 35 kg over distances as much as 10 km. Women's workload is inevitably increased by the falling productivity of agricultural land. Reduced soil fertility leads them to cultivate over larger areas for longer hours, frequently to produce less food. As water collectors, they are obviously also detrimentally affected by reduced supplies, not only in terms of their own health but also increased workloads.

Several authors have recently pointed to the scant attention paid to the development of technology to reduce women's domestic drudgery or the establishment of, for example, childcare facilities, except where productivity on nationally required crops suffer. Ann Whitehead (1985) suggests that the adoption of innovations in women's domestic work has much to do with the extent to which the interests of men and women coincide and the amount of economic flexibility women have. Thus if women want an improved supply of water or a nearer source of firewood '(t)he crude question is: can they pay for it and, if not, what leverage do they have to encourage men to provide the resource?' (Whitehead, 1985, p.51).

Where possible, an assessment of the lack of flexibility built into the gender division of labour has to be made – which tasks are rarely done by men, which never, etc. In most of SSA, women are responsible for a wide variety of tasks which ensure that their families have adequate food stocks, that raw foods are processed and cooked, that there is wood and water with which to cook, that children receive medical attention and continuous care when they are infants, and so on. Men will rarely take over cooking, care for infants and children, but may increase their involvement in crop production or fetching wood and water when women cannot cope. In different societies there will be different arrangements of rights and responsibilities between the sexes, such as male responsibility for providing basic staples or household necessities, female for childcare and socialisation. Such arrangements form part of the marital contract and may also provide the parameters of the types of labour both husbands and wives can call upon for given tasks, from each other or others. Economic (and social) change usually involves the need to reorganise or redefine both rights and obligations. The question for those introducing economic change is whether the changes, as envisaged, privilege one of the genders over the other. And if the answer is yes, what compensatory changes can be introduced before the division of labour is weighted against women.

We have shown examples of the tendency to assume that women can and will provide farm labour as part of their domestic tasks or marital obligation. This is often accompanied by the further assumption that their labour is somehow 'free' in terms of both money and time. This is most marked when the tasks are part of the smallholder farm enterprise, but it may also occur with reference to work outside the household. However, as noted above, there are complex sets of rights and obligations around the supplying of labour (see Roberts, 1988, 1989), and in SSA both male and female labour are frequently exchanged for payment in both cash and kind (see Guyer, 1981, 1984). Failure to appreciate this had led to several planning failures (some of which we have cited above), and in many cases has resulted in intolerable demands on the labour of women (and children). With the modernisation of agriculture both men and women's work burdens have intensified. But despite the fact that men are now putting in longer work hours per day and over more months, their overall labour input is still lower than women's because of women's higher burden of reproductive work, which is additional to their productive work.

Much agricultural policy still assumes a degree of homogeneity and similarity among rural households, and that the respective roles of men and women are roughly similar through time and unproblematic. But the household is not a static entity, nor easily generalisable to one particular form (see Roberts, 1991; Guyer, 1981). A household may include several wives and their children (i.e. is polygamous), several generations and lateral kin (i.e. is an extended or joint family), or is a more restricted unit (i.e. a nuclear family). In many rural areas differences in form and composition of households can be a sign of economic differentiation.

Various factors lie behind changing household form in SSA. The nuclear family form has been encouraged by missionaries, planners and development projects themselves (as well as by the so-called progressive commercial farmers). However, rural out-migration, particularly of men, has increased, whether on a seasonal or a permanent basis. In many countries, colonial policy encouraged male wage labour migration, and this has continued to date (notably countries bordering on South Africa). However, its effects have not been uniform. In some cases, women have taken over farming and agricultural stagnation has ensued; in others the opposite has occurred – i.e. agricultural innovation and production for the market.

One of the more consistent effects of male out-migration has been the increase of *de facto* female-headed households, in which women are responsible for both household livelihood and home maintenance tasks. In many countries female-headed households constitute more than 30 per cent of all rural households. Such households are generally poorer and less able to command resources than others.

The distribution of resources

Another erroneous but widespread view is that households are unproblematic units of pooling and sharing. In reality patterns of intra-household distribution vary widely. Each involves a variety of constraints and incentives to action, given differential control of resources, and culturally and socially formed attitudes (Dwyer and Bruce, 1988; Young, 1990; Sen, 1987). Two of the most important variables in the distribution of resources are access to and control over income and access to and control over food. Even in poor households not all members of the household are equally poor (Agarwal, 1986). Although evidence is scanty, the suggestion that women and girls tend to be discriminated against is justifiable, particularly when food is scarce. The effects of this will be exacerbated at times of seasonal stress.

The argument is frequently put forward that despite being unequal, intra-household allocations are nevertheless fair because of differential caloric requirements of men as against women, and boys as compared with girls – men are bigger, expend more energy, need more food, etc. There is, however, little strength in this justification. For one thing, women often have a greater energy requirement when pregnant and lactating – a frequent situation for many women in SSA. Secondly, even when this is not the case, women's workloads usually make their calorific requirements significantly greater than conventional wisdom allows. In Longhurst's (1980) study of nutrition in rural Nigeria, he found that women's intake consistently fell short of their requirements while that of men exceeded theirs.

It has been suggested that '(d)ifferential male-female status in the household that leads to sex-selective feeding, particularly (but by no means exclusively) in scarcity situations, is likely to lead to a differential distribution, by gender, of income for other needs as well' (Agarwal, 1986, p.77). Although she is discussing South Asia, even in SSA where women undertake a disproportionately large share of agricultural work, they do not have corresponding control of household cash income. Typically, although women work on men's cash crops and are entitled to a share, their entitlement comes after all other obligations have been met, and is at the man's discretion. Given this, wives may prefer to spend as much time as they can on growing crops which they can market, which gives them unmediated access to cash. But even then, they may not entirely control this cash. Studies of women's income-generating projects in Kenya showed that wives' income was often given *in toto* to the husband. The research concluded that women's ability to control their income is not so much a consequence of having earned it as an indication of the overall pattern of relationships, needs and resources within their households (McCormack *et al.*, 1986). A recent study in northern Zambia showed a variety of arrangements about access to cash: for example, if a man helped a wife (provided labour, seed or fertiliser) in her enterprise he had a right to a share of the proceeds; wives did not enjoy reciprocal rights. However, women had devised a range of ways to lessen the levy – many women bartered their products, or if they sold them immediately spent the cash on needed goods (Evans and Young, 1988). Recent studies indicate that conflict between husbands and wives over allocation and use of cash and labour are frequent and bitter (see Whitehead, 1990; Leach, 1991).

What cash gets spent on appears to depend on who controls it. Research indicates that when women have some income, they are more likely to spend it on children's and other family members' needs than men. In many cultures men are allowed personal spending money (for things like tobacco and beer) while women are expected to spend all their cash on family needs. But again, there are social conventions about who takes care of what aspects of household expenditures (see Whitehead, 1984; Young 1990). It is not always the case that men are improvident just as it is far from the case that women are helpless dependants, with no control over financial resources. What is necessary is an awareness of the fact that firstly, husbands do not always act as egalitarian distributers of 'household' resources; secondly, that control of income is a function of intra-household power differences; and lastly, that households themselves come in many shapes and sizes. Before designing interventions, planners need, as a minimum, to accept the possibility that women act as independent economic agents, and better still to ensure they find out what the common variants in household resource management are.

Access to land, labour and extension services

Land is a vital commodity, not just in terms of the food and crops it provides, but as a means of obtaining credit, access to inputs, and participation in rural development schemes. Obviously to be without clear title to land is to be dependent on those who do control it, even though use rights alone are recognised. Traditionally, neither women nor men had exclusive ownership rights over land in SSA. Instead, a regime of use rights prevailed, allowing people to control what they were able to cultivate. The precise nature of use rights has varied from society to society, depending partly on whether inheritance was through the female or the male line, and whether on marriage the couple lived in his or her parents' village. Men's use rights were often, however, more clearly defined than women's, whose rights often depended on their ability to bear (male) children.

Colonial and post-colonial policies have undermined traditional patterns of land control by developing land registration schemes which assume male household heads and patrilinity. Legal and economic security has thus been bestowed on men, leaving women in a considerably more precarious position. Looking at the impact of land adjudication in Western Kenya, one researcher found that of 135 women farmers surveyed, in only eight cases was the land registered in the woman's name alone; in eight cases sons' names were included as well; in 34 only sons' names were registered and in more than 50 per cent of the cases only the husband's name (Palmer, 1985). The new adjudication gave widows and women with daughters little land on the grounds that they did not really need it. To aggravate matters further, only men were mobilised to assist in the implementation of the adjudication. A critical observation made by Ann Whitehead (1990) is that with increased production of cash crops, women's access to land has become more fragile because the agrarian social relations which give access to land and other rural resources have become highly politicised.

Labour and access to it is also critical for farmers. This involves both the amount of time farmers are able to devote to their own crops as well as their ability to mobilise the labour of others. We have seen that development planners have consistently failed to appreciate the heterogeneity of labour use patterns and particularly the division of labour between men and women. The rapid disappearance of reciprocal labour between kin or neighbours, caused partly by the cash nexus itself and partly by male migration, has reduced women's access to the labour of others. Always less able than men to mobilise wide-ranging social relations to get male labour for their enterprises, women are even further penalised by having so little access to cash, and being unable to rely on reciprocal forms of labour (even among women). Husbands too are reluctant to work on wives' plots when they have work to do on their cash crops. The inability of women to acquire male labour at the optimum time is a factor in lowered yields – as is the fact that women themselves may be required to work on men's cash crops when they should be working on their own.

Kathleen Staudt's 1985 study showed clear differences in male and female access to agricultural extension services and much needed credit. This is supported by evidence from several quarters. For example, 'extension services are often biased towards work with men and neglect the very important role, that of women as farmers in most parts of the world' (World Bank, 1982, p.73). Although women do have access to home economics extension services, the information they provide is seldom relevant. Furthermore, women are seldom trained and employed as agricultural advisers and extension workers. According to FAO sources, while women make up 47 per cent of the agricultural labour force in SSA, only 2.9 per cent of agricultural advisers are women (FAO, 1984).

What lies at the root of women farmers' limited access to resources? The problem is two-fold. It arises both from false perceptions born out of ideological bias which often amounts to a failure to 'see' what women are actually doing, but also from the less often conceded fact that men's and women's interests are not always coincident, and that, in the main, the balance of power lies with men.

The first aspect of the problem has often been attributed to the failure to collect adequate and accurate information on what women are actually doing and what their needs are. The problems around statistical evidence will be examined in more depth in Chapter 7, but at this stage we can note that if ideological bias is the problem, collecting more data but on the basis of the same set of false assumptions cannot be the answer.

The question of potential or actual conflict in gender interests raises the question of whether the assumption is correct that improving agricultural efficiency and meeting women's needs are both compatible and attainable. While men are able to control resources, including women's unpaid labour, what incentives are there which would induce them to give up such control? (see Roberts, 1979, 1989). The promise of an overall rise in productivity seems unlikely to be sufficiently attractive to the individual (although the collectivity might benefit substantially). More often than not, technical solutions are sought to problems which are about relative control of resources because these do not challenge the *status quo*. As Bina Agarwal puts it:

> 'the problem cannot be located in the technological innovation *per se*, since what is often inappropriate about the innovation is not its technical characteristics, but the socio-political context within which it is introduced... . The fact that it is women who often tend to lose more or gain less from a scheme than the men of their class relates less to the technical characteristics of the scheme than to the ideology that legitimises and reinforces women's position, economically and socially, both in the household and in the wider society' (Agarwal, 1985, p.122).

Ingrid Palmer has specifically looked at this question in terms of the likely impact of price changes for agricultural produce, a key element in structural adjustment policies, on men and women cultivators. She concludes that these policies will favour men's crops (Palmer, 1988); women who farm other crops on their own account will be under pressure to surrender more of their labour and even some of their land so that their husbands may take advantage of the price increases. 'Unless there is major institutional reform affecting women's access to variable inputs many of the benefits of market liberalisation will stop at the farm household door. To say that freeing prices will lead to the most efficient use of household resources is to ignore utterly the terms on which separate accounting units work' (Palmer, 1988, p.8, and see also Palmer, 1991).

Development planning for women

With the discovery that women constituted a large proportion of the poorest and most disadvantaged groups in LDCs came the decision to allocate a certain amount of aid funds to special projects for them. A number of international agencies such as the World Bank, USAID and the United Nations Development Programme (UNDP) established formal criteria for integrating women into rural development programmes. Strategies either took the form of special small-scale projects focusing on a particular aspect of women's lives, or of a women's component added on to major projects. Initially, as we noted, improving the material conditions of poor rural women was the aim by providing basic home economics education and teaching them to be more effective in home management, nutrition, hygiene and family planning. While welfare concerns played a significant role in the identification of women's needs, some consideration was given to women's ability to earn an income, for example through small-scale income-generating activities: handicraft enterprises, raising small animals for sale, preparation of dried, smoked or other treated food, marketing of processed and unprocessed food, etc.

The importance to women of meeting the needs of their children and other dependants is indisputable. But of equal importance are their multifarious, independent productive activities. Plans for integrating women in rural development rarely touched upon the implication of women's unequal access to productive resources, credit, marketing advice and technical assistance. Instead, preference was given to short-term palliative measures such as small-scale income-generating projects. Support for rural women was also given within the framework of sets of relationships which subordinate women and their activities to the activities and functions of men. This strategy, as we saw frequently, left women less well off and bereft of many of their traditional sources of power and status.

Small-scale women's projects can be (and frequently are) used as a justification by male development officials that they are 'doing something about women'. However the most honest of them recognise that such projects are marginal and the first to have funding/staffing cut when financial squeezes occur. On the other hand, the alternative strategy, which aims to incorporate a gendered analysis into all aspects of the development process, can result in paying lip service to the idea while pandering to existing vested interests. A third alternative, giving support to women organising on their own account, has provided some useful examples (see for example Muntemba, 1985) but this still fails to address the overall policy question of planning with women.

Development planning with women

What then would development planning with women look like? Here we can only sketch in a few of the necessary elements. First and foremost women would be integrated into the planning process from the beginning. They would not merely be consulted at an advanced stage of planning to ensure their needs were being properly considered, when changes are virtually impossible to incorporate. Rather, women of different ages, social status and involved in diverse economic activities would be able to articulate the diversity, and the similarity, of their interests and needs and these would form the central part of the considerations upon which planning would be based.

Secondly, given this, it would be self-evident that women as farmers, traders, food processors and so on need the same access to land, credit, training and inputs as other farmers, traders, etc. They also need to be given the same incentives to produce more efficiently and effectively. Looking at production from a woman's point of view would result in much more attention being paid to ensuring the long-term viability of forms of production, the provision of more adequate storage to minimise in-field and on-farm crop wastage, and of more sensible distribution facilities to ensure local as well as national markets are supplied. Rather than looking to the quick-fix technical solution, planning with women would look to using the resources to hand in a more thorough and effective way. To work with the land and with nature and not merely to control them. Priority would be given to the rehabilitation of soils, the care and regeneration of woods and forests, the better care and management of water resources. Planning for production of a much wider range of crops so as to spread the risk of climatic variation would require greater resources being spent on research into those crops which are widely eaten but not internationally tradeable – cassava, yams, sorghum, millet and plantains are amongst some of the more obvious – as well as those forest or wild crops which are not nationally traded but widely consumed locally. More intensive research into traditional methods of intercropping, rotation, soil fertility, and pest control would be married to modern organic farming knowledge. Intensive work would also be required on forms of draft power which would lessen a farmer's burden of work but which could also be used for water and wood haulage.

Thirdly, planning with women would look at the totality of what both men and women do in rural households, and look to see where men could be given better training or extension to support their roles as fathers, and where domestic technology is needed to lessen the burden of domestic chores for women and their daughters by a variety of tasks being taken on by men and their sons. The problem of most planning models, and even of some of the current rhetoric about including women in agricultural development planning, is the failure to predict conflict between the genders.[3] There is plenty of evidence that this occurs. Mwea and the Gambian case study show how at the household level, male and female interests clearly diverge.

64

For development planning to be able to respond to the needs of rural women, a closer examination is needed of social and economic relations between men and women, between men, and between women themselves. The different forms of household organisation and divisions of labour need to be understood in more detail as does the division and control over resources such as land and its products. But the ability to resolve such conflict must lie not in strengthening the resource base of the already stronger party, but rather reducing the inequalities, to allow both to negotiate an acceptable solution.

Research methods, and approaches such as farming system research, would need a radical reorientation of focus which will take social relations within the household as much as beyond it into account, and look at how these are affected by gender and age. The variety of household forms and composition needs recognition and the differential access of men and women to markets and inputs. Concepts such as household, production, reproduction, domestic will have to be opened out to reveal the diversity and complexity of the pattern of activity, decision-making, access and control which they hide.

Planning with women is still not an accepted strategy but slowly more governments are taking women's concerns more seriously. For example, an international group of senior women (SWAG) has been set up to advise the United Nations Environment Programme (and indirectly governments) on the implication of environment policies for women and to put forward alternative ideas which might be more likely to lead to sustainable development. Several of these women are on the International Advisory Council of WorldWIDE, an organisation of women founded in 1982 to educate the public and policymakers about the effects on women of the destruction and contamination of natural resources and ecological systems, and to increase women's involvement in the design and implementation of development policies.

Notes

1 The third type is where both sexes work side by side, each carrying out a complementary task – for example the man digs the hole and the woman puts in the seed and covers the hole.

2 Little attention is paid in time allocation studies to the time women spend collecting 'wild foods'. I noted in my own research in Mexico that when cultivated or bought food was in short supply, older women would go to the forest areas, fields in fallow and brooks and bring back a wide variety of edibles: fungus, grubs, leaves, small rodents. At other times most of the women and children would bring back large quantities of grasshoppers (eaten roasted), and bee larvae. The importance of wild foods for survival was raised at the international meeting on food strategies in Paris (1980), but does not seem to have been taken much further.

3 Disturbing the balance of current gender relations is, of course, the classic pretext for not giving women a fair share of resources; but this fear appears only concerned with upsetting men.

5 Women and manufacturing employment: The case of Asia

In the following two chapters we will be looking at women in the non-agricultural labour force. Although a distinction is usually made between regular paid employment in the formal sector and unregulated, often casual employment (or self-employment) in the informal sector, these should not be thought of as distinct sectors since the links between them are crucial. The informal sector is often a critical contributor to the profitability of more apparently organised economic activity, and workers may shift between the two depending on economic conditions, availability of employment or opportunity for self-employment, and their own mobility or survival strategies. In this chapter we will concentrate on women's paid employment in more obviously regulated conditions, paying particular attention to manufacturing employment, especially that geared towards export. This is a sector of rapid growth in which women have been vital contributors, particularly in the Asian NICs.

For many, industrialisation, the fundamental objective of mainstream economic development and the means to improve the standard of living of most of the population, is synonymous with large-scale manufacturing in the modern sector. However, industrialisation can be seen in a broader sense as a complex process involving the introduction of scientific and technological innovations in production and the technical upgrading of all major economic sectors. In this sense, industrialisation is not restricted to manufacturing. Industrialised agriculture is perfectly feasible and indeed agro-industries are now found in most LDCs. Manufacturing industry does, however, usually command the central place in the industrialisation process. In the 'modern' sector this involves manufacturing by domestic firms, foreign owned or based multinational (MNCs) or transnational corporations (TNCs) or a combination of the two.

66

Countries can adopt a variety of industrialisation strategies depending on whether emphasis is on production primarily for export or internal consumption, and how the balance between the two is weighted. The particular choice will depend not only upon economic considerations, but on wider social, cultural and political conditions. We will look at the two main strategies for industrial development and some of the debates surrounding them. We will then turn to gender issues in employment in manufacturing, concentrating on the role of the TNCs in the creation of new sectors of employment for women. Although this emphasis leaves large areas of women's formal employment unexamined, some of the conceptual and policy issues in terms of women's recruitment and insertion in the labour force, and of their assumed abilities and attributes are applicable to other sectors. Looking at the positive and negative aspects of manufacturing employment for women, we shall highlight those areas which should be of particular concern to policymakers and development practitioners. Given the preponderance of Asian countries in manufacturing for export, most of our examples are drawn from that region.

Strategies for industrial development

Strategies for industrialisation have to be concerned both with internal policy supports to promote manufacturing and also the role of external institutions and trade – foreign investment, exports and imports, etc. One of the most critical factors is that of foreign exchange. In somewhat simplistic terms one can say that actual industrialisation strategies adopted by LDCs have given different weight to each of these sets of factors and have taken two major forms: import substitution and export promotion. The former involves the production for the domestic market of many manufactured goods previously imported, thus saving foreign exchange, and the latter the production of goods for external markets, thus earning foreign exchange. Essentially each strategy embodies a somewhat different view of the way a country/economy should relate to the global economic system.

Import-Substituting Industrialisation (ISI)

In theory ISI involves a three-stage process by means of which a country can progressively build up industrial capacity and aim for self-sufficiency (Colman and Nixson, 1986). In the first phase, the LDC uses its foreign exchange to import investment goods (machinery, technology and other equipment), those raw materials and fuels needed to manufacture non-durable consumer goods, such as cloth and clothing, for local consumption, using local labour. This phase of assembly and basic manufacture generally relies heavily on foreign inputs of technology and expertise and on protecting the nascent domestic manufactures from foreign competition.

The second phase involves the use of foreign exchange to import capital goods, such as machine tools, to make more sophisticated consumer durables and capital goods to produce intermediate goods, for example, steel. Since the technological and scientific equipment used at this stage is more complex than before, imports are still needed – capital, technology and managerial expertise – so as to consolidate the new production processes. In the third phase industries expand into replacing imported technology and basic capital equipment with domestic equivalents (or improvements); technological expertise is indigenised, the local pool of skilled, educated labour and managerial capacity expanded. With a firm domestic industrial base, countries can enter the international market as independent exporters of domestic manufactures. That is to say they are ready to shift to an export-oriented strategy.

The choice of ISI as a development strategy may reflect concern over the dependence of developing economies on Western manufactured goods; many people believe that sustainable development must involve a degree of self-reliance. But saving foreign exchange through import substitution was widely seen as a less difficult option than earning additional foreign exchange through producing manufactured exports. An export-oriented strategy requires breaking into new markets and devising and implementing successful export promotion policies: both risky and difficult undertakings. In contrast, finding ways to protect domestic markets and to produce goods for a known and established market seems less complex and risky.

In practice the three-phase sequence proved extremely difficult to follow successfully. Many of the countries failed to pass the first or second phase, mainly because of difficulties in meeting greater capital and complex technological requirements. Criticised for its lack of theoretical coherence and its practical ineffectiveness, academics, politicians and planners alike became disillusioned with the ISI strategy (cf., Little, Scitovsky and Scott, 1970; Sunkel, 1973; Cardoso and Faletto, 1979).

Export-Oriented Industrialisation (EOI)

The rationale of EOI is that the export of manufactured goods will expand the availability of foreign exchange earnings both for investment in industrial production and for meeting increasingly diversified producer and consumer needs. Success necessarily hinges upon the absorptive capacity of the global market for particular goods – primary commodities as much as manufactured exports – and regulation of prices so that LDC exports are competitive without unduly undercutting world prices. Proponents of EOI place considerable faith in the regulatory capacity of markets and envisage a limited role for the state – ensuring the appropriate economic conditions, through export incentives, for unhindered export promotion.

For many countries, pursuing a strategy geared towards the export market has involved giving control over parts of the economy to foreign-owned firms. Special export zones (Free Trade Zones, Export Processing Zones) have been set up which offer financial and other incentives to TNCs, such as low rates of tax, provision of infrastructure, newly-built factories, cheap utilities, and the right to expatriate profits. TNCs are also attracted by the promise of a cheap, plentiful and docile labour force (trade union activity is usually circumscribed if not banned) – clearly critical to those industries which rely on labour intensive technologies. A 1979 report claims that wages for unskilled and semi-skilled work in Asian FTZs were between 1/10 and 1/8 of those in equivalent factories in the West (Elson and Pearson, 1980).

The difficulties encountered with ISI and the success of the export-oriented NICs have encouraged the resurgence of the neo-classical case for the adoption of outward-looking industrialisation policies or EOI in the 1980s. Advocates of this strategy point to the rapid growth in manufactured exports from certain LDCs during the 1960s and 1970s (e.g. Brazil, India, South Korea, Singapore and Thailand) and attribute this to their adoption of EOI.[1] They argue that EOI leads to better growth performance because resources are allocated according to the dictates of comparative advantage, economies of scale can be exploited, and technological improvements generated in response to competition. Furthermore it leads to increased employment.

EOI has been a popular strategy over the past two decades but criticism is widespread, possibly more so among political economists than more conventional economists. They point to its legitimation of the existing pattern of international economic and political relations, LDC's increased vulnerability to the vagaries of international markets, and their lack of defence against the protectionism of Western countries. The strategy of externally induced industrialisation, and particularly setting up FTZ, generates little indigenous employment or output linkages with the rest of the economy, and provides little in the way of export revenues, transfer of technology and know-how.[2]

A more telling argument is that of timing and scale. Although the annual growth rates of South Korea, Taiwan, Hong Kong, Singapore (the Four Little Tigers) and, during the 1970s, Brazil, have been consistently high, and are held up as proof of the success of EOI policies, were these impressive rates of growth the result of the right policies or of the prevailing international situation (Schmitz, 1984)? Further, while conditions were favourable for export manufactures from the few successful NICs, if all LDCs were to follow such policies could the world market absorb the enormous volume of products?[3]

Balance and the world economy

A review of the LDC experiences suggests that it is too simplistic to describe ISI as a failure and EOI as a success. Both strategies involve a complex set of economic relationships, each of which requires detailed evaluation. Empirically, all successful export-oriented economies first went through an import substitution phase. This suggests that both should be employed and the relative weight given to either is likely to alter over time. For example, in the 1950s both Chile and Brazil focused largely on ISI only to shift to massive incentives for exports and encouragement of foreign investment in the early-1970s. In South Korea a much shorter initial period of ISI was followed by an elaborate mix of ISI and EOI to propel the economy through the next two decades. India has always been cited as an example of a sophisticated ISI strategy for promoting and protecting domestic industry; however, export incentives and a degree of outward orientation have never been far out of the picture, and are of growing importance today.

The appropriate balance between ISI and EOI will be determined by, amongst other things, what is considered politically or socially feasible, the country's level of industrialisation, its size and resource base, its overall objectives, the capacity of the state to intervene in the economy and to attract foreign investment, the state of the global economy, and the strategies of other industrial and industrialising nations. Equally, the availability of markets, their location and nature, must rank high in the factors that inform decisions about whether to adopt a more open or closed approach. Lastly, the success or failure of a strategy may depend on the state of the world economy more critically than any other factor. For example, in the 1960s when South Korea shifted to EOI the world economy was buoyant and global demand was positive and steady; when Brazil tried to shift in the mid-1970s the situation was radically different and its experience equally so. The most important lesson to be learned from the past development decades is the close interaction between national patterns of industrial development and the structure and cycles of the international economy.

Gender issues in manufacturing employment

One of the key findings of recent research into gender and development is that in all societies men and women are integrated into economic and social structures in different ways; past patterns influencing future possibilities. As a result gender differences in both economic and social outcomes can be quite marked. What is more contentious is why these outcomes tend to favour one gender over the other, and in many instances actually diminish the economic and political agency of women relative to men. Since industrialisation is one of the key processes through which men and women are integrated into economic and social structures, we should analyse the different experiences of the genders, both in the ways they have been integrated and in the effects of such integration. These vary by country, sector and socio-economic group.

A number of trends within the industrialisation process are hidden by official employment or production statistics, as is the interaction between urban and rural sectors within industrialisation. For example, research shows that certain industrial processes established in urban areas have in fact displaced workers, mostly women, from their traditional occupations in the rural area. For example, the food processing industry – a large 'new' employer of women in urban areas – has put a large number of rural producers, often self-employed, out of business, removing their major source of cash income. Plastic products replace old traditional goods many of which were produced by rural women – such as wood and wicker products and leather goods; ready-made clothes replace handwoven materials made up to measure. The effects of industrial growth are so widespread that intersectoral linkages have to be considered as well as intra-sectoral shifts if we are to begin to understand fully the industrialisation process in LDCs.

Ideology and the sexual division of labour

In all countries there are marked differences between the genders in the sectoral and occupational distribution of labour, in their employment status, in average earnings, and conditions and prospects. Both horizontal and vertical occupational segregation are apparent. Women are generally crowded into a few industrial sectors and within them in a narrow range of occupations. They tend to be in jobs categorised unskilled or semi-skilled, get few if any opportunities for advancement through either seniority or promotion, and have to accept less favourable conditions of work than men. While most observers agree that the dynamic of the gender division of labour is not economic rationality, economic factors tend to reinforce it.

Skill categories are not solely based on objective criteria but are contaminated by gender ideology. Men are ideologically represented as being more skilled or better capable of being trained to carry out skilled work than women. For example, consider the importance given to strength as against dexterity: tasks requiring certain types of strength are often designated as jobs for men and as skilled while those requiring dexterity (good hand to eye co-ordination) are designated as female and unskilled. This suggests that the designation of a task as being particularly suitable for a man or a woman has more to do with gender or socially constructed ideas about masculinity and femininity, than actual physical or mental attributes. Reality is of course complex: most surgeons (requiring skill and dexterity) are male, many tasks requiring great physical strength are carried out by women (lifting hospital patients). Many manufacturing jobs labelled as unskilled women's work in fact entail intricate and extremely rapid assembly work, which has a high cost in terms of permanent physical damage to eyesight and general health; skilled men's work may only involve manipulation of simple mechanical devices.

A refinement on this comes when certain tasks are seen to be intrinsically male – or what we call bearers of masculinity – despite the fact that women are usually perfectly capable of carrying them out. The ideology behind this is that men and women should do the tasks to which they are 'naturally' suited. Ann Whitehead (1979) has argued that gender categorisations can be ascriptive, which is to say that the gender is contained in the term itself – as with mother, brother (whether these are actual or fictive kin terms) – or gender bearing. In the latter case, in relation to employment in Western countries, terms such as those of boss and doctor are stereotypically thought of as male and secretary and nurse as female. Equally important is the fact that gender definitions are never absent, so that, as Elson and Pearson point out, even if a women escapes one particular set of gender ascriptive relations by not getting married, she cannot escape the way in which gender defines all other aspects of her life (Elson and Pearson, 1980).

The material form ideology takes is the exclusion of women from certain types of activity – on the grounds that they are too heavy or dangerous or 'unfeminine'. In this way particular jobs/activities become themselves bearers of masculine or feminine identity. The designation of certain tasks as male also provides a means of job protection; such jobs are often better paid as well as bearers of masculine identity. In both world wars in Western countries, women took over a number of typically male jobs (in munitions, shipyards, steel industry, etc.) but only after long negotiations between the labour unions, employers and government, to ensure that their employment would be ended when the men returned. And indeed, when the men came home the women lost their jobs, despite the fact that many needed to retain them so as to continue maintaining their own households.[4]

The reasons given by employers, male workers and some female workers for occupational segregation are varied: women's lower levels of education and training, of skills and commitment, their preference for undemanding jobs and dislike of management or supervisory positions are all suggested. Most of these reasons, when subjected to careful analysis, have been found to reflect stereotypes rather than reality. For example, women fail in their efforts to enter occupations for which they have appropriate qualifications, precisely because of occupational segregation. Equally, their educational achievements are often discounted; women workers often have higher qualifications than male colleagues doing similar work. Again, although women are believed to have lesser commitment to employment (or greater commitment to their children) than men and thus their rate of absenteeism is greater, studies have shown that their attendance record can be better than or equal to that of male workers, especially in those countries where alcohol dependence among men is high (Anker and Hein, 1986).

Trends in women's paid employment
Taking the developing countries as a whole, women's labour force participation has shown a slow but real upward trend over recent decades, although there are wide variations, from the 45.6 per cent in Thailand to 6.9 per cent in

Bangladesh. At the same time, there has been a relative increase in the employment of women in manufacturing over other sectors as women moved into industry at a faster rate than men.

Substantial regional variations are however evident: women's share of all non-agricultural employment is the lowest in North Africa and the Middle East (12 per cent) and highest in Latin America and the Caribbean (35 per cent); in Asia as a whole the figure is 27 per cent. Women also tend to be over-represented in professional categories relative to their overall representation in the labour force. In many countries this is due to women's predominance in teaching and nursing. For example in India in 1971, women constituted almost 20 per cent of professional workers, but 90 per cent of these were nurses or primary and secondary school teachers. As production workers, women are generally under-represented (less than 20 per cent in most of Latin America, North Africa and the Middle East), but there has been a marked increase in some areas, particularly in East Asia (Anker and Hein, 1986). In Hong Kong, South Korea, Taiwan, the Philippines, Singapore and Thailand, women constitute more than 40 per cent of the manufacturing labour force (See 1986 and 1989 United Nations *World Survey on the Role of Women in Development*).

The integration of LDCs into international markets has had its impact on women's labour force participation: the relatively rapid industrial expansion in the NICs has opened up a range of employment opportunities for both men and women. For women these have been largely in industries producing for export. Changes in the international economy have had their impact on women in two major ways. Firstly, women have most rapidly been absorbed into manufacturing in countries where the rate of growth of total industrial output and employment has been fastest. In most cases this is associated with rapid increases in the rate of growth of manufactured exports; the Four Little Tigers are good examples here. Thus we can say that women's employment in industry is positively correlated not only with the overall level of an economy's industrial growth but also with the degree of its integration into the international market economy.

Secondly, women in both LDCs and IMEs typically work in sectors or branches of industry which use predominantly labour-intensive techniques; in most instances these are traditional consumer goods industries. Manufactured exports from the NICs (although this has recently changed) are largely composed of non-durable consumer goods (textiles, clothing, footwear, electrical goods), produced using relatively labour intensive techniques – for example, in South Korea, where women are 43 per cent of industrial workers overall, they make up 67 per cent of the labour force in textile manufacture. Their significance for LDCs is particularly marked because of their strategic importance in total manufactured exports. Susan Joekes notes that 'Female labour is even more important in the export sector of most developing countries' industry than in the industrial sector as a whole' (Joekes, 1987, p.92). And she concludes that for the NICs industrialisation in the post-war period has been as much female-led as export-led.

A major lesson from the recent industrialisation of the LDCs is, therefore, the connection between the employment of women in certain industrial sectors and the deepening of international integration in manufactured production. Growing integration has not, however, been simply a matter of domestic manufacturers claiming a share of world export markets. As we noted earlier, many LDCs created special conditions to attract foreign direct investment in manufacturing. TNCs have had a major role to play in the increases of manufactured exports of NICs, particularly Singapore, South Korea and Brazil. World market factories were found by Oskar Kreyer in 51 out of 103 developing countries in 1977 (cited in Elson and Pearson, 1980, p.1). The TNCs transferred large sections of their production processes – particularly the labour intensive aspects – to export zones in Asia, the Caribbean and Latin America. They often imported their own technology, management and sometimes raw materials, only using local labour to produce the finished or semi-finished manufactured product which was then exported back to the home country. In the early-1970s, about 40 per cent of the employees of the US electronics industry were in developing countries. More recently, increasing use of technology is leading to cheap labour being a less important factor of production.[5]

The important point to note is that women's labour itself has been the basis of the growing international competitiveness of some NICs. The questions that this raises are: what is it about women's labour that provides such an important basis for competing internationally? Is the situation similar in industries producing for domestic markets? What have the effects been for women workers in the industrial labour force? To answer these questions we must look at some of the characteristics of women's labour, employment patterns, wage and income levels, levels of education and training, and working conditions.

Characteristics of women's labour force participation

Instability of employment

Possibly the most disturbing condition for many women workers is the instability of their work, their lack of job security and of labour protection. Research shows that employers frequently lay off women workers when there is a shortage of work and dismiss them with relative ease when production conditions change. For example, Noeleen Heyzer reports that during the 1974/5 world recession, 75 per cent of the 20,000 workers who lost their jobs in Singapore were women employed in the textile and electronics industries (Heyzer, 1986). Stability of employment within TNC factories, however, is unlikely to be worse than in domestic industry, both of which reflect the overall demand patterns for labour in the economy (Lim, 1985).

74

If technological change actually alters the pattern of production as well as the capital : labour ratio, the composition of the workforce may change permanently. New technologies tend to bring greater labour productivity and allow higher wages, thereby attracting male labour. The ability of men to pre-empt women benefiting from technological change is as much an issue of subjective gender ideology, i.e. the subordinate status of female labour and the ideological nature of many skill categories, as of the objective nature of male labour.

Women's lack of any prospect of long-term employment in industry, and therefore of being able to gain the benefits of seniority or promotion, their lack of on-the-job training and up-grading of skills, have dual effects. They are encouraged to view employment as temporary, outside their 'real' interests. When they are laid off, or have to give up their jobs because they are unable to keep up with production targets, they rarely have marketable skills and indeed may find it difficult even to be re-hired in their old occupations. Studies have shown that skilled production workers find less difficulty in finding work within their industry after a lay off than unskilled ones, and that unskilled workers find that increasing age is a severe constraint to further employment (Humphrey, 1987). Equally, despite years in industry they are likely to have virtually no management, supervisory or other skills which could be translated into self-employment or micro-entrepreneurship.

What are some of the reasons for job instability? Firstly, the nature of the work itself − labour intensive jobs are increasingly being brought under the control of technology. With increased technical levels men tend to be preferred employees. Secondly, because many women's jobs demand very high levels of concentration and hand to eye co-ordination, their productivity declines quite rapidly within a few years. Given that they are likely to be paid piece rates for their work, women's overall take-home pay becomes too low for survival, so they have to leave. Thirdly, the lack of support women workers receive from organised labour − there is a depressing litany of women's labour struggles which are not supported by the organised labour movement.

A number of studies have suggested that trade unions still appear to consider male workers' needs and demands to be their main concern and to view women as short-term and decidedly secondary workers (ILO, 1988). As a result women workers either have to struggle within their own union for recognition, or to fight their own battles without union support (and often without the support of male colleagues either). In many countries, and particularly in FTZs, trade unions are either banned or severely circumscribed. In the Philippines, special laws of 1970 and 1974 prohibited all labour disputes in the economic zones and reduced workers' freedom of assembly, but trade unions themselves were not banned. In Sri Lanka unions are again formally permitted to organise industrial workers in the FTZ but only management appointees are allowed to sit on the joint negotiating committees set up to handle industrial relations. In many areas joining a trade union leads to instant dismissal if known by management, in others those who attempt to get people to join a union are dismissed, as are all labour activists.

Despite these restrictions (argued to be imposed by governments rather than directly required by MNCs or foreign investors), workers have been quite militant in many areas, and women appear to be no less so than male workers. For example, in the first big strike in a FTZ in the Philippines by textile workers, a high proportion of the activists were women. Over 10,000 workers from 23 factories in the Bataan FTZ walked out, three-quarters of whom were women (Chapkis and Enloe, 1983). However, as Elson and Pearson (1984) pointed out, women's struggles are often more likely to erupt outside the trade union framework because of its tendency to exclude them. Their protest may be spontaneous and sporadic, but it may be more important than formal trade union membership in terms of developing the capacities of those concerned, particularly for self-organisation.

Low earnings

Women are not only crowded into few occupations but these are usually low paid, in part because they are categorised as unskilled or semi-skilled. As a result women earn less than men despite having similar qualifications and experience. Women may also complete lower total working hours than men or be unable to work higher paid shifts. Several studies have shown that women's other working day in the home makes it difficult for wives to take on better paid overtime work or higher rate, unsocial hours shifts (both typical strategies used by low paid males to boost earnings). During peak production periods, however, women are often obliged to take on considerable overtime work, but are still paid the same piece rate.

More significant in differential earnings is the fact that women tend to be paid lower rates than men. The 1988 ILO *Yearbook of Labour Statistics* shows that there are still enormous differentials in wages in manufacturing in many countries. For example, in South Korea women's wages in manufacturing are only 50.2 per cent of those of men: ten years ago they were 43 per cent. In Sri Lanka, the figure is 71.2 per cent and in Kenya, 65.2 per cent. It is difficult to draw substantial conclusions on wage rates because information on wages is not disaggregated by sex by many countries. But according to Anker and Hein (1986), the two countries where earnings differentials are most marked – South Korea and Singapore – are those with substantial export processing zones. The differences exist despite the fact that paying women less than men in the same job is illegal in most countries. The ILO's Equal Remuneration Convention (Convention 100, 1951) had been ratified by 103 countries by June 1983. There are some exceptions; women in electronics components companies in Malaysia are among the best paid workers in the country but so are men in the industry.

One of the complicating factors in discussion of differential wage rates is the fact that women and men are often paid in different ways – men typically receiving an hourly rate (i.e. a rate not tied to productivity) and women piece rates. We have already noted that overtime (usually paid at one and a half times the hourly rate) brings little benefit to those on piece rates. In some factories women are paid a low hourly basic rate, but their total wage is made up by bonus payments (again tied to productivity). High levels of self-exploitation are very hard to sustain over years of work, particularly since intense concentration and co-ordination lead to permanent physical deterioration.

Another complicating factor is the division of labour itself: women and men very rarely do identical jobs. Claims that women workers in TNCs actually earn higher wages than men of similar education and experience are found to be based on a comparison between women working in TNCs and men who are not. Within world market factories, women's wages are generally 20-50 per cent lower than those of men in comparable jobs (Elson and Pearson, 1980, p.13). It should also be remembered that while the initial wage rate may be relatively good in market terms, a characteristic of TNC employment is that women workers have virtually no hope of promotion or on the job training for higher level jobs, and seniority brings minimal increases in pay. Researchers have pointed to the fact that many TNCs in East Asia prefer to employ young, unmarried women, laying them off on marriage or pregnancy. For many such women this can have very serious effects on their standard of living, either because they have established consumption patterns or commitments which they are no longer able to meet, or their wages are essential to their parents' or siblings' survival.

Why women should be given lower pay has been the subject of some research. The commonest reasons given are low levels of education and training, but recent evidence shows that even when work experience and qualifications are taken into account, a considerable gap still remains for which there is no explanation other than discriminatory social factors, which are particularly marked as far as married women are concerned. A more sophisticated argument suggests that the mutually reinforcing combination of gender ideology and gender practices keep women's pay low. In other words gender ideology stresses the role of the man as the source of authority within the family, its head. This translates in modern employment terms into his role as chief breadwinner, for which he must be paid a higher, 'family' wage. Women as 'secondary' wage earners can be given a lower individual wage.

Lack of education and training

Women in most LDCs have lower educational levels than men, although the degree of difference varies by region. Largely as a result of parental discrimination and gender differences in curriculum in formal school education, young women start their working life without the same level of human capital investment as their male counterparts. They are thus unable to seek out jobs demanding greater skill and providing higher wage prospects. From the point of view of employers this may make women perfectly suitable candidates for the unskilled, repetitive manual assembly jobs associated with labour-intensive manufacturing, which require high degrees of concentration but little formal education or on-the-job training. But even for the women who have managed to go through school, the completion of a certain level of education does not bring a commensurate rise in standard or type of employment or earning. For example, in Belo Horizonte in Brazil, the completion of primary education can signify a 60 per cent rise in earnings for men compared to only 6 per cent for women (ICRW, 1980, p.47).

Susan Joekes has argued that what real differences there are in male and female educational levels are built on by employers in that they tend to set wage rates by nominal rather than real skill categories (Joekes, 1987). A task is first defined as women's work, then the wage rate for unskilled work is set for it. That employers do this and do so successfully, is an effect of the general tendency to undervalue the work that women do.

The perception that the work done by women does not require training is itself worthy of closer scrutiny. As we have seen, gender ideology maintains that women are naturally more suited to tasks requiring dexterity (women's 'nimble fingers'). Another aspect of this is the implicit assumption (usually correct) that young women will have already acquired some training in the course of their socialisation into womanhood. Sewing is a good example: women are preferred for employment in textile industries because they already know the basics of sewing. Many of the skills required in the electronics industry are very similar to sewing and are thus quickly and easily learned by women, but only because of prior, informal, training. This belies the idea that women's work is unskilled – it is just that their skills are taken for granted. Ability to do careful work requiring minute observation is also a result of girls' socialisation and gender relations: girls and women learn very early on to read the moods of adults and children and to adjust their behaviour accordingly.

In addition, there is a common belief among many employers that women, particularly young women, are self-effacing, deferential to authority, and preoccupied with the social obligation of finding a marriage partner. These qualities are seen as being inherent rather than the result of socialisation processes. When combined with actual characteristics – close hand to eye co-ordination, attention to detail, considerable powers of concentration in noisy environments, ability to tolerate monotonous work – they make young women prime candidates for highly intensive, poorly-paid jobs with no prospects. Women's 'feminine' qualities, and their commitment to the family, are thought to keep the expectations of women for training and promotion very low. From the employers' point of view the apparently submissive qualities of a female workforce not only strengthen the unit labour cost advantage of female over male labour, but also allow for easy implementation of organisational changes in production processes and the flexibility to hire and fire labour in accord with booms and slumps in cycles of economic activity. Including on-the-job training for women workers would bring no particular benefit to employers in these circumstances, and is unlikely to be a feature of employment practice in labour intensive industries. For women workers these assumptions and the practices built upon them present formidable barriers to advancement through the workplace.

Poor conditions of work

Working conditions are rarely given high priority by other than very stable manufacturing companies. Indeed many employers retain their competitive edge by cutting down on costs relating to the working environment, such as health and safety regulations, provision of lavatories, rest-rooms and places where workers can relax.

Most studies note that working conditions in export-oriented industries vary according to what is produced – electronic enterprises being cleaner and freer from dust and noise than garment or textile factories. On the other hand, the fast pace and the monotonous and repetitive nature of assembly work exerts a heavy toll on workers' physical and mental health, which is exacerbated by the rigidly disciplined environment. Workers complain of heightened nervousness and stomach complaints as well as back and eyestrain (particularly the case amongst electronics workers using microscopes in microchip welding). Forced overtime and imposition of ever higher production quotas increase fatigue and the likelihood of accidents. Some studies show that conditions within foreign firms as against local enterprises are better partly because the former may be under greater obligation to observe labour regulations. Lim (1985) maintains that, as with job stability, conditions are likely to reflect the overall conditions and requirements of the existing economy.

Many of the industries women work in involve the use of hazardous substances – dyes and glues in footwear and toys, various chemicals in pharmaceuticals and even food processing. Recently the electronics industry has been added to the list of high health-risk industries because of workers' exposure to acids, solvents and gases. Medical evidence shows that pregnant workers may well suffer ill-effects from these substances in terms of foetal development. Workers themselves complain of acid burns, dizziness and nausea, skin rashes and swollen eyes, painful lungs, as well as painful kidneys, urinary tract infections and other problems.

Apart from the work environment, many anecdotal reports allude to the appalling conditions and long hours that young women workers are expected to endure if they want to keep their jobs. In many Asian countries the standard working week is 48 hours but in practice there is wide variation with very long hours of overtime when the order books are full at peak periods, and little work, even (temporary) lay-offs, during periods of low demand. Companies employ many techniques to prolong the working day during peak periods such as enforced overtime, quota systems and non-recognition of public holidays. A recent study showed that in the Philippines, on top of an 8 hour shift, 2 to 4 hours of overtime daily is usual. This rises at times of peak production, when double and triple hour shifts are demanded, i.e. working for 16 or even 24 hours straight off (Joekes, 1985). In the same country a recent survey showed that 46 per cent of workers worked almost 60 hours per week and 25 per cent worked more than this. In Malaysia 50 per cent of firms surveyed operated on a three shift basis and about 25 per cent of the women worked more than 48 hours a week. In Sri Lanka 46 per cent of the workers clocked up more than 48 hours and 17 per cent more than 55 hours a week.

Intense periods of long overtime are most common in the clothing industry, which also suffers from periods of little or no work during which workers do not get paid. In neither case do the workers have any choice in the matter; as we noted, frequently overtime does not even attract additional pay. Quota systems, which set the number of items a worker must produce in a working day, are enforced by disciplinary sanctions and fines, or the competitive pressure of bonus payments.

Protective legislation

Many countries have special regulations covering women's working conditions. These may deal with the hours during which women may work or the type of work they may do – placing limitations on particularly heavy or physically demanding work – or they may be aimed at meeting specific needs such as the provision of crèches or maternity leave. For example, ILO Convention No. 89 (1948) limits the amount of night work that women can do. It is, however, ratified by less than half the LDCs; many repeal the prohibition on night work when economic necessity requires women workers. South Korea now allows women to work in 24 out of 30 occupations which were previously prohibited (Anker and Hein, 1986).

The restrictions on night work have been condemned by many people as discriminatory: they make women less attractive to employers, and the ban can become an element in women's lower wages since night work often commands higher wages. Arguments in favour of the ban do have a somewhat paternalistic tone but there is considerable evidence to show that women are vulnerable to physical attacks when going to or leaving work in darkness.

Legislation may be a mixed blessing as it can work to justify forms of discrimination against women, particularly excluding them from certain jobs. It may be more protective of male jobs than of women. For example, Paraguay maintains a legal code which prevents women access to work that might be dangerous to their morality (unspecified). Even provision for women's dual role as productive workers and mothers can be detrimental. The ILO Maternity

Protection Convention of 1952 had, in 1983, been ratified by only 22 member countries, indicating employers' unwillingness to give maternity leave or make allowances for nursing mothers. Where legislation is in force, it can provide a justification for not employing women. For example, compulsory provision of workplace crèches may make the employment of women uneconomic in management eyes. 'Social legislation which has a protective purpose proves to be too costly to employers and encourages preferential hiring of males' (ICRW, 1980, p.52).

Few if any studies report the provision by employers of such things as crèches for children, transport to get the women to work, medical services, subsidised canteens, savings facilities. All of these are an additional non-wage cost which could make employing women less attractive, particularly if there is a labour surplus. None the less the division of labour ensures that some women will be sought as workers. One way employers can avoid the problem of childcare is to give jobs only to young, preferably unmarried women. And in fact, most of the women workers in the EPZs tend to be relatively young, and in manufacturing they are generally between 17 and 25 years of age. Worldwide it has been estimated that 85 per cent of female export processing workers are under 25 years of age. There are interesting differences by geographic region and by type of industry; electronics employs the youngest workers and garments the oldest. Marital status also varies: 80 per cent of workers in export-oriented TNCs in Asia are single (the range is between 70 and 95 per cent regionally). In the Caribbean and Central America the majority of women tend to be older, in some form of marital union, often have children and have sole or major financial responsibility for their households.

Conclusions

A review of the by now copious literature on women in manufacturing employment leads to the fairly obvious conclusion that, across regions and even within specific countries, women are integrated into the industrialisation process in different ways. Women industrial workers do not all experience all the conditions described in this chapter. None the less, women's employment tends to be in jobs which are designated as low skill and paid accordingly, and in an occupational hierarchy which usually provides few or no opportunities for promotion.

The increase in numbers of women working in export manufacture has sparked off a debate on the advantages and disadvantages of this type of employment for women (see Elson and Pearson, 1984 for an early example). Some writers argue that transnational export factories expand job opportunities for women, offer higher wages and better working conditions than domestic firms, and promote sexual equality by integrating women into the modern labour market. Their opponents contend that the jobs on offer are usually unskilled, dead-end and poorly paid; women put themselves at risk of permanently damaging their health for only half men's wages; they learn no transferable skills and enjoy no labour rights or benefits. A recent report on this for USAID concludes that the reality is complex.

On the basis of women's actual employment alternatives, export manufacturing employment unquestionably provides steady incomes, at least for a short period of time. Working conditions, though harsh and unyielding, are at least no worse than those in other sectors. However EPZs perpetuate occupation and wage discrimination by sex and may also subject women to particular health hazards in some industries. In addition, employment in a zone may represent only a short-lived opportunity for improvement in individual women's economic position (Joekes and Moayedi, 1987, p.1).

On balance the authors conclude that such employment provides short but not long-term economic benefits for women in LDCs.

From another angle, wage work may bring benefits in terms of an increase in women's power and status within the family. Amartya Sen (1985, 1987) has discussed how the ability of individuals within a household or family to meet their own wants ('preferences') is to some extent dependent on their 'perceived contribution' to family income. While women's domestic labour continues to be taken for granted and not perceived as a specific contribution to family well-being, an ability to command a regular income through wage work may add to their ability to have more say within the family. However, working women may also have to face considerable difficulties in cultures where the prevailing ideology maintains a 'breadwinner' ethic for men, including resentment about their ability to command wages, possibly because men's perceived contribution is being eroded.

Development planning for or with women

What then are the lessons to be derived from this? Firstly, policymakers and planners need to recognise that women are *not* 'secondary' workers. This of course has implications for the type of education, formal and vocational, offered to women, and for in-service training. That development should involve growing levels of learning and education in the population as a whole is widely recognised – although reality falls far behind the theory. Most research also shows that a woman's level of education is a critical factor in children's acceptance of and enthusiasm for learning; furthermore, the more educated the woman the more likely she will be able to negotiate limiting family size. The combination of education and access to forms of employment which have some prospect of advancement almost everywhere are the greatest stimuli to later marriage, smaller family size and better child welfare. The implication here is that a low wage, dead-end job strategy for women workers pursued by employers, is of great disbenefit to society as a whole. Yet the effects are paid for in the end by everyone in society, including local business.

Secondly, given that women will continue to have children and be responsible for their well-being for a number of years, planning with women would assess the implications of women's double work shift, and face up to the need for (and cost of) provision of childcare facilities, and a system of early education. Experience has shown that both can be of benefit rather than a detriment to society, given that early mixing with other children and early learning can help children adapt more readily to school at the appropriate time. But should such childcare provision be the responsibility of individual business enterprises, or of the state itself?

Most evidence to date shows that employers only provide such facilities when there is an acute labour shortage, and are reluctant to employ women workers with dependant children. The obligation to provide a crèche etc. is often used by employers as a reason for not employing women ('too costly'). One way round this would be to make all enterprises of a certain size provide crèche facilities whether or not they employ women – men after all are fathers. State provision also spreads the cost across all sectors of society. It can be argued that government has a duty to provide the best conditions possible for the socialisation of the younger generation. Low-income working mothers are a feature of modern society, and ignoring their needs is likely to be at the risk of prejudicing the future generation.

Thirdly, opening up a wide range of jobs to women should be a planning objective. This is a more contentious proposition with the new emphasis on private enterprise. While it may not be the planners' responsibility to create job openings, it is their business to. ensure that women are not discriminated against in employment. A key issue is the role of the state itself as employer of women; in most LDCs it is a major employer of women (albeit not in manufacturing). By providing the best conditions possible (within economic constraints), including training for women so they can enter a range of jobs and skills, the state can give a lead to private sector employers.

Lastly, the point has to be made again that without women's involvement in planning, and without widespread consultation with women workers, many of the changes required to make employment for women both feasible for them and profitable for the employer will remain ignored or even unknown. Families in developing countries, particularly poor families, require both mothers and fathers as income earners; less poverty is likely to lead to greater individual planning and effort, fewer unwanted children and sickly adults. Poverty is a terrible cost to developing countries, both socially and economically.

Notes

1 In fact in the early-1980s, primary commodities accounted for 70 per cent or more of the total exports of 42 out of 59 countries for which the World Bank gave data (Southall, 1988, p.15). Where there has been an increase in manufacturing for export, this has been limited to relatively small geographical areas. In 1977, 14 countries accounted for 90 per cent of LDC industrial exports (Southall, 1988, p.15).

2 Attitudes to the activities of TNCs in LDCs have ranged from seeing them as leeches, draining the host country in an entirely parasitic and exploitative way, to valuable generators of employment, technical know-how and foreign exchange. In reality, direct employment effects are not particularly significant: the 50 or so EPZs world-wide, employ about one million workers, 80-90 per cent of whom are women engaged primarily in manufacture for export, who work for a short period of their lives (ILO, 1988).

3 By 1990, South Korea, an early NIC and proponent of EOI, was in serious economic difficulties, in part because of sharp competition from the newer NICs (Malaysia, Thailand, Indonesia). The competition is severest in those segments of manufacturing industry which brought the country to a high level of prosperity in the 1980s – electronics and electrical household goods.

4 The film, *Rosie the Riveter*, provides an excellent portrayal of the manipulation of the ideology of the gender's natural capacities. It was made with a number of women who took part in the US war effort in the 1940s.

5 The importance of TNCs for women's employment should not be overemphasised though: Lim points out that women's employment in TNCs represents less than 1 per cent of their overall labour force participation in developing countries (Lim, 1985, p.8).

6 Women and the urban informal sector: The case of Latin America and the Caribbean

The last chapter focused on formal employment and looked at some trends in women's employment in manufacturing. For example, while women's employment in manufacturing has increased in South-East Asia, it has declined in Latin America. However, declining rates of growth in female employment should not be interpreted as meaning that women are being pushed out of or are leaving the labour force. In reality they may well be moving into other sectors or types of activity. In almost all regions over the past decades women's employment in service industries has expanded rapidly. The expansion has been so significant that some researchers argue that, in general, women's employment has been more resilient to global recession than men's (Joekes, 1987). It appears too that the number of women engaged in domestic outwork (making goods for the manufacturing sector within the home) and the informal sector has also escalated in recent years.

In some regions the apparent increase may be due to a greater understanding of (or research into) the ways large sectors of the population gain a livelihood – although these activities still do not show up in official statistics – rather than to an actual increase in the proportion of people engaged in them. Nevertheless, a distinct feature of industrialisation in most Latin American (and some Asian) countries has been the growth of light manufacturing and service activities in the unorganised or informal sector. Women are major actors in this sector and in many diverse ways support the formal industrialisation effort by providing complementary services to industrial enterprises (and their employees), through domestic outwork, making and selling street foods, the simple domestic manufacture of garments and footwear; and by garbage collection and recycling. It is likely that economies increasingly directed to production for export, are as dependent on these unofficial female (and male) workers, providing low cost services and contributing cheap goods to the domestic market, as on the official labour force, to ensure their competitive edge.

Over the last twenty years debates on the so-called informal sector have spawned a vast literature. Dozens of case studies and policy documents discuss both its form and how and whether it should be supported by government policy, aid agencies, etc. (*Redistribution With Growth* being one of the first – see Chapter 2). There is, however, no agreement as to what is actually being referred to by the term informal sector. Many argue that its descriptive – let alone explanatory – power is negligible; that using the term at all merely perpetuates a misleading dichotomy; that a conceptual tool which gained prominence in the 1970s is now, in the 1990s, obsolete. Others firmly declare its relevance – some indeed claim that it is the form, par excellence, that economic activity takes in the LDCs.

In this chapter we will address some of the conceptual and methodological issues, but our main argument is that gender is a critical dimension of the analysis of the processes of casualisation or informalisation of labour. Equally, the conditions under which women are incorporated into the informal labour market will help to illuminate further why gender matters. Though the limitations of a strict informal/formal sector dichotomy will become clear, policymakers and planners need to look at patterns of labour use and income generation that are ostensibly less regulated in order to grasp the complexity of linkages within the economy as a whole. In this chapter we will largely concentrate on evidence from Latin America where much research has been carried out into the informal sector and casualised labour. There is, however, a wealth of literature on these topics from almost every region of the world (including Europe).

Background and methodological issues

In Chapter 5 we pointed to the fact that among the presumed benefits of industrialisation was its potential for creating employment and absorbing ever larger proportions of the available labour force. In Latin America reality did not match expectations: not only was the new industrial sector unable to provide a sufficient number of jobs, the displacement of the rural population was much more rapid and severe than had been anticipated, in large part because of the economic changes industrialisation brought with it. To illustrate this point briefly we will take Mexico, which adopted Import Substitution Industrialisation in the 1940s, as an example.

Firstly, the process of domestic industrialisation had unexpected effects: although the light consumer goods produced in first stage ISI were intended to replace imports, many of them actually displaced a good deal of existing domestic production. Much of this was located in the rural areas and formed an essential part of the household economy. Machine-made textiles replaced handwoven cloth, ready-made factory clothing replaced that produced by artisans or in small workshops, cheap factory china replaced terracotta goods made by local potters, mass-made aluminium pots and buckets replaced earthenware pots and iron buckets, and so on. With the destruction of much domestic industry, many rural families found that their survival was undermined, and the younger generation had to migrate to the urban areas in search of work (Young, 1976). Secondly, an unfavourable price system which privileged manufactured products over agricultural goods also led to an outflow of peasant producers impoverished by the unequal exchange. Thirdly, the existence of schools in towns drew many of the brighter and more ambitious young men (few girls being allowed to go) out of the rural areas and into the towns.

In all there was a considerable exodus from the countryside to the town, from the agricultural sector to the industrial, at a rate much faster than that planned for. And, as in many other Latin American countries, even under best conditions, the nascent industrial sector did not have the capacity to absorb this massive quantity of labour. Urbanisation outstripped industrialisation.

In many LDCs a contributory factor to labour surplus was rapid population growth. In Latin America, as elsewhere over the past 50 years, this has been fairly spectacular. By the 1980s, however, growth rates were slowing down, although not at the same speed everywhere. In Latin America, until the 1980s, levels of education, industrialisation, and urbanisation were quite advanced and provision of health services tolerable (except in the remoter rural areas). As a result, child and infant mortality had declined relatively fast, and birth rates fell faster than in other developing regions. The annual rate of population increase in the first five years of the 1980s was considerably less than in the equivalent period in the 1960s. However, the rapid rates of population growth of the 1960s and 1970s are now reflected in the expanding labour force, as those born in the earlier decades reach working age. As a result, the labour force grew from 113 million in 1980 to 131 million in 1985, without a corresponding increase in available jobs.

The population not only expanded, it shifted spatially. Between 1950 and 1980, population doubled in the LDCs, but the urban population rose 3.6 times. Again, rates of urbanisation were uneven, the greatest increases being recorded for Latin America: while in 1940 19.6 per cent of the population lived in urban areas, by 1960 32.8 per cent did. Between 1980 and 1985, the region's urban population rose at an average rate of 3.9 per cent annually, while the rural population remained almost unchanged (Europa, 1987). The resulting visible manifestations of poverty, shanty towns – *villas miserias, favelas,* or *pueblos jovenes* as they are variously called – indicate the gap between the hope of regular, adequately paid employment and the reality for most of the urban poor. Cities in Latin America are now among the biggest in the world. Mexico City, the biggest of them all, with roughly 3 million inhabitants in

1950, now has around 18 million, and is projected to be the home of a staggering 31 million people by the year 2000.

In short, as a result of the restructuring of the economy, the movement of population from the rural to the urban areas and the growth of population, the provision of formal, regulated wage employment for the bulk of the population has become a virtually impossible dream for the majority of Latin American countries. But since people must survive they have themselves sought income-earning opportunities and have created a variety of economic activities which probably provide the source of livelihood for the majority of the population. The types of informal economic activity are extremely heterogeneous and have for many years defied neat categorisation by development academics and policymakers alike.

The working poor

By the early 1970s, as we saw in Chapter 2, development economists began to be worried by the poor distribution of the benefits of what economic growth there was, evidenced by growing mass poverty, and the rapid and distorted growth of Third World cities. Concern focused on unemployment, most research centering on the problems of city dwellers without regular work. Partially in response to these concerns, the ILO established its World Employment Programme (WEP) in 1969.

The WEP strategy, *Towards Full Employment*, involved sponsoring missions to investigate the nature of urban labour markets and the conditions of labour participation in a number of LDCs. The missions, at both country and city level, were charged with evolving development strategies which would increase overall levels of employment. The first mission in 1970, to Colombia, was followed in 1971 by one to Sri Lanka. Both missions found three distinct but related dimensions of the problem. Firstly, most people were not strictly unemployed; rather they were working in very intermittent, low-productivity, poorly-paid jobs. The lack of work opportunities offering a reasonable livelihood led to quite high levels of frustration amongst the working age population. Secondly, a significant proportion of both the urban and rural labour force lacked an adequate source of income to meet their basic needs. Thirdly, a great deal of the economic potential of both countries was being wasted through the amount of underutilised as well as unutilised labour.

The 1972 Kenya mission differed from the previous missions in defining its central problem not as unemployment but the nature of employment. In the standard economics literature the term unemployment is defined as being without gainful work (individuals are categorised as being unemployed voluntarily – preferring not to work – or involuntarily – unable to get work). Development economists began to realise that such a narrow definition of unemployment was inappropriate for LDCs because it disguises chronic labour underutilisation – just as the term employment disguises the dreadful conditions and poor wage levels of much of the employed workforce.

The Kenya mission researchers made the point that most people simply could not afford not to work. Most people were struggling to survive on inadequate incomes, but had no alternative but to continue working: 'in addition to people who are not working at all, there is another – and in Kenya more numerous – group of people whom we call the working poor' (ILO, 1972, p.9). The term informal sector (originally coined by Keith Hart [1973] in his study of employment among the urban poor in Ghana) was used to describe the sector of activity of the working poor. Their enterprises were small in scale, largely escaping recognition, enumeration, regulation, government protection or support. According to the Kenya mission, the Informal Sector (IS) absorbed between 28 and 33 per cent of all those working in the urban areas.

Methodologically, the term was used to classify urban activities often without identifiable and analytically useful common characteristics. Part of the fascination with the IS was the difficulty of neatly categorising it and fitting it into existing models of the economy. But equally intriguing was the question of whether the state should support the sector to provide the source of livelihood that its industrialisation strategies had failed to do. The ILO report on the Kenya mission – *Employment, Incomes and Equality* – notes that the sector has great potential for growth and could provide the solution to Kenya's employment problems (ILO, 1972). And it recommends that the government should cease trying to get rid of IS operators (clearing the streets of vendors, destroying their shanties) and instead should recognise the capacity of the sector both to provide employment and to expand the economy. The Kenya mission researchers argued strongly that most IS employment is economically efficient and profit-making, and that the IS is a crucial component of the socio-economic system in that it offers a form of livelihood to a wide range of people who could not hope to get employment in the formal sector. Support for the IS would thus provide a cost effective way to solve one of the most pressing of the LDCs problems – poverty.

But other development practitioners criticised this policy recommendation since promotion of the IS was considered to dissolve rather than resolve many problems for governments. For example, according to Manfred Bienefeld: (by adopting this strategy there would be) 'no massive unemployment since the allegedly unemployed labour was working in the informal sector' (Bienefeld, 1981, p.9, and see also Leys, 1975, pp.267-8). The policy recommendation of encouraging small-scale entrepreneurs, was, however, acceptable to many international institutions and middle of the road governments.

The ILO report identified the family-based household as being an important economic actor in the IS, and noted that women predominated among the working poor. However, it failed to make any systematic analysis of intra-household relations nor the relationship between these and the local informal or formal economy. It did not look at how paid and unpaid tasks are allocated nor to whom, nor at the organisation of work directed to immediate family consumption and that directed to its long-term survival. What other studies of those living in poverty have shown, however, is that it is essential to look at the activities of all members of the household and see how these fit together before one can begin to understand how households survive, or what their relationship is to both the formal and informal economy (Dwyer and Bruce, 1988; Beneria and Roldan, 1987; Moser and Young, 1981). This fact is highlighted by the widespread evidence that women constitute a substantial part of those working in the so-called informal sector and that they are frequently recruited under conditions very different from those of men. We will examine this in more depth later, after discussing some of the criticisms of the IS concept itself.

Problems with conceptualising the Informal Sector

From the very beginning the lively debate which followed upon the ILO sponsorship of the IS focused on two main issues: the characterisation of the economic activities and actors involved, and the adequacy of the dualist framework. The two are linked in the analyses of those who perceive the informal/formal sector relationship as being essentially exploitative. We shall look at both in turn.

As a number of writers point out, there is tremendous confusion about what is meant by the informal sector; the term is applied in different contexts at different times to different referents (see Tokman, 1978; Moser, 1984). The initial ILO distinction between formal and informal economic activity was on the basis of the characteristics of the enterprise. Other researchers, however, concentrated on the differences in the nature of the labour market. Still others emphasised the nature of employment (see also Mezzara, 1989, for a conceptualisation based on surplus labour and lack of productive resources, especially capital to complement labour). As a result, the informal sector can be synonymous with the urban poor, immigrants to cities, people living in slums, or small-scale entrepreneurs (Moser, 1978). In other words, the term is used equally to describe individuals, households, enterprises and activities. Today, size of the enterprise (less than five employees), as well as individual self-employment seems to have gained favour as the main criteria of informality.

Using different criteria, the size and nature of the IS has been very variably presented. For example: 'In many developing countries, the sector as a whole occupies between 50-70 per cent of the urban population' (Cornia et al., 1987, p.93), or 'the micro and small-scale enterprise sector represents 85-95 per cent of the total number of establishments in LDCs' (CIDA, 1987, p.7); the Kenya mission estimated the sector comprised between 28 and 33 per cent of all urban workers (ILO, 1972). In Costa Rica, defining the IS in terms of self-employment, it was claimed that it grew at twice the rate of the formal sector in the early-1980s (Chacon, 1987). In São Paulo State (Brazil), IS activity, calculated in terms of labour units, was held to have increased hugely relative to regular employment – an increase of 1.8 million units out of a total of 2.4 million (Macedo,1987, p.34). In Lima, Peru, it has been estimated that the urban IS represents 39 per cent of the economically active population of which more than 70 per cent are in commerce and services (Pinilla-Cisneros, 1987, p.6).

The problem with such confusion is not merely that the definition used determines the target group selected for policy intervention, but depending upon the relationship of that group to the wider economy, the policy benefits may in fact be subverted by a quite different set of economic actors. To make sense of this we need to look at some of the issues around conceptualisation of the formal-informal sector relationship.

The ILO formulation envisaged the informal sector as an arena of autonomous free enterprise interacting little if at all with the formal sector and relatively independent of it. However, this places arbitrary and artificial boundaries between various productive activities, thereby compartmentalising activities which are in reality organically linked to each other. The links between formal and informal sector enterprises are in fact often complex, and the boundary between them not easily ascertained. Birkbeck's example of the garbage picker in Cali, Colombia, illustrates this point well (1979). The man was one of the city's 1200 to 1500 garbage pickers who collect domestic waste paper for a local factory where it is recycled for re-use by the paper industry. The poverty-stricken garbage pickers are a vital source of raw materials for the industry but are paid extremely low piece-work rates. They appear to be self-employed but are actually a vital part of a multi-million dollar transnational enterprise that stretches vertically from casual labourers, whose poverty derives from the fact that they work for the factory but are not part of it, through employees receiving average wages, to highly-paid salaried executives.

Many such casualised labourers can in fact be described as subcontracted outworkers, and much research hints at the existence of a vast number of outworkers in LDC cities – there are estimated to be 20,000-25,000 garment industry outworkers in Mexico City alone – but hard data are difficult to come by.

The rationale behind subcontracting for entrepreneurs is that it provides a way to lower production costs and spread risks. Subcontracting can be to firms or to individuals. Instead of having a large factory-based labour force (relatively easy to unionise and thus with the possibility of labour militancy over wages and conditions), entrepreneurs can divide their labour force into two segments, an internal and an external one. The external work force – those working at home or in small unregulated workshops – can both be paid less than the going rates for similar work on-site and denied benefits (health or unemployment insurance, or paid holiday time). Equally, when there is little work the out-workers absorb the cost of no pay, when there is too much, they can bear the physical and mental cost of long hours of overtime work. This flexibility helps spread the risks of producing for very volatile and choosy markets. Some commentators are now suggesting that household industry – classified on ILO criteria as informal sector activity – is actually a growing part of the new international division of labour that includes large-scale industry, TNCs, and EPZs (see Beneria and Roldan, 1987).

With more research, it has become clear that although IS employment is in the main associated with poverty, not all those in regulated employment are better off than those working in less well regulated conditions. A substantial number of people work in the formal sector simply to acquire know-how and capital so as to be able to start up a family-based IS enterprise. This may give them a better standard of living and greater social status (see Schmitz, 1982; Bromley, 1978). In the Latin culture there is a strong link between the ideology of man the breadwinner and family head, and that of man the independent self-employed producer and head of the family firm. It is less clear whether, when the family is the unit of production, only the male household head is better off than he was, other household members being as poor or even poorer than before.

Nowadays small-scale, largely unregulated, resource-poor enterprises are usually located conceptually within the general structure of all economic activity as it extends from the large-scale factory to the household. The nature of links with the market, levels of skill and technological expertise, the intensity of use of capital and sources of capital, do vary considerably, but that variation does not imply the existence of separate economic sectors. None the less, many of the issues raised by the attempts to theorise the IS and the nature of LDC labour markets are still relevant today, as is reflected in current concern with flexible specialisation and the trend towards increasing decentralisation of production.

Flexible specialisation

Recently, a major wave of technological modernisation based on microelectronic technologies has taken place in the IMEs and some of the NICs. In the main, the new intelligent machines or computer-based technologies promise to reduce capital costs and at the same time to increase the flexibility and the variety of production. This means that small-scale production has become a much more viable proposition and that firms can become involved in what is called flexible specialisation. By this is meant that small-scale production (and distribution) units can shift their production rapidly to suit the demands of increasingly choosy and selective markets. One of the implications of small-scale production is that avoiding unnecessary labour costs is a top priority. Indications are that firms will increasingly rely on labour located outside the firm – that is on subcontracting and domestic outworking.[1] But these outworkers will be rather different to the unskilled outworkers of the past. They are likely to be quite specialised workers using high-technology machines. They may also earn substantial incomes from their involvement in small-scale special-ised production units.

Will women benefit from these new directions in production and labour use? The major danger is that of the weakness of individuated labour relative to the contractor/employer in a system where maximising profits is the major aim (Lyberaki, 1988). Individual women will have to become much more knowledgeable about their rights and the contractors' obligations, while women workers as a group will have to devise forms of organisation through which to gain protection and to exert the political force to get appropriate employment legislation passed in their own countries.

Gender and the informal sector

We saw in the last chapter that men and women are incorporated into the formal labour force in different ways. During periods of expansion of the labour force, women may be absorbed at rates equal to or faster than those of men but usually into jobs at the lower end of the occupational scale, with less autonomy, greater insecurity and frequently poorer wages. Is this also the case in the casualised, less regulated labour force? Despite great heterogeneity, certain patterns can be discerned. For example, in Sylvia Chant's study of Queretaro, an industrial town in Mexico (Chant, 1987), the extent of social security protection was taken as a measure of formality of employment. She found that two-thirds of men, but only a quarter of women were in protected employment. Women also consistently outnumbered men in services and commerce, but, since they did not own their own businesses and spent more time producing items than trading, their earnings were consistently lower than men's: the average net weekly income from informal commerce was 1741 pesos for women and 3232 pesos for men.

Although many of the problems faced by women in casual work are also faced by men – insecurity, lack of capital, poor incomes, government harass-ment – women invariably face additional burdens related to their reproductive roles and lack of control over domestic resources and limited access to social resources. In this section we will look more closely at women's informal work, then go on to examine what lies behind its characteristics. We will examine the question of how do gender ideology and changing labour market conditions interact?

Characteristics of women's informal sector work
The first point to be made is that much information on women as casual workers is sketchy and frequently unreliable. The lack of data partly reflects

assumptions about what constitutes work (see Chapter 7), and partly the considerable difficulties in collecting data. For this reason, we rely mainly on information from case-studies rather than on statistics.

In general, women's informal work tends to require lower capital outlay than men's (Bunster, 1983), and to reflect and accommodate itself to their family responsibilities (Heyzer, 1981; Moser and Young, 1981). Women also tend to be concentrated in very specific and limited areas of employment; one study of women's employment in Lima, Peru showed that only 11 per cent were in activities which did not already have a marked female concentration (MacEwan Scott, 1986, p.344).

There is an intimate relationship between women's work in the household and family and their acceptance as specific kinds of wage and income-generating workers. Women turn their domestic skills into market skills (as do men but to a lesser degree) – they commoditise their domestic labour. As Nelson put it: 'The boundary between women's unpaid domestic labour and the paid labour they perform in the informal (and even the formal) sector is often a tenuous one. Both in the domestic realm and in the market place, women provide food, childcare, domestic services, charm, companionship and sex' (Nelson, 1979, p.299). A Ministry of Labour survey in Lima, Peru, showed that 55 per cent of women worked in activities which can be described as untransformed domestic work, such as washing and cleaning, dressmaking, food production and sales; a further 11 per cent were in somewhat more professionalised occupations based on domestic skills: domestic service, nursing, social work (cited in MacEwan Scott, 1986). The reasons for this are varied and each has a different weight at different stages in the life cycle. They include the practical appreciation of the sense of making use of existing skills, the need to combine income generation with childcare (men rarely take this on, even when they have no other work), the pressure to remain near the confines of the home, and women's exclusion from certain areas of work that are deemed culturally unsuitable.

As a result women become involved in food processing, cooking, childcare, washing and cleaning, healing and counselling, mending and making clothes for the market. Women's own domestic budgeting skills and making do with what is available, can be transferred into the occupation of professional seller, higgler, market woman, trader or trading intermediary. However, not all domestic skills are transferred to the market – women are not easily accepted as managers despite their notable domestic competence in this area; selling sexual services on the market is not considered appropriate, and women who do so, either because they are forced to or consider it legitimate to do so, are considered bad women. Despite this, sexual servicing may well be one of the commonest forms of income earning for women, whether it is done occasionally to get the family out of an economic fix or as a permanent full or part-time occupation. Men too can sell their domestic skills, but more often they apprentice themselves to relatives, neighbours or even strangers to learn a trade.

We will look at these patterns in two broad sectors of activity: firstly manufacturing, with women as both managers of their own enterprises and subcontractors, and secondly in services, including domestic work, trading and providing catering services.

Manufacturing

Many small-scale enterprises as well as individuals are involved in producing goods for the market whether these are to eat, to wear or to use. A census of small manufacturing enterprises in Jamaica showed that equal numbers of men and women were owners/operators of small-scale enterprises. When non-manufacturing small enterprises were included, the proportion of women was greater because of their strong representation in commerce and service activities (Van der Wees and Romijn, 1987). It is difficult to say whether specific types of production are more likely to be undertaken by men, partly because so many of the small-scale enterprises are categorised as being family based. Statistical evidence is hard to come by, precisely because of their unregulated nature. Even when studies of micro-scale businesses are undertaken – as is increasingly the case – data are often still not given by the sex of the business owner or operator. But on the whole women appear to predominate in food processing, making women's and children's clothing, handicrafts (pottery, baskets, etc.) while men work more with metal, wood and leather, and are often concerned with repairing electrical goods, machines, bikes, cars, etc. Women's enterprises usually require extremely small amounts of working and capital investment, men's slightly greater.

Smallness is a general feature (some would say a major characteristic) of IS enterprises, but women's enterprises are noticeably extremely small – often now called micro-enterprises – and based either on the woman herself or herself and her children. This raises a number of questions: are women less able than men to command non-family sources of labour or are they less concerned to expand their enterprises than men? If the latter is the case, is it a result of their more reduced access to resources or some other factor?

All the evidence points to the fact that women experience greater difficulties than men in getting access to institutional sources of credit, savings and investment, information about markets, etc. (see Berger and Buvinic, 1989). As a result, they have to rely to a greater extent than men on local, household and kin resources. However, studies also show that they may have great difficulty in getting hold of household resources other than those destined for immediate and familial consumption purposes, what has been called the collective aspect of the household budget (Whitehead, 1984). In most cultures men have easier access to (household) resources for personal expenditures than their wives (Pahl, 1983; Dwyer and Bruce, 1988; Young, 1990). They may also invest money from the household budget in their own enterprises without question. Sometimes this even involves an indirect transfer of money from a wife's enterprise to her husband's. Depending on cultural norms and the nature of intra-household relations, the profits from his enterprise may or may not be directed to enhancing household welfare.

In some cultures, for example, husbands are under no obligation to maintain wives, nor do they have sole responsibility for children's welfare. Depending on how his responsibilities are defined, a wife may find that the resources of her own enterprises are in fact maintaining the household, while her husband is able to invest his resources in expanding his enterprises. This is not problematic unless she is unable to call upon him for support, or on his death she is excluded from inheriting his wealth (the case in many patrilineal societies). The differential responsibility of father and mother for children may have a similar effect. For example, if the father pays for the rent and upkeep of the fabric of the house, electricity and cooking fuel, and the mother the family's food and clothing, her expenses will almost inevitably rise as the children grow older whereas his may not. In this situation the economic burden of having a large family is unequally borne, since his are fixed costs and hers variable by family size.

We noted in Chapter 4 that women experience much greater difficulty in getting hold of household and non-household labour than men for ideological reasons. It is often considered improper, even in town, for women to work closely with non-kin, particularly male, even though husbands cannot readily be called on (see Goddard, 1981). Women are also unlikely to be able to acquire male apprentices. Women can, and do, call on their own children's labour and frequently are dependent on their daughters for support if not in income-earning activities, in taking on household tasks. Women's poverty of resources thus leads to daughters' disadvantage. It is probable that some of the gap between boys and girls in levels of schooling is due to the mothers' need for labour.

Men on the other hand can command household labour with greater facility and, given their control over resources, they may also hire labour or take on apprentices (a common form of getting labour very cheaply – apprentices may even have to pay for the training). Lastly, given their lack of responsibility for day-to-day household maintenance, childcare and cooking, men have a much greater ability to concentrate on the development of their enterprise than do women. Men who work at home can also call on household resources in a different sense – they can require that a part of the house be set aside permanently for their activities or use household resources to build a special work space. Women can rarely do this: most studies show them working in the kitchen or another room, and personal accounts almost always stress the inconvenience of having to tidy work away when the husband or children come home. In conditions of poverty and where people live in very crowded circumstances, running a productive enterprise out of the home requires very careful management of space, time and resources.

What this indicates is the need to look at the constraints to women's entrepreneurial activity using a two-pronged approach. Firstly, those constraints which are located in the form of organisation of the household, and in the ideological representation of intra-household and marital relations. In other words, the relations of production and reproduction embedded within household relations. Secondly, those located within the wider environment – the ways in which resources are allocated to men and women with greater or lesser impartiality in society as a whole.

We noted earlier that domestic outwork (or homeworking) is thought to be widespread in LDCs and that much of what is categorised as household industry is in fact subcontracted outwork. The recent trend for large firms to contract out much of the production process has accentuated this. Furthermore it is suggested that women are predominantly engaged in this type of work, given the widespread ideology of women's place being in the home. For some women, homeworking has many benefits – not least of which is the ability to dovetail childcare and domestic work and productive activities.[2] However, they are also aware that wages and conditions are poor and that their ability to remedy this is virtually nil, partly because of the difficulties a fragmented and dispersed labour force has in finding ways of organising, and partly because of the large number of women who will accept such work as a way out of their desperate situation. Women's powerlessness within the family is all too clearly replicated within the social arena.

One study which examines subcontracting and household dynamics in Mexico City found that homeworkers not only sewed clothing but also sorted metal pieces for batteries, assembled cartons, fitted rings on carpet cleaner bags, and produced electronic coils (Beneria and Roldan, 1987). The latter, produced by women on their kitchen tables, go on to become parts of many different products from radio and TV antennae to microphones, undergoing as many as three or four levels of subcontracting. In 25 per cent of the cases, the work the women carried out required no specialised tools. Although there was great variation in the hours worked and the form and amount of pay, the work was generally unstable, and offered little security. Uncertainty about amounts of work, time of delivery and assurance of continuity was widespread. The average wage for a 48 hour week was US \$19.39, less than a third of the official minimum wage of US \$63.90. Outworkers' incomes and employment depended on the overall health of the subcontracting local firms, many of which worked directly or indirectly for very large MNCs.

Most of the outworkers were relatively poorly educated and unskilled in formal terms, and most of them undertook the work because it allowed them to augment the family income and still keep up the tradition of the non-working wife and full-time childcarer. In some cases the husband's income would have been sufficient to keep the family but his pattern of personal consumption (usually on drink but sometimes on maintaining a second family) meant that the housekeeping did not meet all household expenses. In almost all the women's personal accounts there were disagreements between husbands and wives about what should be considered essential consumption items –

from party shoes, to school books, to financial help for kin. Many of the women said they took up paid work to avoid the humiliation of having to beg for money from a husband who considered his wage to be his not theirs (Beneria and Roldan, 1987).

Services
The service sector covers a diverse range of activities from large-scale tourism to itinerant street vending. Such activities may be well regulated and covered by legislation over pay and conditions, but a vast number are casualised. A large proportion of women in LDCs gain their livelihood from work in services, particularly in Latin America and the Caribbean. High rates of urbanisation combine with existing labour market conditions to make this the obvious sector for women to seek incomes in. In the mid-1980s, while women were 23 per cent of the overall labour force, they constituted 39 per cent of those in services.

We have noted that women's income-generating work tends to reflect domestic responsibilities. This is particularly the case in domestic work performed as part of the service sector, where women clean, wash clothes and cook as they do at home but for money (MacEwan Scott, 1986). The work, using women's traditional skills, generally involves little or no capital outlay and gives low returns. Caroline Moser's study of survival strategies in a squatter settlement of Guayaquil, Ecuador, provides a good illustration (Moser, 1981). Thirty-nine per cent of women worked in some form of domestic service – by far the most significant category of employment. The exact type of work depended to some extent on the stage in the life cycle and the marital position of the woman concerned, those without dependants having a greater degree of choice. Women living in free unions (the commonest marital arrangement) take up work such as laundering as and when the household needs money and in direct relation to their husband's employment, which is frequently sporadic. Although there is some social pressure against women taking on such work, this is readily offset by economic necessity. A woman with dependants but no partner is forced to work full time, again usually as a washerwoman. She is paid piece rates for travelling across town, picking up the laundry from middle-class families, washing it in her own home (with the added problem of unreliability of water supply), and returning it at the end of the day. Moser noted that although unemployed, men do not take on any of women's domestic tasks to help them in their income-generating activities.

Trade is another important source of employment and income, with women playing a key role in the occupation. Yet if one looks at standard labour force participation figures, the proportion of the active female population engaged in trade is small. This is rather puzzling since observational evidence from most LDC markets appears to suggest otherwise. The probable explanation for women's lack of visibility in official data is the problem of statistical enumeration of informal activities and the likelihood that many women are only part-time traders. It is impossible therefore to quote worldwide statistics for women's involvement in trading activities, for the same reasons as there is little data on informal manufacturing. However, case studies can give some clues. In Lima, Peru, more women than men were classified as independent workers, but the majority worked in small-scale commerce – mostly retailing street foods. In this, the largest occupational category for both men and women, women constituted 54 per cent of workers (Pinilla-Cisneros, 1987). In Queretaro, Mexico, as we saw above, women predominated in services and commerce but tended not to own their own businesses (Chant, 1987).

Studies indicate that, while both men and women are involved in trading, there tend to be considerable differences in what they trade, and how they trade. Men tend to trade in more expensive (often manufactured or imported) goods, which produce a better margin of profit. They tend to sell from stable sites or use more elaborate stalls or carts than women. They are often involved in long-distance trade which allows for greater profits from unequal exchange, or in contract trade (providing specified goods to customers such as hospitals, hotels, restaurants, and schools in large quantities at specified prices following the terms of duly signed contracts) which requires both widespread business contacts, but also relatively large amounts of capital and the ability to take a high level of risk. Female market sellers tend to be found in those areas requiring the smallest capital investment; they suffer from inefficient buying mechanisms and harassment from the authorities, compounded by the pressures of juggling childcare roles and simply getting enough sleep (Bunster, 1983). As a result their operation remains very small.

Among women traders themselves there are differences, in terms of scale and of what is sold. There are three basic types. First, petty traders: in rural areas these are usually subsistence farmers and part-time traders who are involved in small-scale retailing of processed and raw foodstuffs, handicrafts and other essential non-food items. Illiterate and unskilled urban migrants undertake similar types of retailing. Second, specialist retail or wholesale traders in farm and marine products: these traders regulate the major part of the food supply to urban areas, manage sizeable amounts of capital and travel extensively. They may be illiterate or semi-literate but are very skilled in keeping mental accounts and clear details of all their business contracts. Third, retail or wholesale urban traders dealing in largely modern type goods and often jewellery. Traders in these goods tend to be literate and are often also middle class.

The vast majority of women traders fall into the first category. Those living in urban areas, having neither capital nor access to storage facilities, cannot buy in large quantities and make very small returns on their labour (some calculations estimate they make less than the minimum wage). Most of them trade within very oversaturated markets, where competition is intense and profit margins minute or non-existent. While most of these women are self-employed independent traders, many of those in towns are commission sellers, who are given products to sell and make a small commission on each sale. For example, in some Latin American cities supermarket owners/managers will give traders date-expired goods to sell in the poorer areas, or wholesalers will give a small army of traders trays of sweets and chewing gum to sell on street corners or to passing motorists (Arizpe, 1977).

In some countries government has a very negative attitude to petty traders and entrepreneurs: they are believed to force up prices, create artificial scarcities, engage in illicit trade, etc. For example, the Jamaican government tried to exclude women street traders from selling basic consumption items on the grounds that the higglers (as such traders are called) were hoarding and thus forcing up prices. Petty traders are often harassed by local officials because their trading sites are considered unsightly or a hindrance to traffic. Rather than seeing such women as a potential resource for the development and enhancement of the economy and the society, regulations are adopted which force them out of business.

New constraints are both hampering the expansion of women's trading and in some areas actually diminishing their traditional trading opportunities. Rapid urban growth has brought increasing numbers of women into trading, causing considerable saturation of the sector and lowering of profit margins. The push to expell the poorest from city centres and respectable suburbs has brought a number of extra burdens to small-scale traders: rising costs of transport and storage, and greater need for unhampered spatial mobility. With the growth of the market economy, and changing consumer demands (both in terms of type and quality), the sector may become attractive to capital. Petty traders find it difficult to survive competition from larger scale and more structured traders. Most do not have the means to prepare and package their goods with greater attention to hygiene or appearance to suit the more sophisticated consumer tastes of urbanites, and yet their products may increasingly be in competition with cheap factory-produced equivalents. The social status element of modern consumption goods also plays a significant role in consumer choice.

As a result of these constraints, as well as limited alternative job opportunities, many of women's traditional trading sectors are being rapidly taken over. This is particularly true of basic foods. Men more commonly act as intermediaries between the big commercial firms and the retailers, or as buyers for the wholesale houses, travelling throughout the country, even region, to establish business links with farmers and fishermen. Farmers themselves, as we noticed in Chapter 4, are engaging more and more in commercial production and welcome fixed contracts to buy up their total production.

Causes of gender differences in casualised employment

Broadly speaking, we can discern two sets of factors behind women's and men's unequal participation. Firstly, physical factors such as migration patterns and labour market conditions, and the development of new technologies. Secondly, ideological factors which influence and direct the first set of factors, and specifically those which define work and 'natural' productive and reproductive roles. We will look at some of these factors more closely.

Migration

In some Latin American countries, Mexico is a good case in point, in the initial phase of economic transformation, women were more rapidly expelled from the countryside in order to find paid work than men. Once in towns, women's employment choices were very limited because of the general lack of stable wage employment, and discrimination within the labour market. As a result women either had to face strong competition for the few traditional women's occupations available – domestic service, caring for children, the elderly and infirm, working in textiles and clothing, or in restaurants – or were forced into the margins of the urban economy, into petty trading, petty manufacturing, or sexual servicing. Male migrants, in contrast, had a wider range of job possibilities, and often came to town to work found for them by their sisters or other kin. Many found the fledgling industries sought labour; equally jobs or self-employment were available in the urban labour market, either servicing the new industrial sector, or the expanding urban population.

Access to resources

Women find virtually no institutional provision for them as potential workers or entrepreneurs. In most countries women from the poorer strata have difficulty in getting effective access to credit, suitable and safe facilities for saving and investment, accessible information about services, raw materials and markets, adequate and equitable access to training and skills acquisition. They rarely get protection, recognition or support from official bodies. Inadequate institutional provision for women derives from the ideology of the non-working wife and mother. But women of the poorer strata can rarely afford not to contribute to household finances

They rarely have the same access to cash as men, either from the family budget or formal credit institutions, and they rarely command acceptable forms of collateral – land, house sites, house, livestock, etc. As a result, if they need credit to run their business, they must either borrow it from kin or neighbours (possibly joining an informal savings/credit club), or take out a loan from a local money lender at very high rates of interest. Given such constraints women entrepreneurs frequently can only afford rather inexpensive lines or to buy small amounts. For example, transport and storage are common problems for most traders, but men involved in higher return activities are more likely to be able to afford the higher cost of both more easily. Studies also indicate that they are also more likely to be able to set aside part of the house or house site for their work needs than women.

Ideological factors

Ideology and the actual material practices associated with the ideology greatly constrain women's economic endeavours. One of the crucial restrictions for women is spatial but individual cultures differ considerably. In some, women (especially married women) should not be seen in public, but in many – even when they can be seen outside the home – women are more circumscribed spatially than men. This is the case in Latin America. They should remain near their home, or only travel short distances, or only travel at certain hours of the day. Spatial restrictions in part derive from the almost exclusive responsibility of women for childcare: having to look after children while working makes going to distant sites problematic. But they are clearly also related to fears surrounding women's sexuality and the desire to restrict or control it. Spatial restrictions can have the effect of constraining women's ability to sell in the best markets, to trade in the most profitable products. They also inhibit women's ability to develop a widespread network of contacts, especially with males involved in the business.

Not all women traders, however, suffer from these impediments. In the Caribbean, for example, some women have become international traders, travelling to one island, bartering or selling goods in demand there for goods in scarce supply in another, taking these goods to another island and so on. In this way they may often act as points of connection between three or four different economies. A variety of factors make it possible for women to engage in this often lucrative trade: their age (they are often older women with fewer childcare responsibilities), the type of their relationship with their husband/father, their marital status (i.e. widowed or deserted women generally have greater freedom), and often a previous history in local trading.

In many households survival strategies are designed around the gender ideology which defines certain activities as appropriate to men or to women. For example, men may undertake casual work which is hazardous, relatively well-paid but intermittent, while their wives take on regular but low-paid work, and children are sent out to take up earning opportunities as they occur. By this co-ordinated strategy, an absolutely minimum level of survival of the family is secured by women's steady but low-paid work. Men's higher but casual income secures basic consumption goods (and sometimes if the family is lucky even the means to acquire luxuries – new secondhand clothing, footwear, meat). Children's incomes may be used by the mother to substitute for the man's share or as a standby for bad days. A woman may, however, concentrate her efforts on reproductive activities, making sure that what little income there is goes a long way; providing services and goods which substitute for market goods, dovetailing these with the productive work of other household members, often giving them unpaid assistance. For example, a woman, in addition to her own household and market goods replacement work, will cook food her man or her children will later sell to factory workers in the industrial area of the city.

Dovetailing can also occur when men's primary jobs become scarce, and they have to take on lower paid work in the meantime. For example, when availability of work on the docks or in construction becomes restricted, a man may take on some form of street trade while his wife will take on laundry and cleaning work to enhance total income (as in Guayaquil – see Moser, 1981). These coping strategies contribute to the casual nature of women's productive work as it responds to the fortunes of male workers, especially in households dogged by insecurity of income and pressing basic needs. Women may, of course, entirely substitute for the man when he is sick, or he cannot find work (when there is a downturn in demand for male labour, seasonal lay-offs, etc.). Equally when the total income of the household is insufficient women may have to substitute paid productive, often home-based activities for time spent in domestic work.

For those women who are not in a household with a male wage earner, the penalties of being confined to certain areas of income generation are greatly compounded. Widows, divorcees, women who have been abandoned by their partners, all live under the constricting terms of the ideology of the male breadwinner which justifies their low incomes and restricted opportunities for improving their businesses, but which is not relevant to their actual situation. In Latin America and the Caribbean especially, marital unions tend to be rather transitory with both men and women having several partners in a lifetime. This can mean that many women at any one time are not in a relationship which gives them (even minimal) financial assistance, within an ideological and economic context in which their opportunities for coping without it are both limited and constrained.

Development planning and policy for and with women

How can policymakers and planners support small-scale, often unregulated, enterprises? Do such enterprises have the potential to generate growth and self-sustaining employment? Does promoting such enterprises merely serve the interests of large-scale capital without redressing the essentially exploitative relationship between the two types of enterprises? Would women be better served by greater expenditure of public resources on provision of social infrastructure rather than support for small-scale enterprise? Clearly the answers to such questions depend to a large extent on how the relationship between large, regulated enterprises and small, unregulated enterprises and even individuals, is thought to operate. Is it benign or exploitative?

Many researchers, particularly those working within the Marxist, dependency or structuralist framework, have argued that support for the IS cannot overcome the main cause of poverty in LDCs: their unequal integration into the global economic system. As a result, accumulation and growth within any individual LDC are constrained by structural factors outside it but inherent in the global system. Because of this, the relationship between large-scale capital and marginal enterprises involves subordination at best and more commonly exploitation, depending on the degree of autonomy of individual enterprises. Even where IS enterprises have been able to create a large enough market for their products or services to gain the profits of scale, capital is likely to enter and absorb the small-scale enterprises, entrepreneurs and sometimes even labour force.

Those who take a more benevolent view of the market system argue that successful IS enterprises become larger and more regulated; they provide the dynamism of the market system. Still others hold that while LDCs have such rapidly-growing populations, there will always be labour surplus to requirement, and that those bearing such surplus labour will have to scratch a living as best they can (see Mezzara, 1989). Support for such casualised labour can therefore only take the form of welfare, not investment, since such labour will always be excluded from regular employment, lacking the means to create employment or to gain access to it.

For those who feel that small-scale enterprises do hold out promise for those with low incomes, little education and a rather traditional set of skills, a first step must be to identify the range of constraints such enterprises and entrepreneurs suffer. The macro-economic environment in many countries is generally hostile to small-scale, unregulated activities. Overcoming this constraint can be in terms of improving access to resources, infrastructure, markets and technology.

Over and above this, planners must be conscious of the fact that whether the entrepreneur is male or female is likely to be a critical determinant of success. As we have seen, there are often marked differences by gender: in access to social resources, physical space; in ability to compete for capital, labour, markets; in ability to retain earnings, or to call upon household resources. Below we will look at typical constraints for small entrepreneurs and for women.

Capital and credit

The most critical constraint is usually access to capital and credit. Existing mechanisms and formal channels for getting credit tend to exclude small businesses; either because they are unable to put up the necessary collateral or to fulfil the bureaucratic requirement of regular interest repayments (because of variable levels of profit). These requirements are often doubly difficult for women entrepreneurs. The appropriateness of interventions to provide credit and institutional support depends on the particular context (Stewart, 1987) and should be judged not solely in terms of economic efficiency and sustainability, but equally on how they affect work demands and the overall position of the majority of those targeted. Women have, as we have seen, particular need for credit, but they also have time, spatial and domestic constraints to face which men may not. Provision of credit must take this into account; many successful schemes for women rely on group accountability.[3]

Technology and information

Technology research and macro-level policies also tend to focus on large-scale techniques for large industries. Yet small-scale entrepreneurs can greatly improve productivity and thereby returns to labour by using appropriate technology. Planners must pay attention to the development of technologies for small-scale and low-capital enterprises and, critically, give support to creating information networks for the dissemination of technology for small enterprises. Particular attention will have to be paid to ensuring that women are included in this, since initially at least most inventors and technology enthusiasts are likely to be male.

Technical training and skills upgrading

Many small-scale entrepreneurs learned their skills through a spell of work in the formal sector. Given the sexual division of labour in-manufacturing, most women gain few such skills when employed in modern, even world market factories. The provision of adequate technical training for women and the upgrading of their skills, whether on the job or not, is a critical issue for planners. Women also need to develop their managerial and organisational skills, but often this may have to be preceded by concerted efforts to enhance their feeling of self-worth, and to change public attitudes to women in management. Here planners can consider general public education programmes which raise awareness of women's capacities and contributions to society, and specific programmes directed to the women entrepreneurs.

Organisation

Both men and women face constraints in terms of lack of institutional support and government intolerance of their activities (either as entrepreneurs or workers). But, because women's casualised labour is more often than men's based in and around the home, they are less able to organise together. Yet such organisation is crucial for practical reasons such as reaping the economies of scale of bulk purchasing of raw materials, and for creating solidarity in the face of official harassment. Support for women's organisational efforts should be high on planners' agendas.

Savings

Many small-scale entrepreneurs barely make enough for their daily needs, but equally many have the capacity to make very small weekly savings. Enabling small-scale entrepreneurs to save and to invest these savings in medical or other forms of insurance can often be the critical factor in their ability to survive a crisis. Some research shows that the ability of women IS actors to expand their undertakings is very limited, but if they are grouped within some form of organisation, and the organisation can provide some form of insurance for members, not only are standards of health and family welfare greatly improved, but small investments in the enterprise become possible.

Social infrastructure

Since women also bear the double burden of productive and reproductive work, there is a danger that support for income-generating activities will merely result in a greatly increased workload if it is not complemented by increased support in terms of childcare. Programmes designed initially to help women generate income run the risk of degenerating into unsustainable welfare programmes if no attention is paid to the demands on women's time and energies of reproductive work. Some commentators would argue that direct financial support for income-generating activities should take second place to investment in social infrastructure since this would both benefit low-income women and their children.

Household

One of the difficulties in trying to understand how small-scale enterprises based on the household survive is that, as we have stressed before, intra-household relations vary widely both by culture and by class. In some regions there is little concept of the household as a common economic enterprise. Rather it can be seen as a congeries of independent enterprises with some sketchy ground rules as to basic responsibilities for children's upkeep, and what support can be expected or demanded and by whom. In other regions both dovetailing and substitution are common strategies, involving using women and children's income-earning labour to replace or supplement men's.

Understandings also differ as to what proportion of different household members' earnings belong to the collective aspect of the household budget; the length of time parents should be responsible for children and the age at which children should begin to collaborate in economic activities or should indeed become virtually independent agents. There are differences too in the intensity of responsibility household members have for wider kin or affines.

The most that can be said is that given the wide range of ways in which families and households organise their economic affairs, policymakers must eschew the notion of a uniform, corporate, collaborative and pooling unit.

They should concentrate more on identifying the specific constraints that face different types of enterprises and particular categories of the population in their struggle to survive and to bring up the next generation, and finding the means to lessen or eradicate them.

Notes

1 Studies show how surgical instrument and specialised engineering firms are choosing the path of flexible specialisation as well as the clothing industry and some car firms (Schmitz, 1982; Hoffman and Kaplinsky, 1988). In the service sector too, the new technologies are opening up employment possibilities for women at home as it becomes possible for them to work on computer terminals for data entry and processing work. There is also the capacity for off-shore sourcing for labour. For example, much routine clerical work can be done for US businesses by homeworkers in Mexico, Santo Domingo, the Bermudas or Bahamas (Posthuma, 1987).

2 Empirically homework/domestic outwork often takes precedence over household and childcare work – usually goods have to be produced by a deadline and defaulting can mean losing the job. If fathers cannot take on some of the domestic responsibilities, then daughters are likely to have to.

3 The credit programme for micro-entrepreneurs of the Banco Popular in Costa Rica is judged to be an outstanding success (Stewart, 1987). The programme had 447 clients after one year and average incomes were up by 240 per cent; in addition, group solidarity and savings increased, the dependence on money lenders was reduced, new jobs were created, and the pay-back record on loans was good. But a number of questions remain: who are the beneficiaries – are they predominantly men or women? Have men's increased earnings led to improved collective (household) or individual income? What has happened to the sexual division of labour and women's workload, and in particular, have expectations of unpaid labour contributions of women and children increased? Without answers to such questions, conclusions about the success of a policy may be premature.

7 Making women visible: Problems with concepts and assumptions[1]

Planners, policymakers and development practitioners rely heavily on statistics in their work. They are powerful planning tools, used to assess changes in the economy and to make further planning adjustments. While the disciplines, economics in particular, provide analytical models, planners and policymakers have to transform them into workable tools and flesh them out with empirical data – data which are collected on a more or less regular basis through censuses and surveys. An enormous range of data is collected on numerous aspects of people's lives, on health and education, the household and wealth for example, but probably the most critical data for planners are those to do with economic activity. Until recently, most statistical data made no distinction between men and women as far as labour force participation or economic activity was concerned.

Early on in the Second UN Development Decade, as we saw in Chapter 2, it was argued that lack of concern for women's economic participation was reflected in the absence of statistical data on it. The call then was for statisticians to provide disaggregated data because the 'invisibilisation' of women was not only detrimental to women themselves, but was having a negative effect on development itself. By disaggregation and improving data collection processes and techniques, women's contribution to development could be quantified (and women more efficiently utilised): 'Women who comprise half the population, can and do make enormous contributions to development in all nations. Without adequate statistical description, their current contributions remain invisible and the barriers to promoting their future contributions to the development process remain hidden' (INSTRAW, 1984, p.6).

Considerable efforts have been made since then to overcome the difficulties in collecting data on women's activities, and an enormous amount of data at national and local levels is now available to researchers and planners. None the less a number of problems still remain: like other 'hard data', much of the information is unreliable, inaccurate and often out of date (see Evans, 1990). Definitions can vary between censuses, making comparisons over time difficult. For example, in India a change in the definition of economic activity reduced the female labour force participation rate by an estimated 23 per cent between the censuses of 1961 and 1971. The lack of standardisation across national boundaries also makes comparative work hazardous. Although there are international conventions on the collection of much macro-level data, different countries still adopt different definitions and ways of measuring economic activity, employment and underemployment, income distribution, and so on. The minimum number of hours or minimum age to count as active labour varies, there are differences in the precision with which the boundary between productive and either reproductive or unproductive work is defined – a problem we shall return to in more detail below.

By the 1990s it is recognised that despite having disaggregated data, women's contribution to national economic well-being is still not being adequately recorded. This is for two main reasons. Because women work in non-market, informal and subsistence sectors, it is still very difficult to record and quantify their participation; it remains largely invisible. But more critically, because the bulk of what women do (i.e. household and family work) is not recognised as productive work it goes unrecorded. In other words, the way economic activity is conceptualised has a profound affect on what is measured and what is not. Concentration on amassing disaggregated data led to the neglect of a more critical task – uncovering the stereotypes about women (and men), which inform the conceptual categories used in the creation of data. These stereotypes, which come from looking at the world as if all economic actors are male and with archetypal male characteristics, are held by planners, economists and statisticians alike. Yet the categories themselves have the effect of undercounting and undervaluing the activities and economic contribution of women.

Problems with the concepts

Economic activity

Definitions of economic activity – the production of goods and services – turn on a distinction between productive and unproductive work, but the boundary between these is notoriously vaguely set. This poses particular problems when it comes to measuring the nature and importance of women's economic participation. A great deal of what women do, whether in LDCs or IMEs – processing, preparing and cooking raw food; caring for children and old people; cleaning and washing – is not considered productive. 'But why should preparing and processing food for own-consumption be considered any less productive than growing the food? Why should caring for children be considered less productive than caring for livestock?' (Evans, 1990, p.9). Why should a man who works in the water board that brings water to the town be considered a productive worker while a woman who carries water from the well to her family is not?

The standard answer is, of course, that typical women's work does not involve the market. A less common response implicates widely held preconceptions about the economic activities of men and women and the biological or 'natural' basis of the division of labour between the sexes, particularly as regards work around what can be called human resource production and maintenance (Young, 1987a). If this is thought of as activity deriving from women's natural capacity of childbearing, then a whole range of tasks can be subsumed under this, made invisible ('my wife doesn't work, she looks after the house') and thus excluded from the category economic. Stereotypes about women clearly affect the evaluation of their activities.

Even within the category of activities considered productive, there are still further problems. Statistics are collected on labour force participation rates, the available pool of workers and their employment status (own account, employer, employee), and levels of employment and unemployment. But as we saw in the discussion of the informal sector, much of what goes on in developing economies fits poorly into conceptual categories derived from a different economic reality. Recently, further categories have been developed to accommodate more accurately societies where the bulk of the population is not in regular wage work: these include **underemployment**, for which the criterion is either working for abnormally long hours or for disproportionately low wages. However, as yet, categorisations of underemployment are neither consistently, nor widely applied. The economically inactive are all those who cannot clearly be defined as engaging in productive activity or attempting to do so. Unpaid family workers are included if they contribute 'at least a third of normal working hours' to an economic enterprise, but excluded are students, those totally dependent on others, the retired and 'women who are full-time homemakers' (Boulding, 1983, p.288).

There is also no consensus as to the minimum number of hours that an individual has to spend on an economic activity before this gets recognition, and census data in differing countries vary widely. Magdalena Leon noted in 1984 that 'in six Latin American countries no minimum time is stipulated; ... and in seven a period of between one and 18 hours per week is laid down' (Leon, 1984, p.14).Censuses rarely distinguish between principal and secondary activity: of the 145 censuses carried out between 1955 and 1964 by those UN members which collected occupational information, only 27 asked the respondents about their secondary occupation (Dixon, 1982, p.543). If only one activity occupying a fixed amount of time is recorded for each individual, those who carry out multiple activities but spend less time than the defined amount in each (typically a female pattern) will be classified as inactive.

Collecting data on women's activities

Apart from general problems in getting accurate statistical data, what are the major difficulties facing those trying to get data on women? The first major difficulty lies in recording women's economic activities. To begin with both interviewer and respondent are likely to hold preconceptions, which will produce an undercount of women's activities – for example fetching wood and water is a household task and therefore not 'work' worthy of recording. As was observed wryly by a UN statistician, the woman hauling a 20 litre drum of water to the house is engaged in unproductive (not recordable) activity; her husband laying pipes to bring water to the village is doing both productive work and a recordable activity. Interviewers may expect and therefore elicit stereotypical answers, for example, 'your wife doesn't work, does she?' 'No she doesn't work, she looks after the family.' Respondents may give the census enumerator the expected answer for a range of reasons including desire to please, perceptions of class difference, and cultural proscriptions. Women themselves may adhere to cultural norms which encourage them to undervalue and underestimate their work: I'm only a housewife. In Sen's terms, their perceived contribution and their own valuation of its worth is low (see Sen, 1985, and end of this chapter).

Then translating census questions into local languages always presents difficulties, particularly if the question implies a way of thinking about the organisation of activity which is foreign to the culture itself. For example, in many cultures no separation is made conceptually or linguistically between activities relating to the home and the farm (see Evans, 1990). An easy way to solve this is to omit the activities entirely. Women's work is more vulnerable to omissions of this kind because interviewers and respondents alike may use a mental mapping which allocates many of women's tasks to housework (i.e. not work) and most of men's to economic activity: consider, for example, the linguistic nicety which allows that women garden while men farm. And even if interviewers do try to get data on domestic activities a second set of problems arises: how to distinguish household activities which are 'economic' from the daily processes of living or even leisure. Should making crafts, knitting, going to the market with a few bunches of herbs or growing vegetables in the garden, be regarded as leisure despite the fact that they have an income or income-replacing component?

The second difficulty is how to measure and give a value to activities usually described as domestic? For example, home production. Should it be measured in terms of inputs or outputs; the volume or value of the goods or services produced; the market wage foregone (for further discussion see Goldschmidt-Clermont, 1982). One strategy would be to include only those activities that correspond or contribute to market-directed activities – e.g. food processing, collecting firewood and water, making tools, utensils and clothing, making crafts. Another would be to define active labour 'in relation to its contribution to the production of goods and services for the satisfaction of human needs. Whether this production is channelled through the market and whether it contributes directly to the accumulation process ... should not bias our understanding of what constitutes economic activity' (Beneria, 1982, p.129).

When Lourdes Beneria's recommendation is heeded and home production is acknowledged and added to market work, women's and children's contribution in work time to household welfare is often greater than men's. Using this method on data from the Philippines, King and Evenson (1983) produce some thought-provoking results: husbands contribute most in terms of average market income, but when full income (a combination of payment for market work plus the value of time devoted to home production) is considered, the picture changes dramatically. While men contribute 58 per cent of market income, they only contribute 34 per cent of full income, the remainder being made up by women and children. King and Evenson note that: '... the importance of non-market production to household welfare and income cannot be overemphasized' (King and Evenson, 1983, p.51).

A third problem is the fact that men's work pattern is taken as the norm. Census enumerators generally only ask about the primary or main activity a person undertakes; but women's work patterns are more likely to be multiple, part-time and involve moving between economic and non-economic spheres. As this pattern is unlike men's, these activities are often by-passed. This gives rise to a fourth problem: the minimum number of hours that has to be spent on an activity per day or per week before it can be officially recognised as economic. Because women frequently carry out various activities in parallel (cooking food to be sold later while washing clothes for money; caring for own children while making clothes for sale), it is impossible to keep accurate records (even mental records) of time spent on any one activity. The easiest way for census takers to solve the problem is to ignore the activities and to categorise the woman's status as 'housewife'. It is thus theoretically possible for a woman who works a 35-hour week but in seven different activities and for only five hours a week in each to be classified as economically inactive.

Fifthly and closely connected to this point, are the issues of the reference period and time-scale used when collecting data on economic activity. In most rural areas, production activities vary widely by season, yet census takers come in one season, usually the dry one since travelling is then easier. In that season little work may be being done as far as cultivation is concerned, except possibly harvesting. People are asked to give details of their economic activities over a relatively brief reference period (one or two weeks is the standard). Recording only dry season low-activity rates, a great deal of crucial activity is excluded from the record. Research indicates that collecting information on women's activities is particularly badly affected if their work at the time of the census is not on-farm but in household/domestic work (confirming the stereotype). Even if the census takers do ask about rainy season activities (when people are often busiest), the problem of respondent recall enters (and how people are prompted). Studies on this show both under- and over-reporting. Both unseasonal time of year and limited reference periods are among the technical explanations for the under-reporting and misrepresentation of women's work in agricultural statistics. Some evidence of urban annual labour patterns would suggest that seasonality of work may also be a feature of urban labour markets but as little systematic work has as yet been done on this, the degree of under-reporting is not yet an issue.

Lastly, as previously touched on, many (especially urban) informal sector activities may be overlooked in data collection because they are small-scale, highly mobile, seasonal, or culturally disapproved of. As we saw in Chapter 6, women are not only often disproportionately represented in this sector, but they also will tend to be at the most casualised, least regulated and most insecure end of the informal continuum – thus even harder to capture in aggregate statistics.

What can be done to rectify the situation? Statisticians have been trying to modify their census categories, adding new ones and so on. Clearly they have to walk the tightrope of simplifying without over-simplification. They have to exclude certain activities if the term 'economic' is to have any meaning. However, to exclude all the work that goes into producing the human resources without which no economic activity would occur seems perverse unless one accepts the premise that what women do in this regard is a natural aspect of their condition of being a woman. It is in this sense that what is most needed is for the conceptual model that lies behind the census categories to be brought out into the open, contested and changed.

Once it is agreed that producing human resources is a productive economic activity, then ways will be found to categorise it for inclusion in censuses, and a means to collect data systematically will be devised. We have ourselves suggested that all the tasks associated with the rearing, care and socialisation of children should be recorded (categorising them as human resource production), and given an imputed economic value. The same should be done with those associated with direct daily personal and house maintenance activities – cooking, washing clothes, processing food ('human resource maintenance') and the range of activities such as fetching wood and water, family food farming, making items for domestic or farm use ('activities supporting human resource production and maintenance' – Young, 1987).

If the time spent by women and men on the different aspects of human resource production and maintenance is recorded in census and other statistical records, given an imputed value and shown in national accounts, considerable policy benefits accrue. For example, having a record of the amount of labour spent on the different aspects of human resource production and maintenance would highlight critical labour bottlenecks and facilitate discussion of how they are to be reduced; by direct state investment (i.e. on infrastructure), or indirect investment (i.e. providing credit for acquiring domestic technologies) or encouraging private sector involvement. Furthermore, the contribution of work in the home to socio-economic development will be put on a par with work outside it and a more balanced view achieved of the totality of economic potential in the society.

The household

Households are generally used as the basic social and economic unit on which information in censuses and surveys is collected. However, what constitutes a household unit poses considerable conceptual problems. In large measure this is because of the conflation of the household (a residential unit) with the family (a social unit based on kinship, marriage and parenthood). To help resolve this, international guidelines have been devised which broadly define a household as a number of individuals who live together and provide the basic needs for themselves, their children and relevant others (i.e. those who live under one roof and share a common pot). A family, on the other hand, is defined as those who are related by blood or marriage, though not necessarily living together. Certain assumptions in fact underpin the guidelines: that households are constituted around relationships centred on marriage and parenthood, that co-residence is a defining feature, that the housing unit and the consumption unit are co-extensive, and that members of the unit pool and share economic resources. As a result many of the assumptions made about the nature of intra-household relations are informed by assumptions about the marriage relation itself, and by assumptions about relations between parents and children (see Roberts, 1991).

Household composition in fact depends on a number of factors including rules of residence on marriage, the nature of kinship (patrilineal, matrilineal, bilineal, etc.), marriage rules (polygamy, monogamy, polyandry), inheritance rules (single, multiple or joint inheritance, post- or pre-mortem) and rules of residence for inheritors (the son destined to inherit the land may have to co-reside with his parents, unmarried siblings and his own wife and children), class (are live-in servants employed?), the availability of housing (particularly crucial in towns) and so on.

Composition changes not only with the development cycle of the domestic group (as children are born, grow up and leave to marry or bring in their spouses and begin to have children themselves, as old people and parents age and die), but also in response to other economic, social and political factors. Kinship still remains a politico-economic and social resource in LDCs to a much greater extent than in IMEs – providing a welfare net, a support group, and a political force – and this is reflected in residential patterns and in the constantly shifting location of people residentially.

As a result, the assumption that the household, particularly when viewed as an economic unit, has defined boundaries and does not overlap with others, and that people are clearly allocated to only one household unit, is invalid.

Family members may sleep under one roof but neither eat together nor share a common budget; they may share a common budget but not live under the same roof; adult men, even though in recognised heterosexual relationships with specific women, may never live with them but reside in their mother's house or a men's house; some household members may share production tasks but what they produce may be consumed by other family households altogether and so on (see Roberts, 1991).

In much of the Caribbean, the basic set of people living together is a woman, her daughters and their children, with adult men – sons and children's fathers – spending a varied amount of time in the unit but rarely remaining stable members. Children's fathers usually contribute something to their up-keep, but a woman maintains herself and looks to her brother as her main economic fall-back resource. Children may also be sent to live with their mother's mother or sister as much to help them as to relieve pressure on their mother's budget.

In sub-Saharan Africa, where kinship ties remain quite strong in many areas, and where polygamy is also relatively common, household composition is highly varied and complex. In urban areas a man may live in a common residence with his wife or wives, their children, some of his (or her) siblings and/or siblings' children, and members of the parental generation or their children. In the rural areas, if a man has a plurality of wives, each wife will probably have her own huts and cooking place, and will be visited by the husband in rotation.

In Latin America many men are also involved in simultaneous multiple unions but unlike sub-Saharan Africa polygamy is not legal nor officially recognised. A man may recognise one household as his main place of resi-dence (where he keeps his working tools), but provide some economic support to two or more units, and share his time between them. A woman with children by a previous union may not be able to keep them when she joins with a second husband – they are either dispersed among her own kin or may take to living rough, joining the bands of street children found in almost all large cities (see Jelin, 1991).

In south Asia the joint family still predominates in areas of patrilineal kinship, although to a greater extent in rural than urban areas. In this system a man and his wife, their sons, wives and children, and all unmarried daughters co-reside. The patriarch is the ultimate authority in the household, and its economic head, although much of the day-to-day management may be carried out by his wife.

Inter-household relations
In many areas relations between households are crucial determinants of house-hold and individual decision-making. In rural SSA all the wives of a common husband (each living in a separate hut with her children and each with her own fields, a separate budget and cooking pot) may be involved in deciding how

much land to dedicate to the basic staple, or the decision may be made by the husband or the senior wife. Yet this will set the pattern of their activities for the year. Having a wife's brother in town who can sell household produce may be the crucial determinant in the decision to grow a crop, and proceeds may be divided equally. In rural India, sons may work on the family land under the direction of the father-patriarch but major production decisions may in fact be made by an absent urban-dwelling son who provides the capital needed for the inputs.

Units of production and consumption may coincide or do so only occasionally. For example, in Cameroon, Jane Guyer (1984) observed that wives produced most of the basic staples and relish crops while husbands produced an export cash crop. The women were careful to ensure they had sufficient basic household foods stocks, but also sold vegetables at the market and special delicacies to their husbands and their male kin (thus acquiring some of the men's export crop cash). Women and their children formed the production unit for staples, men and sometimes wives but usually wage labour the production unit for cocoa. Parents and children formed the basic consumption unit, but men also ate with their own matrikin.

All this points to the complexity of household composition and organisation. To make the task of identifying and measuring households manageable, especially in censuses, some simplifying assumptions are, of course, needed. However, over-simplification is misleading in circumstances where complexity prevails. In fact, many of the measurement problems that arise come from the lack of fit between diverse household characteristics and the simplified categories of household type used in censuses and national surveys. Household surveys should be able to reveal diversity and change in household composition and the relationship of this to changing socio-economic conditions. For example, examination of the number of households with dependant children managed by a woman will throw light on female labour force participation. Collecting data on changes in household composition due to migration (of both adults and children) will throw light on labour market pressures and opportunities – and how both men and women are able to respond to them.

Household head

Statisticians work with the convention that all households have a single authority source – the household head – despite the fact that in most societies both husband and wife have their own areas of responsibility and authority. By designating one person head of household (the reference person), census enumerators can identify all other household members in terms of their relationship to the head. However, the criteria by which to select the reference person are quite unclear. Stereotyping usually ensures that a male (not necessarily adult) is chosen whether or not he is the main source of authority. Often the census enumerator decides arbitrarily that an adult male in a household is its head, even though in reality he contributes little to family welfare (Evans, 1990).

Male headship bias leads to the underestimation of women's economic and management activities in a number of ways. Firstly, the male chosen as household head becomes the chief respondent of census questions. But, as much research has shown, men are rarely knowledgeable about women's activities, either because of separate interests and spheres or because of cultural norms – if these dictate that women should not undertake certain activities men may turn a blind eye but are unlikely to record them. Census enumerators are not encouraged to ask women directly about their activities. Secondly, the economic activity of the head 'is used to identify the activity status of the household as a whole irrespective of what other household members may be doing and how much income they are contributing' (Evans, 1990, p.28). Thirdly, in a great many households which nominally have a male head, women have complete economic responsibility, either because the men have migrated or they are unable (because of age, infirmity, etc.) to earn a livelihood.

Some of the ways round these problems would be to indicate clearly the criteria for choosing the reference person – chief economic provider, senior adult, chief economic manager; to collect and present census information on all adult members of a household; to collect detailed information on the characteristics of each (adult) household member in surveys.

Intra-household economic relations

A major problem in policymaking is the prevalence of stereotypes in economic models of how intra-household economic relations should operate. Commonly, marriage is conceived as a partnership between two persons with reciprocal (but not necessarily equal) rights and obligations to each other, with similar rights over and obligations to the children of the marriage, and with a common set of interests. As a result, it is assumed that marriage gives rise to a unit marked by jointness of control and management of resources, and similarity or coincidence in interests and goals. Often there is a tendency to conflate household with couple, this being perhaps most marked in discussions about household resource management (see Young, 1990). Pooling and sharing are assumed to be characteristics of household economic behaviour, in large measure because marriage is supposed to create a joint domestic economy. However, research shows that even where jointness is a social fact, the degree of economic jointness varies. In SSA there would appear to be little notion of the jointness of marital economy; in the south Asian joint family conjugal jointness is positively discouraged.

In SSA where polygyny is common, an in-marrying wife is seen as a wife to the lineage rather than the male alone, and as such may be inherited on her husband's death by his actual brother or a close agnate. Wives are expected to provide for their own children and to feed their husband and his kin when necessary. While it is a husband's obligation to provide his wife/ves with the means by which they are to do this, and to provide her/them with labour at certain points in the production cycle, he is in no way obliged to maintain his wife, and indeed a woman who is a poor cultivator or cannot bear children is likely to be returned to her kin. Where matriliny prevails, a man's obligation is as much to his mother, and his sisters and their children (who are his heirs), as to his wife: he may not even live with his wife but reside with his maternal kin, visiting her from time to time. If she lives nearby she will send food to him at his house. Elsewhere on the continent women are responsible for providing basic food and clothing for themselves and their children, while the men provide the rest. Where marriage is unstable a woman may be receiving some support for children from her ex-husband(s) or may be using her income/wage to support her 'own' children, while getting money from her present husband for the basic housekeeping and support of their children. In Latin America women try to help their mothers and sisters financially, often because they have to leave their children with them while they establish a new relationship with a man.

Where there is no concept of jointness in marriage, husband and wife may well have different strategies for survival and advancement – and sometimes these may be in opposition to each other. For example, a good deal of recent research from SSA attests to the struggles that can take place around the control of women's labour (Roberts, 1989). A married man can call upon his wife's labour for cultivation; she may gain little or no direct benefit but none the less it is her duty as wife to assist him. The contrary does not seem to hold; that is a woman may ask her husband for assistance but usually he is rewarded by a share in the proceeds whether in the form of cooked food, or cash payment. Where men have their own crops (for example, export crops) women can expect little benefit, but wives involved in market-oriented production frequently have to give a share to the husband or indeed hand over the whole of the proceeds (a proportion being returned to them). Studies show the variety of ways in which women attempt to capture some of their husbands' cash income as, for example, the women in Cameroon noted earlier who sell their husbands small cooked delicacies (Guyer, 1984).

This pattern of independent economic activity for men and women, but mutual responsibility for children is also common in the Caribbean where a woman may have children by a number of different men, each of whom should be responsible for the upkeep of his child/ren (but not the mother). In India the joint family system reveals another pattern; all household income is given to the patriarch for redistribution among family members. There would appear to be no concept of even shares, rather sons are preferred above daughters, and eldest son above other sons. Married sons and their wives contribute their income/resources but do not necessarily get a return commensurate with their input.

What are the practical implications of these different patterns? Because of incorrect assumptions about intra-household economic relations, policies on, for example, taxation, child and marriage allowances are often misdirected and can sometimes be positively harmful. Married women in some African countries pay a higher rate of tax than their husbands because it is assumed that husbands take care of household expenses and wives' income is to cover additional or luxury expenditures. Yet the assumption of jointness is not borne out in the case of marriage goods. In many SSA countries with patrilineal kinship systems, all the property of the marriage, however acquired, belongs to the husband. A widow can be completely dispossessed of the marital home and its contents, whether she contributed financially to their acquisition or not. To date, changes in traditional inheritance rules (i.e. customary law) have not been easy to introduce into largely male legislative bodies. In some cases, wives have taken steps to protect themselves and their children by getting husbands to agree to recognise their ownership of goods they have bought, such recognition being ratified in the presence of representatives of both sets of kin.

Even where jointness of economy is the case, questions still have to be asked about the degree to which all members of the family get equal access to its resources. Research shows that a distinction is made between the collective ('family') aspect of the budget and the personal (see Whitehead, 1984, and Pahl, 1983). Men have a far greater call on household resources than women since they can claim personal spending money as well as a share of collective resources. The 'right' of men to take household resources (whoever earned them) for personal consumption items, beer, alcohol, cigarettes, and items of conspicuous consumption (from bicycles, to dark glasses, to shoes) is much commented upon in women's accounts of domestic budgeting (see Dwyer and Bruce, 1988). Women's claims are usually confined to the collective aspect. In the poorest strata almost everywhere the income of each member of the family is vital to survival but often only the woman's income is entirely spent on collective consumption items.

Assumptions behind the models

Mainstream development economics is a version of neo-classical economics and concerns itself with the behaviour of individuals, their preferences or choices, their rationality and their self-interest. Neo-classical economics stems from the basic premises of liberal philosophy which developed in Europe roughly at the time of the emergence of capitalist forms of production. This philosophy may have contributed to the demise of earlier forms of production but was principally concerned with the need to eradicate forms of centralised political power within society. It assumes that all human beings are capable of rationality, that they are primarily motivated by self-interest, that they make choices between competing activities in pursuit of or to maximize self-interest (i.e. choosing that action or set of actions most likely to achieve a pre-determined desired goal). As a result, society operates in a relatively smooth, self-regulatory way precisely because while each person is out to maximise their own utility s/he has to choose goal-oriented strategies which are not in direct conflict with those of others since this may lead to inability to achieve the goal. The role of centralised political power (the state) is to act as arbiter between irreconcilable competing interests, protecting the rights of individuals.

Neo-classical economic theory focuses on markets which are assumed to be sites of free and voluntary exchange between individuals – unless both parties benefit from a transaction it will not take place. It has been said that it offers a universal theory of economic behaviour; however, it assumes the existence of markets while abstracting them from any wider institutional context. In this world, individuals are not embedded in and thus constrained by relationships such as those of kinship or parenthood, nor are inequality, exploitation or conflict essential features.

The household as a corporate unit

The theory does, of course, encompass the fact that individuals marry and bear/father children and form household units. Households are assumed to be composed of a couple and their offspring, and to allocate their labour to market and non-market work on the basis of their 'natural' comparative advantage – women specialising in motherhood and housecare, men in economic activities outside the home. Despite these natural differences, the individual tastes and preferences of spouses and other household members are lumped together so that the household is assumed to have a 'joint utility function' (a common set of goals which maximises household welfare). In other words a simplifying assumption is made about the characteristic behaviour of the family/household: that it behaves as if it were an individual, makes choices, has tastes and preferences, and maximises utility (or welfare). It is assumed that the characteristic behaviour within the family is animated by notions of co-operation, reciprocity and sharing.

This view of the household as a corporate unit does not encourage most economists to analyse the internal structure of the household, to investigate how it actually works as a collectivity, or to enquire into the ways in which joint welfare comes to be arrived at in the interest of all family members. Indeed, it has been argued that economics can bypass all these awkward questions by the assumption that the family is a natural unit in which sharing, reciprocity and co-operation prevail over self-interest and competition (see Folbre, 1986). The family and the family-based household can thus be firmly allocated within the realm of 'the private sphere' (in contrast to the public sphere of the market), which allows them to define intra-household relations as being beyond the remit of the discipline of economics.

In this model it is assumed that the basic form of household survival is through selling labour on the market. However, in most LDCs the majority of households are also family-based enterprises, producing not only for the market but for their own consumption as well. Production decisions have to aim to reach a balance between market and non-market activities. The main problem in analysing this behaviour for economists lies in the fact that relations between household-enterprises and the economy cannot be defined in terms of market forces alone (Evans, 1991). To cope with this a specific branch of economics was developed to provide better tools and concepts for understanding such economic behaviour – the New Household Economics (NHE) (Becker, 1965, 1976).

The household as a decision-making unit

Becker (1965) argues that the household as an economic entity behaves in a way analogous to the firm. It makes both production and consumption decisions which are guided by the need to minimise the costs of production and maximise family consumption. Labour is deployed in response to various pressures: differences in cost or effort between producing something at home as against buying it; the difference between the wage that a household member could get on the market as against the cost of replacing the services/activities foregone within the household (the opportunity cost of labour); and the price of goods.

Becker links the family as a 'natural' kinship unit, motivated by co-operation and sharing, and the household as an enterprise, operating much as the neo-classical theory of the firm predicts. His household is, however, clearly situated within a capitalist market economy; it is bound into markets for labour and goods/services and influenced by prices therein. But his analogy between household and firm is very strained since many exchanges between household members cannot be compared to those involved in buying and selling in the market and many activities cannot simply be dropped because another activity is more profitable (see Evans, 1989).[2]

There are other problems with the theory. What justifies the assumption that husband and wife share tastes/preferences? If behaviour within the market is characterised by natural selfishness (or self-interest) yet in the family selflessness (or altruism) naturally prevails, is there not a problem of theoretical coherence (see Folbre, 1986)? In other words, are human beings by nature somewhat schizophrenic? How are we to understand both relations of conflict and competition and those of sharing and reciprocity? 'Traditional models of price theory and market behaviour are silent on the family. When the silence is broken the old myths and views turn out to be very insecure. While they can be preserved by some special – and typically far-fetched – assumptions, that is hardly the way to face a real challenge' (Sen, 1983, p.25).

The curious contradiction between presumption of self-interest as the principal motivator of market behaviour, enabling the efficient allocation of resources within it, and of altruism within the family, ensuring the efficient allocation of familial resources, appears to have troubled Becker. In later works on the family influenced by the then recent theories of sociobiology, he suggests that the paterfamilias acts as a benevolent dictator to ensure that every family member acts in the interests of the collectivity (Becker, 1976). This poses another puzzle in that, according to this model, husbands, despite their economic power, do not act as selfish tyrants, whereas children (and wives) despite their economic powerlessness apparently do. In other words the model is based on a rather odd prediction of the likely outcome of unequal power relations. But then relations between individuals are not, according to Becker, relations of power, least of all those between husband and wife. In this he differs from John K. Galbraith who has a much clearer view: 'The household, in the established economics, is essentially a disguise for the exercise of male authority' (Galbraith, 1973).

From the point of view of analysing household behaviour in LDCs the assumption in the NHE approach of fully-developed market economy presents serious difficulties. Some of these have been subsequently dealt with by other economists. Allan Low, influenced by the work of the Russian economist Chayanov (1966), for example, showed the need to include both market and non-market opportunities in his analysis of the economic behaviour of farm-households in LDCs (Low, 1986). He showed that factors such as household composition (including the ratio of workers (adults) to consumers (children, elders and adults), and the household division of labour, were important as were differences in labour force participation of all household members (see Evans, 1990).

Low uses the logic of comparative advantage to explain the different allocation of labour but does not address the question of possible conflict of interests between different household or family members. In this sense his vision does not greatly differ from that of orthodox neo-classical economists. Yet research into intra-household relations show that conflict of interest as much as convergence inevitably occur over labour allocation and the distribution of other resources within the family-based household.

Theories about human nature
Studying the household and trying to make sense of observed organisational and behavioural patterns almost inevitably raises questions about the correctness of assumptions as to universal and unchanging human nature. Have neo-classical economics and liberal philosophy got it right – are human beings primarily motivated by individual self-interest? Or do the values of co-operation and reciprocity play as prominent a part in humankind's make up?

Anthropologists would argue that the evidence shows that both co-operation and competition, altruism and self-interest, are potential forms of behaviour, and that the way in which the economy is organised plays a key role in whether individualism and self-interest predominate, or co-operation and altruism. Most previous forms of social organisation have not encouraged the

122

pursuit of economic self-interest in the way or to the extent capitalism does. Indeed, tendencies to economic differentiation were often culturally proscribed (witchcraft accusations being one means of preventing marked economic differentiation), or certain social mechanisms ensured that those who succeeded economically gained social prestige by giving their wealth away, often in grand displays of conspicuous but collective consumption. New analytical tools are badly needed which will allow us to develop theories of co-operative behaviour which can be compared to those of self-interest so as to see which have more predictive power.

Economics appears to be alone among the social sciences in largely discounting the importance of the ways in which individuals are embedded in social structures, the ways in which a variety of institutions, including the family, shape appropriate behaviour towards others; and how these are different for boys and girls, with ideas about masculinity and femininity playing a strong part in defining appropriate behaviour, preferences and expectations. Women are socialised from very early on to be more selfless than men, less personally ruthless, less experimental and daring. Boys may be socialised to behave in ways which appear completely counter to the dictates of self-interest. Furthermore, cultural conditions also shape individuals' responses to given situations – many jokes turn upon the differing responses of people from different cultures to the same situation.

Studying the household also makes one question the stereotypes built into the way we see the world; to stand back from the ideological representation of the family as the supportive bulwark in a heartless world, to ask what relations between men and women are like in reality, what underpins them, what transforms or distorts them. Rather then seeing these relations as effects of unchanging human nature, or of set patterns of roles, they can be seen as dynamic and changing, with men and women bargaining with each other as they seek to further their own advancement as well as the collective good. As David Sahn puts it 'there is a need to determine ... how household members with divergent preference orderings reconcile their differences through some sort of bargaining process' (Sahn, 1985, p.16).

A number of analysts have looked at household dynamics in terms of bargaining theory. Amartya Sen (1985, 1987) suggests that the intra-couple dynamic is most usefully represented as one of **co-operative conflict**. He constructs a model which he suggests is widely applicable. In this, there are a number of potential solutions (he calls them collusive agreements) to differences of goals and strategies, the one finally adopted being the result of the bargaining ability of individuals. Ability, however, in this sense is not a personal negotiating skill: while household members may have divergent views on how to invest resources, use labour and so on, they do not all come with equal power to the bargaining table.

One important component in bargaining power is the perception of self-worth, which differs widely between family members (particularly men and women), and which influences perceptions of advantage and legitimacy. This is based in part on the 'perceived contribution' that the various household members make to household well-being. In modern society, two factors enter here: actual ability to earn income or bring valued resources into the household, and the value given to different members' contributions. As we have seen, since men often get privileged access to income-earning opportunities, and women's contribution to both household and external labour is generally underrated, the idea that the person providing the main inputs to the family or society should make the decisions as to resource allocation is reinforced in men's favour.

Sen's concept of co-operative conflict nicely captures what I have noted above as a more realistic interpretation of human behaviour: the mixture of co-operation and competition, of seeking own aims and furthering those of others. His analysis points to the need to be aware of the factors which throw the relation out of equilibrium and balance into one of inequality. Sen argues that a number of forces have conspired against women's bargaining position over time and that: 'Asymmetries – however developed – are stable and sustained, and the relative weakness of women in co-operative conflict in one period tends to sustain relative weakness in the next' (Sen, 1985, p.13). Until women's contributions are recognised and made visible, until women themselves have a sense of social worth, their bargaining power will remain weak.[3]

Planning with and for women

Once families are brought into economic analysis explicitly, a variety of questions of economic theory and policy emerge (Sen, 1983, p.26).

In this chapter we have argued that the nature of economic models and concepts, the tendency to aggregation and to making simplifying assumptions, make it all too easy to exclude women's activities and contributions. We have also looked at the ways in which statisticians, who provide the data with which planners and economists work, are hampered in producing a better picture of reality, because of assumptions and stereotypes built into their conceptual models. As a result many of the most dynamic processes taking place in LDCs cannot be captured numerically, and women's economic contributions fail to gain proper recognition.

People concerned with developing policies which build on women's social and economic contributions to society as well as to the family face another major obstacle. There is a contradiction between what has been called the seamless web of women's lives and the compartmentalised and gendered mode of conventional thinking about society and social processes in general. Thus, for example, the conceptual separation between the public and the private, productive and unproductive activity, between work and home does not accurately reflect women's reality. It is a male perspective. Linkages need to be made conceptionally between various aspects of women's experience: between family and employment, between unpaid work and paid work, between production and reproduction. So too the link must be made between the production and maintenance of people, and the capacity of an economy to produce goods and services for a variety of markets.

We have also argued that economic theory still cannot help us understand the interlock between household as family and as enterprise and the economy. Since household enterprises are very widespread in LDCs, particularly among the poorer strata, policy instruments are needed which will support these enterprises. Support for poor households is essential both for economic growth and the relief of poverty. But policymakers need to know under what conditions they operate as bounded units, and when they do not, what the wider aggregations are; they need to know what the major constraints to economic viability are – labour, inputs, markets, credit, training, and which household members are the key operators, entrepreneurs or managers.

They also need to know what work women do in the market and in the household, how the two interconnect, and what influences women's ability to participate in economic activity. They also need to understand the time-constraints under which women operate and ask questions about whether increased paid labour force participation is at the cost of unpaid household work or (already scarce) leisure time. When they see that women are moving out of one type of activity and into another they need to know to what extent this reflects a shift from part-time to full-time work, from temporary to permanent employment or vice versa; whether the shift is complementary to or in conflict with trends in male employment (see Evans, 1990). They need to know too whether these shifts are long- or short-term and if the former what additional services need to be provided to women to ensure stability of availability.

Further, they need to know about intra-household distribution of income. Some information is gathered on income but, as Baster (1981) points out, information on income is in fact often missing from macro-level data; when it does appear it tends to refer to households' total monthly and annual cash income, regardless of source. Reliance on money income leads to distortions given the importance in many LDCs of payment in kind and the production of goods for own consumption. Source of income can also be relevant, particularly if there is extensive reliance on transfers from kin or the state. Lastly, little information is given on the control of the various factors determining access to actual or potential income: land, labour, credit, training and paid employment, or to the extent to which the person earning an income controls it.

Given the lack of jointness of marriage as an economic relation, a wide range of policy measures need to be rethought. It may be useful to do this by conceptualising the relations between men and women within the family as characterised by co-operative conflict as we have outlined above. Because of women's weak access to personal money, their greater commitment to and dependence on the collective aspect of the household fund, and the constraints on their ability to build up assets despite their entrepreneurial skills and vocation, policymakers need to consider ways to strengthen the collective aspect of household resources, as much as to support women's enterprises. The aim should not be to reinforce women's dependence, but to enhance the interdependence of men and women to the benefit of both.

Notes

1 This chapter draws heavily on papers written by A. Evans for the IDS Short Courses, and her module for the EL/IDS Training for Trainers series.

2 For example 'There is a limit to the extent to which women can switch from human resource production and maintenance to crop production . . . children will not be left unattended because another crop becomes more profitable' (Vickers, 1991 p.22 quoting Diane Elson's paper 'The Impact of Structural Adjustment on Women: Concepts and Issues.').

3 Gail Wilson has used Sen's model in some research on relative position of household members (see IDS Bulletin, Vol. 22, 1, 1991).

8 Frameworks for analysis

By the end of the 1980s, women in development or WID had become an institutionalised aspect of most international agencies and many national governments have official programmes for women's advancement. The Decade for Women, the conferences, the exhortations, have raised the profile of women's concerns and the importance of their economic and social contributions. At the same time, women themselves have become more organised: whether through grassroots groups working on specific issues, national organisations or umbrella organisations. Women of all classes and races are making demands for recognition, consultation and a greater degree of equality in diverse aspects of their lives with increasing persuasiveness and strength. This activism is further promoted through extensive networking at national, regional and international levels.

But what has actually been achieved? At one level, there have been marked gains in terms of women's health, access to education, and political participation. As health standards throughout the world have improved, so female life expectancy has improved correspondingly, both absolutely and relative to men. In terms of education, women have made noticeable gains, with rises in female literacy and school enrolment. In most countries now, women have, at least officially, political equality – i.e. they can vote or stand for public office. In many countries violence against women is now taken as a serious social matter; in some it is treated as a crime. However, such statements disguise the fact that women still constitute the majority of the poor, the illiterate, and the disenfranchised. The number of women in public office at a high level is still too slight to give one confidence that the diversity of women's voices is beginning to be heard.[1] Furthermore, as was shown in Chapter 3, considerable evidence has accumulated throughout the 1980s of increasing material poverty, in terms of access to food, health care and basic housing, of much of the population in sub-Saharan Africa, Latin America and certain areas of Asia as a result of debt and structural adjustment policies, and that this has been accompanied by a feminisation of poverty.

In Chapter 2 it was argued that the more negative effects of structural adjustment policies tend to hit women first: because of the sexual division of labour, reduced expenditure on social infrastructure and increased privatisation of areas of state assistance increase women's burden of unpaid work. At the same time, when men lose jobs and paid employment opportunities are reduced, their wives have to provide the family income. Those already in some form of paid work will probably have to increase their workload, and those not yet earning an income will have to accept whatever opportunities are available. When women lose regular paid employment, waiting at home until an acceptable equivalent turns up is rarely an option.

The evidence from Chapters 4, 5 and 6 also gives a less than optimistic picture. Women farmers are still largely ignored, and their calls for a change in those policies which lead to environmental depletion and degradation are not heeded. Despite the fact that more than 100 countries now have legislation guaranteeing equal pay for women factory workers, this has had little impact since women continue to be clustered in activities for which there is no obvious male equivalent. As we noted in Chapter 6, the tendency for women to replicate their unpaid domestic labour in the paid workforce, whether formal or informal, has led to their economic contribution being undervalued and their labour being underpaid. Even when they don't, most women are still integrated into the lower levels of the labour hierarchy in occupations that tend to be lower paid and less secure although often more strenuous than those of men. Last but not least, virtually all women continue to face the double day because of a sexual division of labour which automatically assigns domestic and reproductive labour to women.

In Chapter 7 we discussed some of the difficulties of getting women's economic contributions recognised as long as prevailing economic theories make a distinction between productive and unproductive work, and base this distinction largely on whether the activities involved are mediated by the market.

Behind the contradictory observations as to how women have fared lies the question of the terms on which the assessment of improvement is made: is the principal concern the material condition of women or their position in society (Young, 1988)? Despite some obvious improvements in material conditions (with the caveats as above), there is room for doubt that any significant change has come about in the underlying structures that determine women's relative social standing and their share of social resources. Yet it is unlikely that a sustainable improvement in women's material condition is possible without radical changes in these structures. This has led to doubts as to the long-term effectiveness of institutional WID for women, and the questioning of its objectives and strategies for the future by the international women's movement.

While WID is probably the best known approach to the issue it is not the only one. In a recent article Eva Rathgeber suggests there are three basic positions: Women In Development (WID), Woman and Development (WAD), and Gender and Development (GAD) (Rathgeber, 1990). Although these do not share a common theoretical base or perspective, in practice there is considerable overlap and common ground. Indeed, there has been some convergence in the last decade between the WID and GAD approaches. In practice WID is still the predominant institutional perspective. More confusingly, terminology is now no indicator of perspective; the word gender is widely used either to mean women or sex (but not the social appropriation of biological sex), gender roles or gender division of labour commonly replaces sex roles or the sexual division of labour.

In this chapter we shall look at the three approaches, giving the most detailed account of the basic premises of the gender approach, which is the least well-known and has informed discussions throughout this book. In the following section we will discuss the usefulness to planners and policymakers of the two main approaches.

Women or gender – alternative analyses?

Women In Development

Mainstream WID lies squarely within the framework of what has been called liberal feminist theory (see Alison Jagger, 1983). Liberal theory is based on the premise of the rational individual seeking his (almost invariably) own self-interest, virtually free from social encumbrances (children, family, community). Liberal feminism attributes women's unequal status and social position to their exclusion from the public sphere, largely due to the sexual division of labour. Liberal feminists seek to ensure women get greater access to a wide range of occupations and within them to positions of decision-making power. To integrate women into the mainstream of economic, political and social life, laws and institutions must be reformed, and attitudes changed. Women without the right level of qualifications have to be persuaded and aided in getting into higher level education and training. The approach accentuates the fact that women can do everything men do as well as men.

WID is informed by sex role theory[2] and, in terms of development, by modernisation theory and the linear notion of development (see Chapter 1); existing social and economic structures are taken as givens (see Rathgeber, 1990). With economic growth and modernisation, it is assumed that better living conditions, wages, education, etc. will be within the grasp of all and that the grosser elements of patriarchal traditional belief systems will be dissolved by the more progressive attitudes inculcated by modern education. The WID approach gives little importance to a historical perspective or structural divisions among women – whether those of class, caste, race, or creed. It focuses on women and their experience, and places its major emphasis on individuals and their capacity for self-betterment. It therefore emphasises the importance of 'role models' or outstanding women who have gained social recognition in the public sphere.

Early on WID practitioners pointed to women's invisibility, the lack of data on their activities, and argued that women were excluded from development processes. They concentrated their efforts in trying to ensure women's (better) integration into development, and the alleviation of work burdens through provision of appropriate technologies, of lack of access to modern knowledge and other resources through credit programmes, agricultural extension or other training. The recognition that economic development was not benefiting women, led to the legitimation of a women only focus, whether in terms of research or of delivery of benefits via projects. With the poverty alleviation emphasis in the 1970s, WID practitioners focused on the needs of poor women in developing countries.

There are several weaknesses in the original WID perspective. Firstly, the almost exclusive focus on women appears based on the assumption that women can become sole agents of their destiny, without any corresponding change in or reaction from men. Yet women's lives are shaped in very great measure by their relations with men. None the less WID gives scant importance to understanding how gender relations actually work on the ground; how changes in the economy give men (or women) additional options or destroy support systems and weaken the relative standing of individuals or a gender itself; how men (or women) are able to recruit support in moments of tension or dispute. As a result little thought was given to how women were to be enabled to withstand the outright opposition or covert but by no means less disruptive resistance of men to any change in gender relations and the distribution of the benefits of development. Secondly, with its emphasis on equity strategies and getting women into the public sphere and non-conventional forms of employment, that other aspect of women's lives – the private – was neglected.[3] Yet for the bulk of the world's women who live in the rural areas these efforts would have little impact on their lives. Thirdly, the neglect of the ideological aspects of gender meant that many women were unable to respond to WID programmes. The unequal balance of responsibilities, work and value was seen as perfectly 'natural' if not god given, and therefore unchangeable. Lastly, the emphasis on poverty also had the effect of masking the structures of gender inequality; poverty rather than oppressive male-centered social structures became the main cause of women's disadvantage. The relation between women's differential poverty and their subordination was not adequately analysed.

The emphasis on poverty also helped to create a separation between first world 'feminist' demands and Third World 'development' demands. WID became concerned with the needs of women 'out there' in the developing world – indeed development is itself of concern only to those 'out there'. Feminists were seen to be a product of Western culture and were concerned with parochial, even sectarian, issues based firmly in specific national or regional realities (i.e. Western issues), usually social in nature. For women in the developing world, their lack of agency relative to men was not the issue, bread and butter concerns were. As such, the potential strength of largely middle-class feminists in the LDCs and their usefulness as allies to WID were not initially recognised.[4]

The poverty focus also led many to assume that the differences in interests between poor women and wealthier women are inevitably irreconcilable. This made it difficult to see the necessity of distinguishing between differing groups of women, and the need for facilitating alliances between poor women and wealthier, professional women. Yet in strategic terms, it is essential that women with professional training such as lawyers, doctors, scientists, and accountants use their skills to the benefit of the advancement of women as a gender, if the structures of subordination are to be dismantled. It may seem contradictory to claim that a more complex analysis less focused on the individual but comprehending the cross-cutting strands of the potential unity of and the structural divisions between women, would have helped to pinpoint the need for a women's movement as a means of bringing about long-term structural change. In other words, the need to create the conditions for the forging of alliances between women of different social classes and ethnic or cultural background so as to create and consolidate a women's movement powerful enough to challenge structures of inequality.

Perhaps the greatest weakness of WID, at least initially, was that there was little questioning of the aims of development or the processes by which development is to be achieved. The pressure on those working within development-oriented organisations is to go with the current and try to find openings for women; to find manipulable variables which can bring small (incremental) changes (personal communication, Ingrid Eide). As we have noted, throughout the period this book is concerned with, the focuses and strategies of institutional WID derived from the concerns of the mainstream, so that WID proponents moved from concern with welfare to poverty to efficiency as did mainstream development practitioners. As we move into the 1990s the emphasis is shifting from efficiency to empowerment and in some circles to democratisation.

The reasons for some of the perceived weaknesses in the WID approach are thus not necessarily solely rooted in its theoretical approach. As we noted in Chapter 3, some of the recommendations from the 1975 Mexico City Conference were quite bold in their implications. The need to change relations between men and women within the domestic sphere – so as to ensure a redistribution of domestic chores – was explicitly recognised in the Mexico Plan of Action, as was the need to recognise the value of women's unpaid labour. The need for a profound redistribution of social resources from men to women was not mooted at that point, but equity strategies did form part of the demands of institutional WID, at least for a short period after the world conference. But as Mayra Buvinic (1983) notes, these demands had to be abandoned because of the hostility they aroused among development 'experts'.

The hostility arose in part from deeply entrenched male resistance to change in long-established patterns of behaviour and thought or to accommodate women's views and concerns (see Staudt, 1990). But there was another element too. Most development practitioners (not all of them male) are concerned with not violating what they see as deeply embedded cultural practices and values.[5] In this they are reinforced by the vocal objections of many developing country representatives – politicians, planners and others – to focusing on women. The absence of women at high levels of their governments and the lack of women's active involvement in policymaking, allows them to represent such concerns as being 'Western impositions' of no interest to 'our women'.[6] Women's absence also means that development practitioners, planners and negotiators are often unaware of (or have no means of hearing) women's actual concerns and needs. Cultural imperialism is obviously a critical issue, but all too often it is used as a justification by (Western) practitioners for doing nothing to question, far less weaken, structures of subordination which women in the LDCs are not anxious to preserve. Until steps are taken to remedy the absence of women in consultative fora, it is difficult to be entirely convinced by the practitioners' protestations.

Rather than pursue the equity issue and risk professional marginalisation, those in institutional WID opted for a pragmatic strategy which would enable them to continue to work with male colleagues while trying to shift the climate of opinion in the development industry. Even this strategy of accommodation did not prevent powerful and committed women from being increasingly marginalised and their WID bureaux starved of funds (for an analysis of the case of USAID see Staudt and Jacquette, 1988; see also Buvinic, 1983; Staudt, 1990).

The institutional practice of WID looks to reforming the social and economic system to be more 'user friendly' to women. Strategies largely focus on technical solutions to the problems of inequality: training, access to resources, incorporation in the market. Early on WID practitioners argued for the inclusion of a women's component to international aid programmes (promoted by a number of aid agencies such as USAID after the 1976 Percy Amendment), and the employment of more women in development-related agencies. The UN's WID strategy was to promote the establishment of national machinery – women's bureaux, cells or ministries. And as we have seen (in Chapter 3) a great many countries did set up national machinery. In many countries too, laws enshrining grosser forms of gender discrimination were changed, and new laws introduced to facilitate the equalisation of the sexes.

However, experience has shown that these strategies can all too easily be subverted. At the project level women's components are usually poorly financed and either limited to welfare areas of decision-making, re-emphasising women's reproductive roles, or focus on forms of income earning which are marginal, unstable and poorly rewarded. While possibly meeting some of women's practical needs, the piecemeal approach often adds to women's overall work burden. Gender relations, and the distribution of rewards and burdens of development, are rarely if ever addressed. The alternative, to incorporate women's needs into all development programmes, has its own difficulties.[7]

The UN strategy has also been criticised on the grounds that it has served in many cases to isolate and marginalise women's issues. In the summary conclusions to Chapter 3 some of the constraints facing women's bureaux and personnel at women's ministries are briefly discussed. With the incorporation into the mainstream of government of the 'woman question', the voices of some of the strongest advocates for women have paradoxically enough been stifled; the concerns of bureaux personnel have to take second place to 'political and economic realities'. At the same time those in control can claim they are doing something about women – while in reality pushing them to the bottom of the agenda. The language of women's special needs also all too often masks political expediency; it is rarely if ever accompanied by any commitment to changing structures of discrimination and subordination.

These failings, of course, cannot be laid at the door of WID practitioners, but they illustrate some of the difficulties facing those who wish to incorporate WID into the mainstream, and point to the need for a clearly thought through and determined strategy for change.

Women and Development

The form of analysis which Rathgeber calls WAD, concentrates more on the inequalities between IMEs and LDCs within the development process, and the nature of development itself, as the prime overarching determinants of women's poverty, marginalisation and inequality. If we take DAWN (an international network of Third World women researchers – see Chapter 3) as a representative of this perspective, they argue that:

> We are now more aware of the need to question in a more fundamental way the underlying processes of development into which we have been attempting to integrate women. Throughout the Decade it has been implicit that women's main problem in the Third World has been insufficient participation in an otherwise benevolent process of growth and development. Increasing women's participation and improving their shares in resources, land, employment and income relative to men were seen as both necessary and sufficient to effect dramatic changes in their economic and social position. Our experiences now lead us to challenge this belief. (Sen and Grown, 1987).

The DAWN group has more recently been active in analysing the impact of the debt crisis on women, the women's movement in various countries, and certain members are involved in research into the effects of militarism on developing countries (DAWN, 1991, Vols. 1 and 2). This position reflects that of many radical thinkers and practitioners who maintain that unless and until there is a more equal international economic system (set in motion by a redistribution of global resources from the IMEs to the LDCs), there can be no real development, economic or otherwise.

Gender and Development

That relations between men and women are at the heart of the development problematic was the starting point of analysis for a group of women working on issues of women's subordination within the development process at the Institute of Development Studies, University of Sussex, in the mid-1970s. Initially at least, the group set out to contest the WID approach from a perspective which was informed by the marxist analysis of social change, and a feminist analysis of patriarchy. Most of the group had experience in living and working overseas, and had been involved in women's struggles in the UK as well. One of the group's first activities was to organise an international conference to start to build a network of people in both developing and developed countries working from a similar perspective.[8] This reflected the group's view that without international solidarity in struggle, lasting change would not be possible.

The conceptual framework of GAD was constructed around several key propositions: that women are incorporated into the development process but in very specific ways; that a focus on women alone was inadequate to understand the opportunities for women for agency or change; that women are not a homogeneous category but are divided by class, colour and creed; that any analysis of social organisation and social process has to take into account the structure and dynamic of gender relations; that the totality of women's and men's lives has to be the focus of analysis, not merely their productive, or their reproductive activities; that women are not passive, nor marginal, but active subjects of social processes (see Young, 1979).

From this perspective the basic problematic is not women's integration into development, or their invisibility, or their lack of training, education, credit, self-esteem, but the structures and processes that give rise to women's disadvantage. One source of disadvantage is the pervasive ideology of male superiority, physical and intellectual, which appears to be found, in different degrees, in almost all cultures and economies, and which also shapes women's view of themselves and their capacities. Another is the control men as a gender exercise over valued political, economic and social resources, and thus over the distribution of power. From this perspective, changing the symptoms of disadvantage – giving women training, credit, etc. – is not a solution but only a useful first step in women's empowerment. Dismantling the structures which support women's disadvantage – changing laws, religious and political institutions, systems of thought, socialisation practices – will involve a tremendous struggle for both women and men as they negotiate and adapt to changes in the nature of gender relations in the public and the private spheres. A salient feature of these relations is that they are structured in inequality. As Ann Whitehead put it: 'We use the term subordination ... to make the general point that the character of gender relations is that of male dominance and female subordination' (Whitehead, 1979, p.12). In other words the relation between men and women is one of the sets of power relations in society. A corollary of this is that since relations between men and women within the family share this general character, they cannot be assumed to be harmonious and conflicting. Another salient feature of these relations is the heavy ideological burden they bear; their character as relations of unequal power is masked by the ideology of complementary interdependence.

The GAD approach attempts to be holistic. That is, it tries to comprehend the main features of social organisation, economic and political life, in order to understand the shaping of particular aspects of society. While it assumes that gender – a hierarchical ordering – will be a relevant aspect of social organisation, it does not assume it will be the most important or powerful, nor that gender relations will necessarily be the principal determinant of women's situation. Rather, it seeks to analyse culturally specific forms of social inequality and divisions, to see how gender is related to or interlocked with other forms of social hierarchy. As such, the position of a given society within the wider international system must itself be part of the analysis.

Given the emphasis on the structural underpinnings of women's subordination the IDS group looked at the nature of the economic development being promoted as a key component in the gender equation. We understood the term development to be a shorthand for the process of social and economic change involved in the creation of a (global) market economy and a class society. This form of economic organisation was not seen in a positive light for two main reasons. Historically, capitalism in the IMEs has used women as a reserve of labour, to be sucked into and ejected from the labour force when expansion and contraction of the economy required. Further, women's unpaid labour underpins the system's ability to create wealth and is a key but neglected aspect of the unequal distribution of the wealth created by the combining of capital and labour. Socialist development strategies on the other hand suffered from a productivist bias which was almost as inimical to women's struggle towards equality.[9] However, within socialist theory women's inequality was at least recognised which allowed for the possibility of greater public support for women's emancipatory struggles. The main difficulty within socialism for women was the lack of questioning of the socialist version of sex role theory, the lack of value given to reproductive work, and the absence of structures allowing for challenge and dissent.

True development was viewed as a complex process involving the social, economic, political and cultural betterment of individuals and of society itself. Betterment in this sense meant the ability of the society to meet the physical, emotional and creative needs of the population at an historically acceptable level, and to free human labour time from the incessant treadmill of basic needs production. It thus involves raising standards of living but not conspicuous consumption, and it implies a form of organisation of society which allows for equal distribution of social wealth. In other words one in which all citizens have a voice in decision-making processes.[10]

Within this process, women and men were viewed as active agents in and not passive recipients of development. However, as men and women are differently located within the socio-economic structure, they tend to have different sets of interests and needs. The approach thus recognised the existence of contradictions between the genders but made no assumptions as to whether these are antagonistic or not. The approach also recognised that differences between women can give rise to sharp contradictions, which make the task of creating a movement that incorporates diversity but also shares a common vision a difficult one.

The IDS Subordination of Women Collective (SOW) emphasised the need to move away from the focus on women to looking at the relations between men and women. In this SOW were building upon a very crucial point made some years before by feminist thinkers: that our basic identities as men and as women are socially constructed rather than based on fixed biological characteristics (Oakley, 1972; Rubin, 1975). Thus the need to get away from the term sex with its connotations of biological fixity to using a term which connotes malleability. In this sense, it is possible to talk about the historical differences in masculinity or femininity in a given society, as well as the differences in them between societies

Gender

Since the 1970s a copious literature has become available (see e.g. Tolson, 1977; Archer and Lloyd, 1983; Connell, 1987; Brittan 1989) but the SOW group was then feeling its way toward a useful perspective. We used gender to refer to the social meanings given to being either a man or a woman in a given society, and to the expectations held as to the characteristics, aptitudes and likely behaviour of men and women. As such it involves both **ideology** and **material practices**. When we say that a certain type of behaviour (e.g. crying, expressing emotion) or certain activities (e.g. washing dishes, cooking, caring for babies), are unmanly, we are basing this on our expectation as to how a 'real' man of our culture (and often class) would behave in a given situation. But it also implies that such behaviour/activity is the hallmark of femininity – and as such, behaviour or activity becomes itself impregnated with gender.

136

In large measure such judgements are based on cultural understandings, but these also turn on gender stereotypes. One of the puzzles in analysis is the pervasiveness of such stereotypes (across cultures) and by extension their origin. In part they clearly derive from what might be called the commonsense theory about differences between men and women. This has a number of more or less explicit principles: that men and women differ fundamentally (i.e. that the differences are categorical or that there is little overlapping of traits); that men are superior to women both physically and intellectually (or in a softer, post-feminist, version that men and women think differently and are naturally drawn to different forms of intellectual and other activity). Behind these notions lie a number of assumptions; that physical difference (bodily characteristics) influences mental traits, which in turn influence aptitudes and predispositions; that such differences are both natural and unproblematic.

The commonsense approach provides, in fact, a popular theory about human nature and a justification for existing relationships between men and women which is **essentialist** and derived from a biological model of human nature. The popular model has been given academic credentials by a number of writers (usually writing in popular style – for example Ardrey, 1977; Morris, 1967; Lorenz, 1967) and by the discipline of socio-biology.[11] The gender approach contests this. One of its basic premises is that rather slight physiological and psychological differences between the sexes can be, and in some societies are, construed as categorical differences, and that such construction is supported by ideologies representing gender differences as natural or indeed divinely ordained. Such ideologies are supported and reinforced by a wide range of material practices from the sexual division of labour, exclusion of women from positions of religious, political or military command, to male avoidance of touching a menstruating woman (and her seclusion during this period, the prohibition on her cooking, etc.). In contrast, the gender approach holds that 'gender difference is not absolute, abstract, or irreducible, it does not involve an essence of gender. Gender differences, and the experience of differences, are socially and psychologically created and situated ...' (Nancy Chodorow, 1979, p.53).

If masculinity and femininity are not given by nature, then how are they acquired? This is clearly a complex subject and requires an understanding of a range of psychological and child development theories.[12] But put at its most basic, gendering (the acquisition of social characteristics of masculinity or femininity) is not a simple, nor a single process, but rather a highly complex set of processes involving both psychological events and socialisation, which start almost at birth and continue well into adulthood.[13] It involves both acquiring an identity (social and sexual) and learning a set of differentiated behaviours and capacities appropriate to the masculine or the feminine.[14] Acquisition of gender identity is not in most societies left to the 'invisible psychic hand' but is constantly reinforced and refined by a wide range of other social practices. This is perhaps an indication of the fact that the acquisition of gender identity and appropriate sexuality is not unproblematic; indeed much psychoanalytic and therapeutic time is consumed in sorting out the difficulties of those for whom the acquisition was either incomplete or flawed. Through continuing socialisation – at school, home, through games and rituals, and even the sexual division of labour – boys and girls, men and women, learn those behaviours and capacities appropriate to their gender and their culture.

Social relations of gender

Gender relations are those socially constituted relations between men and women which are shaped and sanctioned by norms and values held by members of a given society (but not necessarily held with the same degrees of firmness). Central to these relations are culturally specific notions of masculinity and femininity, and around these notions appropriate behaviours for each of the genders are socially constructed.

There are a number of critical arenas in which gender is likely to be a decisive operator. One of these is the domestic arena, another is that of kinship. With this latter field most of the relations between men and women are ascribed, that is their character derives from the position of the parties in sets of relations largely established on the basis of kinship and marriage (Whitehead, 1979). Examples of ascribed relations are those of father:daughter, uncle:niece, brother:sister, husband:wife and so on. For each set there is a socially sanctioned pattern of appropriate behaviour. In many societies these ascriptive relations are marked by behavioural patterns such as deference, subordination, submission, or other forms of social signalling of difference if not inferiority.

Outside the domestic arena lies that of the community or wider society. Here relations are not ascriptive in modern society. But a characteristic of many of these relations is that when they involve male and female, they tend to replicate the order of dominance found in the domestic arena. That is to say the male tends to be the superior term in the relation. Such relations are in this sense gender bearing (Whitehead, 1979). For example, in the economic sphere one can commonly guess the gender of the occupant of a position by its place in the hierarchy of occupational positions – doctor:nurse, boss:secretary, university professor:lecturer; trade union leader:semi-skilled garment worker.

While gender identity is an important strand in any individual's sense of self, it is not the only social force structuring relations. Societies are complex unities involving multiple systems of stratification and hierarchy. As a result, the nature of any given relation involving men and women cannot simply be read off. Gender is but one of a number of differentiators – class, race, ethnicity, religion, age – so that relations that are gender bearing are likely also to be carriers of class or race signifiers. This means that historical and cultural specificity in analysis is always a necessity. An implication of this is that the rather crude rule of thumb that within a single element or set of a stratification system males are likely to be superordinate, can be overridden by class, age or race hierarchy.

When we talk about gender relations we are not generally referring to day-to-day empirical encounters between men and women, the outcome of which largely depends on specific individuals and their unique characteristics. Instead, we mean the ideal or normative set of relations which permits a person to say: in my country men do this (and don't do that), and women do that (and never do this). In other words, a structured set of social behaviour. The behaviour derives in part from the different social identities of the two genders inasmuch as people, at least initially, relate to each other in accordance with given gender codes of behaviour and expectations. But they are also underpinned by ideology (such as the popular version of human nature discussed above) and reinforced by the different access of the genders to socially valued resources, and sanctioned by a range of mechanisms from social opprobrium to death. As such they are relations into which people enter involuntarily.

Obviously, in real life, neither men nor women always live 'by the book', rather in their daily encounters and negotiations both have to balance differences in character, in readings of the actual lived situation, in the nature of the support they can call on from external sources (including the guardians of the norms) and so on. The difficulty this raises for analysis is what weight to assign to **structural coercion** as against **individual motivation and volition** (a problem not confined to the analysis of gender relations alone).

The gender approach assumes that gender identity provides a framework for response to constraints and opportunities, as does the specific structure of gender relations. But actual behaviour is responsive to a wider range of political, religious, racial and economic factors. It is therefore necessary to analyse how these other forces intersect with and dynamise gender relations, provoking in some instances structural rather than individual responses to produce relational configurations which may be reinforcements of old forms or may be quite new ones. Alternatively, individual responses may take on a momentum and massification which leads to structural change. A key moment when relations between men and women are cast in high relief is when rapid economic change throws up new opportunities as well as new penalties and burdens; access to or avoidance of them then becomes a critical site of struggle between the genders.

Comparison between WID and GAD perspective

Possibly the difference between WID and GAD is best illustrated by the way the sexual or gender division of labour (SDOL) is conceptualised. For most WID proponents the SDOL allocates men and women to different tasks; as such the important thing is to analyse the production system to see what women do, how much time it takes, how much control they have over the proceeds, and what is needed to lighten the burden of work and to give women greater control over the fruits of their labour. From a GAD perspective although the SDOL appears to be a form of social separation it is in fact a form of **social connection**. That is to say, by making men and women undertake different activities, and produce different goods and services, they are made dependent upon each other (a point made by Levi Strauss, 1969 but see also Whitehead, 1990). Such separation but mutual interdependence assumes that some form of recognised exchange system exists between men and women and that both co-operate in such a system, but not without conflict, latent or manifest.

To give a simple example, in industrial and market economies the SDOL allocates men to the sphere of wage work and women to that of domestic or household work. A man who spends the bulk of the day earning wages has to have a means to ensure that he is regularly provided with such things as cooked food, clean clothes, a tidy house, emotional warmth and physical relaxation. One means by which he can do this is by marrying a woman and exchanging his wage goods for her services.

A critical area for gender analysis is the precise terms under which men and women co-operate and the specific institutions through which such co-operation is structured. One such institution is marriage, the socially elaborated terms of exchange and collaboration of which are embodied in what Whitehead (1984) has called the **conjugal contract**. The literature on marriage in developing countries is not particularly rich but some attempts have been made to understand one aspect of the conjugal contract – how resources are shared within marriage (see Dwyer and Bruce, 1988; Young, 1990).

It is reasonable to suggest that one effect of the SDOL is to make men and women **artificially separate** – distinct and different – from each other. And further, that it tends to make what they do incommensurable (or non-comparable). But this artificiality – the social nature of the division – is ideologically denied by systems of thought which represent the division as being based on 'natural' biological differences and capacities: that women are naturally more adept at caring for the young, domestic servicing, etc.; that men have a natural capacity for organising, production, dispute resolution, etc. In other words, overlying the division is the gender logic – a set of ideas about natural characteristics of men and women derived from their biological differences. If indeed the basis of the SDOL were natural characteristics derived from biological difference, then one would expect to find a similar SDOL crossculturally and historically. Yet analysis shows changes over time in the SDOL in response to a variety of forces, and furthermore that the nature of the genders' natural attributes also changes.

Why these changes occur is not entirely clear. In some cases it appears to be changes in economic relations, in others political, in others demographic.

What this suggests is that the operation of the SDOL is mediated by other structures or forces within society. And this reinforces the view that the SDOL itself is a social construction operating on sets of relations themselves socially constructed, and dependent upon or affected by the form of society and its economy.

A second feature of the SDOL – that tasks are not merely allocated, but differently valued – is also noted in WID analysis. In other words the SDOL embodies a set of values: some tasks are given high social prominence, others are not – and those who do them are equally differently socially valued. The rationale behind the valuation does not appear to be based on a single criterion – intellectual work is given greater value than manual labour; but headwork and handwork greater value than bodywork (i.e. caring for children, the sick, the elderly; providing food and other forms of nourishment). Equally, work which meets male characteristics and aptitudes appears to be given greater social value than female (i.e. strength rather than dexterity, physical endurance rather than mental endurance). Since in most societies men are thought to be more capable of headwork, and women are largely relegated to bodywork (feeding, cleaning, providing health care, sexual servicing, and giving psychological counselling to children and adults alike), it can in fact be argued that there is but one criterion. Men and what they do are valued, women and their work less so. There is a complex relation between who does a task and the value given to it, which is reinforced over time, so that certain tasks become almost the quintessential expression of the gender performing them.[15]

WID and GAD as planning approaches

GAD, as Rathgeber notes, is weak on practical application; it provides a critical perspective, a different way of seeing the world. If we take the SDOL again, the prescriptions from the analysis would be rather different. WID proponents would look to ensuring the SDOL is understood by project planners or project implementers so as not to undermine women's status or overburden them; they would argue that women need recognition for the work they are doing, and greater value given to that effort. They might argue for the need for appropriate technology to lessen women's burden of drudgery.

GAD proponents would take a different tack. Starting from the premise that the SDOL is a form of social connection, which creates interdependence but also reinforces the system of differential evaluation of masculinity and femininity, they would argue that it is a critical element maintaining and/or recreating gender inequality. As such, changing it must be a key tool in undermining inequality and releasing both men and women's full potential for the development effort. They would thus examine how the specific SDOL division constructs women in relation to men – as their inferiors, their chattels, their helpmeets or their equals. They would look to see whether the gender logic ensures that much of what women are doing gets subsumed under the category of the natural (caring for children, even subsistence farming), while men's work is being categorised as eminently social or cultural, i.e. man-made. If this were the case, they would see whether the unequal burden of responsibility and the unequal system of rewards was ideologically justified or socially invisibilised. With this analysis they would then put forward a strategy which would in the long run undermine the SDOL.

GAD proponents would argue that lessening women's burden of responsibilities and providing greater access to resources is important, but equally important is the need to create spaces in which women can begin to socialise their experience, to break away from the highly circumscribed sphere of family, kin or village, to question common justifications for their situation, to understand the role of ideology in constructing the individual's understanding of her or his experience. In other words, they would try to prepare the ground for change and also to create support mechanisms for women in their efforts to bring about change in themselves and others.

A key WID strategy is getting women access to cash income either as individuals or members of some form of collectivity. To facilitate women's insertion into the market they also stress training and skilling, access to credit, etc. This strategy derives both from the belief that women's economic dependence on men is the primary cause of their subordination and from confidence in the market itself. From a GAD perspective, the market is much more ambiguous in its impact. At the individual level, some women will be able to benefit from entry into the market; some will gain greater bargaining strength within the family because they can contribute to their own upkeep or that of the children. What is doubtful is whether individual gains will translate themselves into the overall empowerment of women as a gender. The market has rarely been shown to be an egalitarian distributor of wealth, indeed some would argue it depends on inequality for its efficient functioning. In general, since the structures of gender inequality are embedded within the market system, there is a degree of scepticism as to whether reforms proposed by WID are sufficient to restructure gender relations on more equal terms.

A GAD analysis too places greater importance on the state as a locus of support for women. Women, because of mothering, are more dependent on socialised forms of support than men, and some form of state provision, particularly in terms of health and care for children and the elderly, is essential for women's well-being. From this perspective children should not be seen merely as the concern of their parents or kin-group, but are the wealth of the entire society, and as such society must provide the best possible conditions for those future generations.[16]

Both approaches accept that if only one gender takes decisions about development options, the choices and solutions arrived at will differ from those agreed upon when both genders are involved. However, if both genders are involved, a much more complex process of bargaining and making trade-offs, negotiating and reaching painful compromises is inevitable. But a GAD proponent would not subscribe to the view that all that is needed to better the situation for women is 'to ask the women themselves'. While women are clearly active in trying to cope with the situation they find themselves in, it cannot be assumed that they have perfect knowledge or understanding of the economic, political and social context of their lives. Nor that women by essence have some greater intuitive power or vision. Women as individuals may well be aware of their subordinate position and powerlessness, but the force of ideology may render this 'natural' or 'god given'. Equally, even when it is recognised as social, the structural roots of discrimination and inequality are not always easily identified. Individual men too may be aware of the social pervasiveness of male dominance, but may themselves feel personally powerless and even oppressed (see Connell, 1987; Brittan, 1989). Discussion, experimentation, feedback and comparison – consciousness raising – is a necessary enabling process, which in time may provide the basis for the empowerment of both women (and progressive men) in their struggle for change.

In examining any potential or actual impact of development programmes on a particular society or group within a society, GAD proponents ask the questions: what economic and social changes are sought, who is involved, with the collaboration of whom, with what objective, for the benefit of whom and against the interests of whom; what is the resultant balance of rights and obligations, power and privilege between men and women? Are men or women the major beneficiaries, which specific categories of men or women benefit and which lose out? If women are to benefit, where will women benefiting get their support from; what trade-offs are involved, what rewards and responsibilities will be available to men to facilitate their acquiescence? Finally, will the development options being preferred lead to sustainable forms of production and distribution? Are mechanisms in place which allow local women as well as men to monitor progress, and in the case of abuse or wastage of local resources, human or environmental, allow them to call a halt to the process.

Conclusion

GAD has in a way fulfilled the role in the women and development field that radical feminism has to feminism. That is to say it has pointed to the deficiencies in the WID approach, constantly criticised modernisation theory, the notion of development, incorporation and betterment. It has argued for the importance of allowing women to find their own feet, and of women defining their own needs and interests, and the need to recognise the challenge of diversity. Yet because of the importance it gives to the role of ideology, it is much less convinced of the view that women somehow inately know what is best; that they have been less contaminated and corrupted by the ideological onslaughts of not only consumerist capitalism, but also intransigent fundamentalisms of a variety of faiths. It therefore places emphasis on organisation as a space in which women can share their views and learn to dissect the competing untruths and mystifications of the human condition.

It is a much less coherent view than WID, in part because it is more dynamic; and much less acceptable to mainstream development because of its emphasis on gender as a relation of power. Like WID it emphasises the importance of women's involvement in decision-making and political power, but given the differences between women, and the cross-cutting loyalties of women, it would argue that women need to organise around a range of different and often conflicting issues before they can make a long-term and lasting impact. While prominent individuals are important as trial blazers (or 'role' models), women's organisations can ensure a longer term base for struggle, and a means whereby individuals who aspire to political power can be held accountable to the women they represent.

The GAD approach 'leads, inevitably, to a fundamental re-examination of social structures and institutions and, ultimately, to the loss of power of entrenched elites, which will affect some women as well as men. ... It demands a degree of commitment to structural change and power shifts which is unlikely to be found either in national or in international agencies' (Rathgeber, 1990, p.495). But this fundamental re-examination may have to be undertaken as more and more development planners, policymakers and people of influence come to recognise the links between women's subordination and continuing poverty, population crises and unsustainable forms of economic organisation.

Notes

1 Of every 100 ministerial-level positions worldwide in 1989, only four were held by women. Regional differences are quite marked: Asia and Pacific 1.6, Africa 2.5, Latin America 4.0, socialist block 4.6, northern industrialised countries 8.9.

2 For a critical discussion of sex role theories see R. W. Connell, 1983, 1987 and Brittan, 1989.

3 Equity strategies largely emphasised getting women into formal employment and ending discrimination in the labour force – there was little questioning of the male pattern of much employment, nor the fact of the double day. It became obvious, however, that while women can do men's jobs, there is still that other – woman's – job to be done. Who is to care for the children, the old and the infirm? One answer was to professionalise women's domestic services. Better-off women who wanted to take on (well-paid) work in the public sphere should employ maids, cooks, nannies, etc. to free them to do so. Another was to provide collective facilities, such as crèches for children. The big question was then whether this should be undertaken by the state or the private enterprises. Those who argued for state provision saw this as representing a transfer of resources from men to women as well as a recognition of the social importance of the care and socialisation of the next generation. The argument against state provision was both the poor quality of the service offered, and, as with the professionalisation of women's domestic skills, the

fact that workers (very largely women) in the caring professions received very low wages and benefits, and little social valuation. Private provision, of course, discriminates against the poor, and represents a transfer of resources from women to men, inasmuch as it is almost always from the woman's pay that the expense of childcare is taken, enabling men to retain a higher proportion of their own wages as personal money (see Chapter 7).

4 The relation between middle-class and working-class women is obviously a complex one. None the less many social reformers and inspirers of working-class organisations have middle-class origins but have attempted to subordinate their 'class interest' to a larger cause. This raises the question of the main components of identity which is discussed later in this chapter.

5 It is curious how Western development experts are happy with the notion of changing economic behaviour and attendant relationships (as well as other 'harmful' traditional practices and values) but relations between men and women are considered sacrosanct, despite the fact that the very economic relations being fostered are changing gender relations often to women's detriment.

6 Ingrid Eide (erstwhile WID programme director at UNDP) notes the tendency to 'externalise' concerns which threaten the status quo; i.e. civil rights – northern ideas; environmental concerns – foreign impositions; WID – concern of donor agencies, Western obsession.

7 Barbara Lewis, *Women in Development Planning*, provides a discussion of the separate vs. integrated debate (in O'Barr, 1982).

8 Discussions at the conference were organised around three main themes: production, reproduction and struggle (IDS Bulletin, 1979; Young *et al*, 1984; Young, 1989).

9 A key debate at the time was whether entry into wage work (of socialised production) is a sufficient condition for liberating women; the group considered this to be misplaced. 'Marriage and the social relations between women and men which flow from this contract, almost everywhere give men privileged command of women's labour, and the product of that labour, as well as exclusive right to women's sexuality. ... When women are incorporated into wage work, this gender hierarchy is not broken but replicated' (Young, 1979, p.4).

10 This, of course, is a fine vision but we did not get down to conceptualising the nuts and bolts of the political and economic system that would make the vision possible.

11 Essentialism has also been adopted by certain versions of feminism (although the stereotypes are reversed – see Lynne Segal [1987] for a critique).

12 There are a number of theories of socialisation; two appear most common. Social learning theory suggests young men and women learn the appropriate behaviours, attitudes, values, etc. by imitating their parents, teachers, etc. and through reinforcements (i.e. rewards and punishments). Furthermore, these behavioural sets are organised into a system of sex roles which young people fit into, and to which, as they grow older, are added new sex appropriate roles.

The cognitive development approach assumes the progressive interaction of the child and the environment, and that children (like adults) need a framework to organise and recall experience. A child's initial experience of learning that two categories of people exist and that s/he belongs to one of them helps it to develop a gender schema through which to process information about gender, and which is a prerequisite for learning more about it. Children tend to recall information in terms of gender stereotypes – a function of the child's gender schema – and this may help to explain the prevalence of stereotyping despite the reality of considerable diversity. The cognitive development approach allows children a more active role in the construction and ordering of knowledge, and leaves the possibility of change and adaptation, for example, as gender relations themselves change (for extended discussion of these and other theories see Archer and Lloyd, 1983; and see also Brittan, 1989, Connell, 1983, 1987, for critiques of socialisation approaches).

13 In one reinterpretation of mainstream psychological theory, feminist psychologists suggest that initially the acquisition of gender identity is deeply intertwined with the processes surrounding the individuation of the infant and the construction of its sense of self (see, for example, Chodorow, 1979). So that to some extent to become a person separate and distinct from the mother involves simultaneously becoming a female (like mother) and the bearer of those attributes considered feminine by her society, or a male (unlike mother) and the bearer of a masculine set of attributes. Usually these are constructed in oppositional terms: strong-weak, hard-soft, etc.

14 Many people experience acute discomfort when they are talking to or confronted by someone whose gender they cannot establish.

15 Connell (1987) suggests the sexual division of labour 'must be seen as part of a larger pattern, a gender-structured system of production, consumption and distribution' (p.103).

16 This does not necessarily mean that the state itself should directly provide the support services – childcare, early-learning centres, pre-natal counselling – but rather the means by which women can organise the forms of support they most require, at different points in the life cycle.

9 Planning from a gender perspective: Making a world of difference

One of the questions raised by the last chapter is whether concern with women and development is in fact a matter of social justice or of development pragmatism. We would argue that involving women at all levels of development thinking, planning and implementation will make a world of difference not merely to women but to the capacity of society to envisage and carry out planned social change which will permit humankind to live in harmony with nature and itself. To bring women to centre stage, however, will require profound changes in the way that societies conceive of relations between the genders and the dismantling of centuries-old structures of thought and practice. Such changes will take a long time to bring about but as has become increasingly clear over the past decades, women are a tremendous social resource which no society can afford any longer to undervalue or underuse. But women will no longer accept being treated as workhorses for development strategies planned by others; they require to be treated as partners in development practice and planning. As such, planners have a great responsibility: both to listen to women but also to build their vision into planning strategies.

Listening to women

The failure of many development plans and their implementing instruments, development projects, has been blamed on a planning process which neither involves people in the decision-making process nor in the identification of their own needs. At a minimum, consultation of local people about projects or programmes is now argued to be a pre-condition for successful planning outcomes, particularly when innovation is concerned. Greater involvement of the wider society in decision-making through democratic processes is also argued to be central. But consultation and involvement are not unproblematic;

social heterogeneity raises complex questions of how consensus is to be achieved. All too often, in fact, consultation is confined to those who are wealthier, more articulate and educated. And these in many developing countries will be male; when asked, they may give their views as to women's needs. But more commonly it is assumed that women's needs will be identical to those of men or broader groupings such as farmers or indigenous entrepreneurs. As we noted in Chapters 3 and 4, many development projects perform poorly precisely because of such false assumptions. When women are actively consulted the differences in men and women's lives, needs, and concerns are thrown into sharp relief, but so too may differences between women (as we saw in Chapter 8).

Active consultation, however, must take into account the fact that simply asking women to list their needs is not enough (see Pareja in Young, 1987 and 1988). Women, particularly if they are from a different class, caste or community segment than the planners or their researchers, may well be very reticent about their needs because of fear of offending powerful persons as much as of negative or unsympathetic male reaction. But more critically, women in many cultures are socialised in such a way as to lack any sense of having rights or needs except in relation to others; women typically want things for others – their children, their family. Powerlessness not only impedes the powerless from getting their demands placed on the agenda, it often makes articulating such demands unimaginable. A first step has to be creating the conditions which enable such demands to be imagined and then expressed.[1] This is frequently the task that women's organisations set themselves; we return to this point later in the chapter.

Planners themselves largely see women as providers of family well-being or as conduits for the well-being of others. Thus they will be more attuned to accepting the material condition of the majority of women – their illiteracy, ill health, lack of training – as their priority needs. As such they find it difficult to explore the extent to which women's social weakness (if not political disenfranchisement) contributes to their material ill-being.

It is important not to limit consultation to exploring women's perceptions of their needs; their perception of the constraints they face is equally relevant. Frequently development planners fail to do this or examine carefully their own assumptions as to motivating incentives. A good example of this is the failure of many attempts to get rural women in Africa and Asia to buy improved cooking stoves to reduce woodfuel consumption. While planners saw patterns of woodfuel consumption as leading to critical shortages, they failed to investigate whether women, the supposed beneficiaries, felt shortage of fuelwood was an equally crucial issue to them. Given that lack of cash is a major constraint for rural women, a woman is unlikely to spend her precious store of money on a new technology of uncertain benefit to her.

In situations where the consultation is around planned projects or programmes, intended beneficiaries should also be asked about implementation procedures so they may alert planners to potential blocking tactics, or subversive strategies. Time and again, project designers have met with resistance from men (and some women) when attempting to include specific benefits for certain categories of women, or they have found that the supposed benefits for women have been subverted and chanelled to men. Yet women themselves often have a clear, but indirect strategy by which to overcome the difficulties imposed by gender relations. For example, in Bankura (India), women complained of men's violence but when the project designers suggested tackling this, the women responded: you give us economic strength and we'll take care of the men ourselves (ILO, 1988a).

What these reflections point to is that if planners are to meet women's needs they must first be able to have these needs identified; then, wherever possible in consultation with women or their representatives, they must assess their capacity to meet them, and, again in consultation, prioritise those that are amenable to a planning or policy solution. The impact of such consultation has been shown to revolutionise more profoundly planners' views of women than vice versa (see, for example, Bankura, ILO, 1988a), but none the less such consultation is an important aspect both of women's sense of empowerment, and, at the project level, of project ownership. Lastly, a strategy for achieving planning objectives has to be devised and a clear timeframe for achievement set out. The strategy should also include markers along the way which will enable planners – as well as beneficiaries – to assess how well aims are being achieved within the time envisaged. These markers, or pauses for re-assessment, must also be framed in such a way that women's views are essential inputs into the revision of the strategy in the light of their experience.

But can one plan for women?

The first requirement of consulting with women immediately poses a theoretical as well as a practical problem; can 'women' be used as a general category at all? Is it useful to assume common problems when the reality is of such great diversity? Society is stratified in numerous ways – by gender, class, caste, race, ethnicity, age. These forms of stratification cut across each other and interact in complex ways. We have argued that it is impossible to prioritise any one of them in the abstract: in particular situations women will experience one or more of them as critical. This ranking will change as the situation changes. Again, though most women share the experience of gender subordination, the form it takes may differ significantly. Equally, the common fact of subordination may not lead to unity among women, other factors serving to divide them along lines which are perceived or experienced as more crucial.

To give an obvious example: the interests of a rural cultivator selling produce in the market will differ from those of the wage labourer who has to buy her food. Although both women may be suffering from similar levels of poverty, the first wants high prices for her products, the second, low cost food for her family. In this case class as such does not play a key role, since both women are equally poor and neither may own her means of production, but location in the overall economic system does. Another example is that of divorce: while no woman (or man) would choose to remain in a relationship which has irretrievably broken down, older women may find legislation permitting divorce a threat, since it makes it easier for their husbands to abandon them for younger women. Given the social tolerance of older men consorting with much younger women, and the common strategy of young women to seek out older men for the economic and status advantages they are thought to provide, it is easy to understand the older women's reservations. Furthermore, the unequal distribution of resources between women and men means that for most women divorce inevitably results in greater poverty as well as loss of social status. But most young women would prefer to have the freedom to divorce as it enables them to try to find a more tolerable partner the second time round, or enjoy unwedded bliss.

The practical implications are great. Given the diversity, is it possible to devise policies or plans which can benefit a wide range of women without causing others difficulties? One answer might be that while the majority of women can be benefited by one policy option, the minority who are likely to suffer can be helped through special provisions. For example, in the case of divorce, special provisions can be made for older women who fear divorce and are quite likely to be cast off by husbands. The total cost to the state of such provision may be quite minimal and it can be phased out over time.

Policymakers and planners

Throughout the book we have referred in rather general terms to 'planners and policymakers'. But to whom are we actually referring? In the context of this book, policymakers are those who wield the power, both financial and political, to bring about major economic, social and even political change within a given country. They may be national bureaucrats at a central or local level (but not necessarily in the planning unit of the government), or high ranking politicians of the party in power, or they may be the representatives of international organisations such as any of the United Nations Agencies, or multinational organisations such as the World Bank and the IMF. A wide range of groups, organisations, political and otherwise, seek to influence policymakers. Women's organisations themselves are increasingly seeking to intervene in the decision-making process, though the extent of their political clout is a subject of contention (considered below).

Planners, on the other hand, execute the decisions of policymakers as to the general economic, social and political direction of the country by using a variety of political, economic and social levers. The degree of intervention and strength of the guidance depends on the political system itself, and varies from tight control on all aspects of the economy (pervasive planning) to a greater reliance on market forces but with some incentives being given to direct outcomes (parametric planning). None the less, there is always some degree of macro-economic management and the provision of critical aspects of infrastructure (White, 1984).

When we come to discuss the role of policymakers and male dominated bureaucracies in promoting women's needs or interests a number of questions arise. Firstly, to what extent is it reasonable to expect that planners or policymakers, the overwhelming majority of whom are men incorporated into the present system and deriving benefits from it, will be prepared to work for a more equitable sharing of power and resources in society? By what means can they be persuaded to work towards meeting women's interests?

A recent book edited by Kathleen Staudt looks at the experience of women trying to bring about change within aid and other bureaucracies (largely but not entirely in the north). Her conclusions are somewhat disheartening: 'grim resistance has been faced by those working with women's programmes in national and international agencies. It is becoming increasingly clear that a key source of this problem is to be located in bureaucratic institutions and in the ideologies officials use as they act on gender issues' (Staudt, 1990, p.10).

Staudt maintains that gender in equality has become embedded and institutionalised in the political and bureaucratic authority of the state. This has led to 'property, income, public representation, and state benefits' being directed into the hands of husbands or fathers as household heads, women being seen as reproducers and mothers. As a result any attempt to bring about a redistribution of benefits to women meets with resistance from men, loath to lose traditional privileges, and 'those women who have a stake in existing male privilege.' The struggle for redistribution at the best of times is difficult, but gender redistributive politics 'are subtle in the personalised resistance they incur and complex in their confusion with cross-sex interpersonal relations' (Staudt, 1990, p.10).

Resistance takes many forms; we have noted the strategy of setting up women's units but placing them where their ability to influence critical decisions by government is nil; giving them few and untrained staff; depriving them of funds; cutting them off from their constituency (see Alvarez, 1990). Even within the United Nations, which many see as a firm promoter of women's advancement, the resistance to real change for women is stout. Hilkka Pietila and Jeanne Vickers, in their book on the role of the United Nations in promoting women's advancement, document the ways in which the Decade for Women meetings differed from other UN meetings in the time given for their preparation, as well as the importance given to their findings (Pietila and Vickers, 1990). They note that the International Development Strategy (IDS) for the UN's Third Development Decade (largely based upon the various Plans of Action adopted by world conferences of the 1970s) incorporates neither the Mexico (1975) nor the Copenhagen (1980) Plans of

Action – they are only referred to in a small paragraph at the end of the chapter on social development. Women are mentioned only in connection with social objectives and social development. Preparatory papers for the new IDS for the Fourth Development Decade (1990-9) do not even mention the Forward-Looking Strategies of the Nairobi Conference (1985). Set against this fairly obvious obstruction through forgetfulness is the system-wide Medium Term Plan for Women and Development (1990-5) which was prepared by those within the system determined not to lose the impetus of the Women's Decade.

None the less there are positive examples of individuals within state bureaucracies who have been able to create greater space for women. For example in the Philippines the head of the Civil Service Commission was able to bring in changes to promotion procedures to lessen the gap between middle level (predominantly female) and executive level staff (overwhelmingly male) (see Santo Thomas, 1991). But despite the critical role that active and courageous individuals can play in bringing about change, depending on individuals alone is not a position of strength. Individuals, whether men or women, need both to feel supported by and accountable to the women outside the bureaucracy if they are to continue to bring change and further build upon it. The strategic aim must eventually be to change bureaucracies and institutions and make them more responsive to women's concerns. Where women find it difficult to enter in the first place, an equal opportunities employment policy is the first step (see Cockburn, 1991). But bringing a large number of women into the bureaucracy (whether this is the state bureaucracy or another form, such as a trade union) is no guarantee that women's concerns will be given a higher profile; new forms of relating to those who are served is also needed. Often existing structures and organisational cultures are not conducive to new ideas and new forms of working with constituencies. But with determination it can be done.[2] For those in state bureaucracies, a strong political groundswell may impell responsiveness, although this probably works more effectively when activists identify allies within bureaucratic structures and target key positions to ensure the groundswell is converted into positive bureaucratic response.

Planning presents a different set of issues. At an apparently technical level, planners may be influenced by misleading and inaccurate information. Data collection techniques are faulty, particularly when it comes to the measurement of women's (and informal) economic activity, as we saw in Chapter 7; conceptualisations of the household can give an erroneous picture of some household members' economic situation. As we argued, behind the technical faults lie biases in what data is chosen as relevant in the first place and in the conceptual framework used. The mass of data on women collected in recent years may help to undermine these inaccuracies, but planners still tend to be more concerned with information reflecting women's mothering and family-centred activities than their position in society. Researchers too choose to study problems they consider to be both important (or for which they can get funds) and about which information is relatively simply ascertained. Hence, with the concern about rapid population growth, accurate figures on fertility are more readily available than those on maternal mortality. Data is available on literacy but not the impact of adult literacy on women's position within the family or the community (Bown, 1990). Although more data are now available on women in paid work, data are sparse on their wages relative to those of men. Women's contribution to the unpaid labour force remains excluded from economic calculations (see Seager and Olson, 1986, p.40).

In one sense then, planning is a technical exercise, but it is also always more than this. Policymakers set the general parameters but planners' own perspectives will inevitably influence the degree of fervour with which they follow policymakers desires. Many a politician's ardour for change has been cooled by the ways in which planners and other bureaucrats drag their feet, or cannot find solutions for certain problems (see Pareja, 1988 for a good example of bureaucratic resistance). Planners are in fact front line agents of state intervention in the economy and as such are not merely technical experts but also political actors.

The choices they make are in most cases profoundly political because they bear within them the potential for a particular type of society and of social relationships; they are born of collective value judgements which derive from social consensus or a given ideology (Comeliau, 1986). As part of the administrative apparatus of government, planners not only have to meet the short-term goals imposed on them by governments which may change (and often with them the economic, social and political complexion of the society which is envisaged), but also to work within the constraints imposed by planning decisions made in the past and by the structure of the national economy, itself embedded in a global economic system. Their room for manoeuvre may be extremely limited.

Practical needs and strategic interests

An interesting example of where policymakers have specifically tried to address themselves to these issues is provided by socialist societies because women's emancipation forms part of the socialist programme. A good number of studies conclude, however, that this commitment is rarely successfully implemented (see e.g. Scott, 1974; Markus, 1976; Stacey, 1983). Maxine Molyneux (1985) looks at the question of what a revolutionary government perceives as women's interests. She suggests that these centre on easing women's delivery of traditional benefits to children and family through a wide range of heterogeneous interventions, while drawing them into the labour force and giving them the right to political participation.

In examining the question of women's interests Molyneux suggests the need to distinguish between two sets of interests: those arising from the fact that women are allocated certain roles by the sexual division of labour, and those from the fact that women as a social category have unequal access to resources and power. The former can be either short- or long-term and derive from the various responsibilities of women for the care and education of children, the elderly and the sick, household maintenance (family well-being), and servicing kin and neighbourhood (community well-being). Women's unequal access to resources results from their exclusion from the arenas of political and economic power, their inequality within the family and the society, and their lack of control over their lives. In both cases women's actual location in the social structure has important implications for the degree of manoeuvre individual women have.

Molyneux has called these practical gender interests and strategic gender interests. In thinking about this, I have found it more useful to talk about practical needs and strategic interests, because a distinction is needed between mundane wants or lacks, and conscious imagining of collective requirements usually involving some degree of change in the existing order of things. The former I call needs, despite the fact that in Molyneux terms they can (and often do) motivate women to collective action (bread riots are perhaps the classic case); I term the latter strategic interests (see Young, 1987 and 1988).[3]

The identification of practical needs produces a great many similarities across cultures: an adequate food supply, convenient access to safe water, a steady source of income, ready availability of reliable and safe contraception, access to education, training and credit, and so on. In the final analysis, no one can do without food, water, shelter, clothing (ILO's basic needs). However, this should not obscure the fact that different practical needs may be prioritised at any one time, nor the likelihood that there will be disagreements about what is a need and what a luxury. Even the obvious starting point of food as a practical need soon runs into exceptions and difficulties: there may be occasions when an apparent 'luxury' is subjectively more of a need to the person concerned than physical sustenance. Equally, the indicators by which people judge their own well-being are not necessarily the same as those of an outside observer. Rural householders in Rajasthan, for example, put self-respect and independence on as high a level as the possession of assets to provide security against unexpected contingencies.

Strategic gender interests come into focus when women's position in society is questioned. According to Molyneux, a theoretical analysis of the processes of women's subordination gives rise to strategic moral and ethical objectives which are in the interests of all woman. Such objectives constitute a 'vision' of the future in which inequalities between men and women are no longer found. This implies that inequalities are neither genetically determined nor sacrosanct and impossible to change.

Although in the abstract, the concept of strategic interests may seem reasonably straightforward, there is considerable uncertainty and debate about what actual strategic interests are. As yet our understanding of what constitutes the bedrock of inequality between men and women is still quite culture, class, race specific. Despite the differences, feminists maintain that women should and can unite around a number of issues arising from their subordination as a gender so as to find ways of transforming the situation. The issues most commonly identified are: male control of women's labour; women's restricted access to valued social and economic resources and political power, and as a result a very unequal distribution of resources between the genders; male violence and control of sexuality.

Given that the identification of common strategic interests is full of difficulties, and involves a conscious effort of understanding and commitment to change, women's activists emphasise the need for consciousness raising and collective empowerment. Once specific categories of women collectively come to understand better the mechanisms and processes of subordination, they are able to identify appropriate strategies for change, which may include forming alliances with a very broad range of other women. Strategies must involve both changing a variety of practices and the way we think about gender and gender relations. Merely changing activities – for example, changing the sexual division of labour, promoted by some as a strategic gender interest – brings little change for women if what women do is still undervalued. In countries such as Britain and the former USSR women have entered all male professions only to see the profession both feminised and devalued within a short time.[4] The pervasive ideology of male superiority has to be changed too, both as an aspect of women's own worldview and that of society at large. And this may involve women in long-term changes in the ways they socialise their own children and grandchildren.

What Molyneux's schema implies is that there is a range of **potentially** common objectives for women which are related to their relative standing to men, their capacity for autonomy and social agency, and a great diversity of more specific concerns which arise from the daily processes of gaining a livelihood which different categories of women experience. The latter do not challenge the prevailing forms of gender subordination, but the former must.

The means of needs identification for development practitioners based on Molyneux's pioneering work is now widely used (see Moser, 1989; Wallace and March, 1991). There is, however, the danger that the usefulness of the distinction between practical needs and strategic interests as a tool of analysis and reflection will be nullified by being used in a mechanical, non-dynamic way: as a blueprint. As such women's practical needs can be listed almost a priori (credit, training, water, etc.) and, particularly in contexts where men are being introduced to WID issues, can be argued to be no more than a women-focused set of basic needs. The question of strategic interests can then be set aside as feminist concerns, i.e. irrelevancies to planners and development practitioners.

Transformatory potential

Yet this either/or categorisation is unhelpful; it neither allows recognition of the potential dynamism of a given situation, nor of the ways in which very practical needs of women are closely enmeshed with their need for structural change. For example, in some cases what would in the blueprint mode be argued to be a strategic interest – the need to end all forms of violence against women, by government, non-government and community means – may in fact be a practical need. If women cannot work outside the home or the village without fear of being physically abused, how can they as mothers ensure family welfare, and indeed how can their economic contribution be realised either at the family or the community level? In trying to ensure that the analytical tool of needs and interest is used in a dynamic way, a third concept may be useful – that of **transformatory potential** (Young, 1987, 1988).

The idea here is to allow the interrogation of practical needs (by women themselves) to see how they can become or transform themselves into strategic concerns. In other words have they the capacity or potential for questioning, undermining or transforming gender relations and the structures of subordination?

A rather simple-minded example of how meeting a practical need can have transformatory potential is that of the need for a cash income. This need can be met in a wide range of ways: by providing piece-work to women isolated within the home; by setting up a small collectivity of some kind which enables women to meet together within a work context which is not highly structured; or by providing factory employment. In the first case, women are left as isolated as before, and the home-based work may merely add to their burden of work. In the third case, the need to fulfil production norms, to complete a fixed and rigid working day, within a context in which men are likely to be in positions of power and authority over the women, is unlikely to add to women's sense of self-worth and agency. Forming a locally-based collectivity – a production group, a co-operative – can provide the conditions for a more empowering experience.[5]

However, provision should be made for space for discussion and exchange of experiences, and an examination of the roots of women's poverty and powerlessness. While this can be empowering in the radical sense of that term, the outcome cannot be predicted just because women are brought together. The stifling of disagreement and the pressure to conform because of an assumed commonality of womanhood can be an entirely un-empowering experience. But with forms of organisation which do enable the women to gain a greater sense of self-worth, agency and common purpose, and the recognition of difference, then they may use this as a springboard to other activities which have a more clearly directed objective of collective empowerment. And this in turn may lead to the formation of alliances with other collectivities of women, or of men and women who are desirous of bringing about structural change.

Another example might be that of lessening rural women's work burden by bringing a mechanical grinding mill to the village. By ensuring that the mill is owned by women as a collective enterprise and that all members learn to run, maintain and service the mill, women will have been helped to own a vital community resource. This should both increase individual women's feeling of self-worth but also bring women collectively greater social recognition. If a proportion of the income from the mill could also be set aside for a community project the women would gain influence and greater decision-making power within the community. This might be further parlayed into getting agreement that women take part in critical decision-making arenas at the local level. And from there wider opportunities may well become available.

The crucial element in transformatory thinking is the need to transform women's position in such a way that the advance will be sustained. Equally important is that women should themselves feel that they have been the agents of the transformation, that they have won this new space for action themselves. But it is also important that they realise that each step taken in the direction of gaining greater control over their lives, will throw up other needs, other contradictions to be resolved in turn.

In the end the aim should be to set in motion a process which is doubly transformatory: women being transformed into conscious social agents, and practical needs into strategic interests. Of vital importance here is the provision of information. Many studies have shown that giving examples of how other women live, how they have struggled to overcome subordinating and oppressive structures, has sparked off discussion of alternatives which are feasible and culturally appropriate. Women's lack of access to information about their own societies, and the range of debate about political and economic matters is often a key element in their hesitancy about change.

The assumption behind transformatory potential is that the process of women working together and solving problems on a trial and error basis, of learning by doing, and also of learning to identify allies and forging alliances when needed, will lead to empowerment, both collective and individual. Experience has also shown that often women involved in what have been called welfare-oriented schemes (providing better nutrition for their children, community improvement projects, etc.) have often, through their collective experience of struggle, become active in questioning their social position and organising to bring an end to discriminatory practices (see Guzman, 1991).

Empowerment

The language of 'empowerment' has, as we noted in Chapter 8, gained prominence in the closing years of the UN's Third Development Decade. The Washington-based Association for Women in Development had 'empowerment' for the theme of its 1989 conference. The World Bank and most aid agencies also claim to wish to empower women. Feminist groups also speak of the need for empowerment. But to what are they referring? Are we all talking about the same thing?

Empowerment was originally a demand made by activist feminist groups. In an obvious sense, empowerment is about people taking control over their own lives: gaining the ability to do things, to set their own agendas, to change events, in a way previously lacking. This may include affecting the way other people act and consciously or unconsciously forcing changes in their behaviour. But for feminists, empowerment is more than this: it involves the radical alteration of the processes and structures which reproduce women's subordinate position as a gender. In other words, strategies for empowerment cannot be taken out of the historical context that created lack of power in the first place, nor can they be viewed in isolation from present processes. Feminist theoreticians and activists, while accepting and even emphasising diversity, nevertheless maintain that women share a common experience of oppression and subordination, whatever the differences in the forms that these take.

Central to the theory is the argument that this subordination is founded on the regulation and control of female sexuality and procreation, and the sexual division of labour which allocates women a heavy burden of responsibilities while denying them control of valuable social resources. Not all women agree upon the nature of the structures and processes which reproduce women's subordination, nor is there consensus that the ideological representation of the social place and activities of women (and men) as determined by biology rather than society is a critical element. None the less, until the structures of male dominance, both those which are external and those which have been internalised by women as much as men, are unmasked and changed, they will continue to reproduce subordination. And as long as laws, institutions and practices are organised from a male perspective, with male life experience as the typical, any changes made can only be superficial. And this includes the practice of development itself: an approach which concentrates on quick economic growth which benefits little the mass of the population, on quick results and technical fixes rather than the slower processes of building up human capacity is not women's one. And as long as gross inequalities exist between nations as much as within them, interdependence structured in equality between women and men is an illusion.

Such a view of empowerment implies collective empowerment not individual empowerment. 'Women become empowered through collective reflection and decision-making. The parameters of empowerment are: building a positive self-image and self-confidence; developing the ability to think critically; building up group cohesion and fostering decision-making and action' (Programme of Action of the Government of India National Policy on Education [1986]). In other words empowerment includes both individual change and collective action. What is meant is enabling women collectively to take control of their own lives to set their own agendas, to organise to help each other and make demands on the state for support and on society itself for change. With the collective empowerment of women the direction and processes of development would also be shifted to respond to womens' needs and their vision. The collective empowerment of women, of course, would bring with it the individual empowerment of women but not merely for individual advancement. This understanding of women's empowerment is a good deal more radical than the more common approach – i.e. that of economic empowerment or getting women in the cash economy generally through self-employment or income generation.

It also implies some degree of conflict: empowerment is not just about women acquiring something, but about those holding power relinquishing it. We have argued that relations between men and women are characterised both by conflict and by co-operation. Just as women must organise together to gain the sense of self-worth and understanding of the wider context of their lives that empower and make long-term co-operation possible, so must men undergo a process of reflection and transformation which makes it possible for them to recognise the ways in which their power is a double-edged sword. It structures their relations with other men in competition and conflict, and makes co-operation and building on advances highly problematic.

As we have pointed out though, the language of empowerment has been adopted by those within the mainstream of development theory and practice. What is this empowerment about? The term appears to mean entrepreneurial self-reliance, and echoes the general emphasis within the mainstream on unleashing the capacity for individuals to be more entrepreneurial, more self-reliant; on entrepreneurial capitalism and market forces as the main saviours of sickly or backward economies; on limiting state provision of welfare, services and employment. It is closely allied to the current emphasis on individualistic values: people 'empowering themselves' by pulling themselves up by their bootstraps; in other words self-reliance in its most narrow interpretation. With the emphasis on individualism, co-operation becomes submerged, and there is no mention of the need to alter existing social structures. In this version of empowerment there is also little emphasis on the necessity for those who wield financial and political power, whether at the family level or within society as a whole, to accept the obligation to change themselves. Without such an obligation, men who largely occupy positions of power in society at all its levels, appear to be going to remain invisible as they have done throughout the development decades. We've heard too long about the need for women to change; both women and men need to change if future society is to be more harmonious than in the past.

Putting pressure on policymakers

'Because women are politically weak in the sense that no government will fall from power based on its policies affecting women, it is rare that the interests of women are explicitly considered in either the economic or political aspects of development planning, and the creation of various women's organisations and national machinery for women during the Women's Decade has not changed this' (Heyzer, 1981, p.xiii).

Policymakers are responsive to directives and pressures from a variety of political arenas and actors of varying degrees of power and persuasiveness. Thus in many cases to get them to recognise an obligation to do something about even women's pressing practical needs, such needs have to be expressed in such a way as to become a critical political problem which is amenable to a planning solution. And this must involve constituting women as political actors of equal weight as men. But almost everywhere women are either absent or excluded from the main political arenas, and as a result have little experience of the operation of the political system. At both the international and the national level women are poorly represented. In LDCs they have only 7 per cent of the seats in national legislatures. It is often argued that a democratic political system is a prerequisite for a modern economy but while much attention has been paid to the representation of a range of class and other interests, that of women as women has been and continues to be lacking.[6]

Women's gender interests are unlikely to come high on politicians' agendas unless women from a wide social spectrum take up the challenge and enter the political arena. In many countries this is not likely to be an easy matter; a number of pre-conditions would have to be met given women's lower educational levels, their lack of experience of involvement in the public sector, their exclusion from a range of political arenas from the local to the national level. These pre-conditions might include: providing special formal and non-formal education programmes; eliminating discriminatory legislation; integrating women into the labour market; providing childcare facilities; organising women in local level, women-only organisations so that they can learn the basics of effective organisation, identification of goals, strategic planning and alliance building, and so on; and making positive efforts to recruit women and men sensitive to gender issues to the ranks of the civil service, planning organisms, etc. (see Pareja in Young, 1988). But many of these pre-conditions themselves presuppose the support of the state, and indeed building women's organisations at a minimum requires the tacit approval of the state, not to speak of considerable financial resources. To date these have rarely been forthcoming from national governments or private national sources in the developing world.

The suggestion that women must constitute themselves as a pressure group so as to make it more likely that their gender interests will be built into state policy assumes a specific form of relation between the state and civil society. In reality, political cultures are very varied, political systems likewise. In some countries the political culture allows space for interest groups to compete against each other (or to form alliances) to influence state decisions, or indeed to mobilise public opinion against certain government decisions without fear of reprisal. And in such countries power is usually relatively widely spread throughout the populace and the political system relatively uncorrupt and effective precisely because of the strength of civil society itself and its ability to act as watchdog over state activities.

But in others, political power is the purview of a small coterie, the main pressures exerted on them being mediated through kinship or locality, the institutions of civil society being weakly developed. Lobbying activity by voluntary associations, or overt and recognised interest groups are not the stuff of the political process in such countries. In such situations, as the last two decades have shown, those in power interpret such pressure as hostile and undermining of state authority, and respond to it by curtailing basic civil liberties. In many LDCs too, civilian government is weak and in the wings the military or militant religious groups wait to capitalise on any mistakes made. Given the nature of gender relations, any attempt to ameliorate even the conditions within which the bulk of women live may give rise to a degree of social unrest which the military, conservative, or fundamentalist groups can utilise to their advantage.[7]

However the 1990s will doubtless see considerable pressure being exerted both by external and internal forces to ensure greater levels of democracy and accountability, and public involvement in a wide range of policy matters. The posture of Western governments and international agencies such as the World Bank on good governance does mean that greater space should become available for a wide range of social forces to mobilise themselves for intervention in the debate/decision-making on social, political and economic change. It will also mean a greater availability of funds – but, as a range of non-governmental organisations and interest groups will be competing for those same funds, organisations with a more radical transformatory philosophy may be no better off than today.

Despite these objections, or perhaps because of them, it is increasingly recognised that women must form their own organisations so as to make women's concerns intrinsic to political bargaining and negotiations. If policymakers are to do more than listen to women, there needs to be some political compulsion behind their demands. Political will flourishes when there is political impetus. The form of organisation and the space(s) within which it takes shape depend in part on the nature of the political system. If women are able to bring about radical change in some more open countries, and if such change benefits society as a whole – facilitating social development and economic growth – this may well act as a demonstration to others of the wisdom of making women's concerns a central aspect of public policy. But in order to acquire sufficient political clout women's organisations will have to look to widening their contacts with other organisations working for social transformation. In so doing many organisations broaden their vision out from what may be quite narrow and sectarian concerns to encompass a wide range of alternatives. It is in this sense that the current debate about women's empowerment is highly relevant.

Collective empowerment as a planning goal

It is now being recognised in development circles that economic growth and social betterment are best achieved when the mass of the population is informed about and involved in development aims and plans, and sees itself as a direct beneficiary of the expanded resources growth should bring. One of the ways to achieve this is structuring the decision-making process in such a way as to ensure widespread consultation at all levels of society about development goals, the processes by which those goals are to be reached and the resources needed to achieve them.

Rather than the 'there is no alternative' single way forward, a range of ways in which goals and targets could be met as well as a range of timeframes in which to meet them, can be put forward for discussion. Other ways include consultation with groups representing capital, labour and the informal sector; and the producers of labour, working closely with grassroots NGOs, especially those involved in development work and education; giving information through the press; having party branches discuss party policy; holding referenda, etc. It can, however, fairly be said that despite these attempts, there are no instances in which economic macro-level policymaking has been restructured so as to include ideas or demands from the grassroots – when this does occur it is around social policy planning and programming. As yet there are also virtually no mechanisms available for communities which have devised policy to have such policies discussed within a wider social framework, nor for them to be incorporated into national planning systems.

The options mentioned above are only available where a variety of institutions of civil society, a free press, a clear and unmuzzled judiciary, a wide range of pressure groups and voluntary organisations, already exist. Where they do not, a strong argument can be made for encouraging the development of such institutions. Government works best when it is responsive to and accountable to the bulk of the population; interest groups as well as private voluntary organisations (PVOs) or non-governmental organisations (NGOs) can play an important role as promoters of the interests and liberties of the citizenry. But in many cases NGOs provide a power base for people from the same social stratum as is in government, whether as politicians, planners or civil servants (see Clarke, 1991). Without the empowerment of their own members, and democratic working practices, such groups are unlikely to act as the watchdogs on behalf of the people. Groups which are truly representative of the grassroots and the poor are quite rare, but their expansion should be encouraged in all ways possible. Their empowerment can be seen as a potential planning goal.

We have alluded to the importance of ensuring that NGOs experiment with a range of organisational forms and practices so as to give their members, as well as the people they serve, the possibility of their own empowerment – i.e. collective reflection and decision-making, developing the capacity for critical thought, and undertaking collective action toward a goal which is of benefit to all. That many NGOs parallel and replicate very top down ways of organisation is not often recognised. The absence of comparative research into a variety of organisational forms in terms of their effectiveness both in service delivery and strengthening of grassroots capacity makes it difficult to draw very firm conclusions. But certainly many of the most vibrant development NGOs and women's organisations have experimented with quite flattened power and authority structures, and a range of mechanisms to ensure frequent consultation with the membership. The toll on staff time is, however, great (see Ford Smith, 1990, for a very interesting account), and informal hierarchies and power dynamics which reproduce inequality actively lead to dis-empowerment. Fear of this in turn can lead to a strong tendency to go for the lowest common denominator in order to get something achieved.

Empowerment can be a planning goal in the sense that government support is given to a range of interest groups and NGOs, by using them as consultative bodies or councils. In this sense too, it is clear that empowerment cannot be of the few at the expense of the many. 'We must recognise the fundamental truth that power is not a scarce commodity but one that can be enjoyed and shared. Power is only in short supply if we care to make it so and create artificial shortage.' (John Eggleston, Professor of Education, University of Warwick in a discussion on racism and education). Until this is clearly recognised and the fear of the widespread distribution of power within society is eradicated, then participation will be half-hearted and people will not feel part of the process of development, and the government itself may come to lack legitimacy.

Funds can, of course, be provided from the public purse to support the initial setting-up stages of those groups who are specially underprivileged in society and who would not find it possible to consolidate themselves without such support. This was a tactic used successfully by the Greater London Council in its attempts to make the consultative and decision-making process within the management of London more democratic and responsive. And London at the time was as large as some small nation states. Such a strategy does not require a vast amount of resources either; indeed, a miniscule proportion of the defence budget would be more than ample in the case of most developing countries. But care has to be exercised to ensure the funds are not used to control NGOs, nor that their removal will lead to the collapse of the groups initially supported.

One such underprivileged sector is comprised of women's organisations. We have, like many others, argued strongly for their recognition and for the need for them to become key actors in the development process. But this is a strategy not without difficulties. In most countries women's organisations are very heterogeneous. Many such organisations are not concerned with change but with preservation of the status quo; many are themselves very hierarchical and concerned with maintaining status differentials, and differential access to resources (Desai in Young, 1989). Many too, are merely seen as a means through which individuals can appropriate resources for their own households (see Betty Wamalwa, 1991). Others, and these are the majority, are informal and depend for their effectiveness on a degree of flexibility and fluidity which is hard to translate into more formal types of associations (see March and Taqqu, 1986). Even those which are more formally organised vary in type. The DAWN group identified six main types of women's organisations; traditional service-orientated organisations, arms or branches of political parties, worker based, project based, research oriented and grassroots groups (Sen and Grown, 1987). The situation in many countries is made more complicated by the fact of little co-ordination or even collaboration between groups.

If women's organisations are to play a key role in participatory planning, three things must be attended to. Firstly, those women's organisations which are concerned with working with the poor and delivering service or other benefits to them, must look very stringently at their own mechanisms of participation, democratic decision-making and accountability. 'Within organisations, open and democratic processes are essential ... the long-term viability of the organisation, and the growing autonomy and control by poor women over their lives, are linked through the organisation's own internal processes of shared responsibility and decision-making' (Sen and Grown, 1987, and G. Young, 1990). They must also find ways of creating means of interacting with the poorest women who are unlikely to be members of organisations (Guzman, 1991). Secondly, women's organisations must get financial resources, training (whether in management, leadership formation, or conflict resolution), and access to information which will enable them to play their part adequately. Thirdly, women's organisations should play a prominent part in wider social movements so as to prevent gender issues from becoming marginalised.

If in the future women's views are to be taken into serious consideration by development planners, then turning to such organisations for consultation and advice should provide planners with a wide range of information. But more than this, women's organisations should not merely be seen as advocates and intermediaries, they should be enabled to take part in creating the mechanisms for policy to be developed by those most affected by it. The greater the degree of involvement of those organisations bringing together those most deeply to be affected by change, the more likely that planning will achieve its aims. But it has always to be remembered that if one of the major aims of development is to strengthen the least privileged and the poorest, then care has to be taken to reach out also to the unorganised since the poorest often have the least structural capacity for organisation.

Conclusion

The implication of this chapter (and the book as a whole) is that while any person now entering into the field of development must, to do a good and professional job, take women into account, the impetus for a change in bureaucratic and planning practice will have to come from those who organise themselves to promote change. Change will not come from above, but from the interaction between the compelling impetus of those who will directly benefit from change and those within the structures of power who have the capacity to share their wider vision. The relationship between planner and those struggling for change will be characterised by that same co-operative conflict we discussed earlier. Such co-operative conflict can only be truly fruitful when predominance is not a foregone conclusion on either side.

Notes

1 'The ability to impose a definition of the situation, to set the terms in which events are understood and issues discussed, to formulate ideals and define morality, in short to assert hegemony, is also an essential part of social power' (Connell, 1987, p.107).

2 Cockburn provides a most illuminating account of the impact on decision-making and strategy of the introduction of ground level democracy by a woman divisional head of her trade union. Making a distinction between representative democracy and participatory democracy, she was able to turn much of her section of the union's focus on the lowest paid and least represented workers. Providing them with training, information, and the means to put forward their viewpoints, led to quite wide-ranging change in union practice and process, including a consultative approach to bargaining. See Cockburn, 1991, pp.125-8.

3 The discussion of needs is not furthered by the confusion in much of the literature as to what a need is; much the same is true of interests. One useful treatment is provided by Connell (1987) who notes that: 'an interest is defined by the possibility of advantage and disadvantage in some collective practice' (p.137). See his discussion on the articulation of interests, pp.262-5.

4 The classic example in Britain is the shift from male clerks to female secretaries; in the former USSR as more women got into the medical profession as general practitioners, so men moved into higher status specialisms. For the example of the banking profession in Australia see Game and Pringle, 1984.

5 I am assuming that the co-operative/collective is making something for which there is a market, and that the women are not involved in a soul-destroying treadmill of low productivity:low reward work which undermines rather than empowers.

6 It is depressing to read in the 1992 *Human Development Report* (UNDP).

7 The backlash against women's attempts to promote more equal gender relations in the USA is documented by Faludi (1991).

Bibliography

References

Agarwal, B. (1985) 'Women and Technological Change in Agriculture: The Asian and African Experience', in Ahmed, I. (ed.) *Technology and Rural Women: Conceptual and Empirical Issues*, pp. 67–114, London: George Allen and Unwin/ILO.

— (1986) 'Women, Poverty and Agricultural Growth in India', *Journal of Peasant Studies*, **13**, (4), pp. 165–220.

Ahmed, I. (ed.) (1985) *Technology and Rural Women: Conceptual and Empirical Issues*, London: George Allen and Unwin/ILO.

Aidoo, A. (1988) 'Women and Food Security', *Development*, **2/3**, pp. 56–62.

Alvarez, S. (1990) 'Contradictions of a "Woman's Space" in a Male Dominant State', in Staudt, K. (ed.).

Anker, R. and Hein, C. (eds) (1986) *Sex Inequalities in Urban Employment in the Third World*, London: Macmillan.

Archer, J. and Lloyd, B. (1982) *Sex and Gender*, Pelican Books, Harmondsworth.

Ardrey, R. (1977) *The Hunting Hypothesis*, London: Fontana.

Arizpe, L. (1977) 'Women in the Informal Labour Sector in Mexico City', in Wellesley Editorial Committee (eds) *Women and National Development: The Complexities of Change*, pp. 24–37, Chicago: University of Chicago Press.

Baster, N. (1981) 'The Measurement of Women's Participation in Development: The Use of Census Data', *IDS Discussion Paper No. 159*, Brighton: Institute of Development Studies.

Bauer, P.I. (1984) *Reality and Rhetoric: Studies in the Economics of Development*, London: Weidenfeld and Nicholson.

Becker, G. (1965) 'A Theory of the Allocation of Time', *Economic Journal*, September, **75**, pp. 493–517.

— (1976) *The Economic Approach to Human Behaviour*, Chicago, University of Chicago Press.

Beneria, L. (1982) 'Accounting for Women's Work', in Beneria, L. (ed.) *Women and Development: The Sexual Division of Labour in Rural Societies*, pp. 119–47, New York, Praeger Publishers.

Beneria, L. and Roldan, M. (1987) *The Crossroads of Class and Gender: Industrial Homework, Sub-contracting and Household Dynamics in Mexico City*, Chicago and London: University of Chicago Press.

Berger, H. and Buvinic, M. (eds) (1989) *Women's Ventures: Assistance to the Internal Sector in Latin America*, West Hartford: Kumarian Press Inc.

Bienefeld, M. (1981) 'The Informal Sector and Women's Oppression', *IDS Bulletin*, **12**, (3), pp. 8–13.

Bienefeld, M. and Godfrey, M. (1975) 'Measuring Unemployment and the Informal Sector: Some Conceptual and Statistical Problems', *IDS Bulletin*, 7, (3), pp. 4–10.

Birkbeck, C. (1979) 'Garbage, Industry and the "Vultures" of Cali, Colombia', in Bromley, R. and Gerry, C. (eds) *Casual Work and Poverty in Third World Cities*, pp. 161–83, Chichester, New York: John Wiley and Sons.

Boserup, E. (1970) *Women's Role in Economic Development*, London: George Allen and Unwin.

Boulding, E. (1983) 'Measures of Women's Work in the Third World: Problems and Suggestions', in Buvinic, M., Lycette, M. and McGreevey, W. (eds) *Women in Poverty in the Third World*, pp. 286–318, Baltimore: Johns Hopkins University Press.

Brittan, A. (1989) *Masculinity and Power*, Basil Blackwell, Oxford.

Bromley, R. (1978) 'The Urban Informal Sector: Why is it Worth Discussing?', *World Development*, 6, (9/10), pp. 1033–9, also in Bromley, R. (ed.) (1979) *The Urban Informal Sector: Critical Perspectives on Employment and Housing Policies*, Oxford: Pergamon Press.

Brown, L. (1990) 'Preparing the Future, Women, Literacy and Development', *Action-Aid Development Report*, No. 4.

Bryson, J. (1981) 'Women and Agriculture in Sub-Saharan Africa: Implications for Development', *Journal of Development Studies*, 17, (3), pp. 29–46.

Bunster, B. (1983) 'Market Sellers in Lima, Peru', in Buvinic, M., Lycette, M. and McGreevey, W. (eds) *Women and Poverty in the Third World*, pp. 92–103, Baltimore: Johns Hopkins University Press.

Burfisher, M. and Horenstein, N. (1985) *Sex Roles in the Nigerian Tiv Farm Household, Cases for Planners*, West Hartford, Connecticut: Kumarian Press.

Buvinic, M. (1983) 'Women's Issues in Third World Poverty: A Policy Analysis', in Buvinic, M., Lycette, M. and McGreevey, W. (eds) *Women and Poverty in the Third World*, pp. 13–31, Baltimore: Johns Hopkins University Press.

Canadian International Development Agency (CIDA) (1987) 'Women in Micro- and Small-Scale Employment (MSE) Development', a paper presented at the International Seminar on Women in Micro- and Small-Scale Enterprise Development, Hull, 26–28 October, 1987.

Cardoso, F. and Faletto, E. (1979) *Dependency and Development in Latin America*, Berkeley: University of California Press.

Cassam, A. (1987) 'The United Nations Special Session on Africa in Retrospect', *Development*, (2/3), pp. 11–13.

Chacon, I. (1987) 'The Development of Women's Small-Scale Enterprises in Costa Rica: ACORDE's Case', paper presented at the International Seminar on Women in Micro- and Small-Scale Enterprise Development, Ottawa, October, 1987.

Chambers, R. (1983) *Rural Development: Putting the Last First*, London: Longman.

Chambers, R., Longhurst, R. and Pacey, A. (1981) *Seasonal Dimensions of Rural Poverty*, London: Frances Pinter.

Chant, S. (1987) 'Family Structure and Female Labour in Queretaro, Mexico', in Momsen, J. and Townsend, J. (eds) *Geography of Gender in the Third World*, pp. 277–93, London: Hutchinson.

Chapkis, W. and Enloe, C. (eds) (1983) *Of Common Cloth: Women in the Global Textile Industry*, Amsterdam: Transnational Institute.

Chayanov, A.V. (1966) 'Theory of Peasant Economy' in Thorner, D. *et al.* (ed.) *American Economic Association*.

Chen, L., Huq, E. and D'Souza, S. (1981) 'Sex Bias in the Family: Allocation of Food and Health Care in Rural Bangladesh', *Population and Development Review*, 7, (1), pp. 55–70.

Chenery, H. *et al.* (1974) *Redistribution with Growth*, Oxford: Oxford University Press.

Chodorow, N. (1979) 'Feminism and Difference: Gender, Relations and Difference in Psychoanalytic Perspective', *Socialist Review*, **9**, (4), pp. 51–69.

Clark, J. (1986) *For Richer, For Poorer*, Oxford: Oxfam.

—— (1991) *Democratizing Development: The Role of Voluntary Organizations*, London: Earthscan Publications.

Cockburn, C. (1991) *In the Way of Women*, London: Macmillan Education Ltd.

Colman, D. and Nixson, F. (1986) *The Economics of Change in Less Developed Countries*, Second Edition, Oxford: Oxford University Press.

Comeliau, C. (1986) *Questions aux Planificateurs*, DEV/EPD/44, Paris: UNESCO.

Connell, R. W. (1983) *Which Way is Up? Essays on sex, class and culture*, Sydney: George Allen and Unwin.

—— (1987) *Gender and Power*, Oxford: Polity Press and Basil Blackwell.

Cornia, A., Jolly, R. and Stewart, F., (eds) (1987) *Adjustment with a Human Face: Protecting the Vulnerable and Promoting Growth*, Oxford: Clarendon Press.

Crener, M., Leal, G., LeBlanc, R. and Thebaud, B. (1983) 'Integrated Rural Development', *State of the Art Review* — 1982/83, Ottawa: CIDA.

Dankelman, I. and Davidson, J. (1988) *Women and the Environment in the Third World: Alliance for the Future*, London: Earthscan.

DAWN, (1991) *Alternatives I and II*, Rio de Janeiro: Editora Rosa dos Tempos Ltda.

Desai, N. (1989) 'Emergence and Development of Women's Organizations in India', in Young K. (ed.) *Serving Two Masters*, New Delhi: Allied Publishers Ltd.

Dey, J. (1981) 'Gambian Women: Unequal Partners in Rice Development Projects?', in Nelson, N. (ed.) *African Women in the Development Process*, pp. 109–22, London: Frank Cass.

Dixon, R. (1982) 'Women in Agriculture: Counting the Labour Force in Developing Countries', *Population and Development Review*, **8**, (3), pp. 539–66.

Dwyer, D. and Bruce, J. (eds) (1988) *A Home Divided: Women and Income in the Third World*, Stanford, California: Stanford University Press.

Edholm, F., Harris, O. and Young, K. (1975) 'Conceptualising Women', *Critique of Anthropology*, **3**, (9/10), pp. 101–30.

Elson, D. (1987) 'The Impact of Structural Adjustment on Women: Concepts and Issues', paper prepared for the Commonwealth Secretariat, London: Commonwealth Secretariat. Also in Onimode, B., (ed.) (1989) *The IMF, The World Bank and the African Debt*, London: Institute for African Alternatives, pp. 56–74.

—— (1990) 'Male Bias in Macroeconomics', in *Male Bias in the Development Process*, Manchester: Manchester University Press.

Elson, D. and Pearson, R. (1980) 'The Latest Phase in the Internationalisation of Capital and Its Implications for Women in the Third World', *IDS Discussion Paper*, No. 150, Brighton: Institute of Development Studies, and in revised form, 1984.

—— (1984) 'The Subordination of Women and the Internationalisation of Factory Production', in Young, K., Wolkowitz, C. and McCullagh, R. (eds) pp. 18–40.

Europa (1987) *South America, Central America and the Caribbean*, London: Europa Publications.

Evans, A. (1989) 'Women: Rural Development Gender Issues in Rural Household Economics', *IDS Discussion Paper*, No. 254, Brighton: Institute of Development Studies, University of Sussex.

—— (1990) Economic Statistics, Module 1 of Gender and Third World Development, Brighton: Institute of Development Studies.

—— (1991) 'Gender Issues in Rural Household Economics' *IDS Bulletin*, **22**, (1), pp. 51–9.

Evans, A. and Young, K. (1988) 'Gender Issues in Household Labour Allocation: The

Transformation of a Farming System in Northern Province, Zambia', *ODA/ESCOR Research Report*.

Faludi, S. (1991) *Backlash: The Undeclared War Against Women*, London: Chatto and Windus.

FAO (1984) 'Women, Food and Nutrition in Africa: Economic Change and the Outlook for Nutrition', *Food and Nutrition*, **10**, (1), pp. 71–5.

Farooq, G. and Simmons, G. (eds) (1984) *Fertility in Developing Countries: An Economic Perspective on Research and Policy Issues*, London: Macmillan.

Folbre, N. (1986) 'Hearts and Spades, Paradigms of Household Economics', *World Development*, **14**, (2), pp. 245–55.

Ford Smith, H. (1989) *Ring Ding in a Tight Corner*, Toronto: Women's Programme ICAE.

Furtado, C. (1964), *Development and Underdevelopment*, Berkeley: University of California Press.

Galbraith, J. K. (1973) *Economics and the Public Purpose*, New York: Signet.

Game, A. and Pringle, R. (1984) *Gender at Work*, London: Pluto Press.

Goddard, V. (1981) 'The Leather Trade in the Bassi of Naples', *IDS Bulletin*, **12**, (3), pp. 30–5.

Goldschmidt-Clermont, L. (1982) 'Unpaid Work in the Household: A Review of Economic Evaluation Methods', *Women, Work and Development Series*, No. 1, Geneva: ILO.

Government of India, (1986) *Programme of Action, National Policy on Education*.

Grainger, A. (1982) *Dersertification: How People Make Deserts, How People Can Stop*, London: Earthscan.

Griffin, K. (1989) *Alternative Strategies for Economic Development*, London in association with OECD Development Centre: Macmillan.

Guyer, J. (1981) 'Household and Community in African Studies', *African Studies Review*, **24**, (2/3) pp. 87–137.

— (1984) 'Family and Farm in Southern Cameroon', *Research Studies*, No. 15, Boston: Boston University African Studies Centre.

Guzman, V. (1991) 'Desde los proyectos de desarrollo a la sociedad', in *Genero en el desarrollo*, Guzman, V., Portocarrero, P. and Vargas, V. (eds) ediciones entre mujeres, Lima.

Hanger, J. and Moris, J. (1973) 'Women and the Household Economy', in Chambers, R. and Moris, J. (eds) *Mwea: An Irrigated Rice Settlement*, pp. 209–44, Munich: Welforum Verlag.

Hart, K. (1973) 'Informal Income Opportunities and Urban Employment in Ghana', *Journal of Modern African Studies*, **11**, (1), pp. 61–89.

Hassan, M., Pitt, M. and Rosenzweig, M. (1989) *Productivity, Health and Inequality in the Intra-Household Distribution of Food in Low Income Countries*, Minneapolis: Economic Development Center, University of Minnesota.

Hegedus, A., *et al.* (eds) (1976) *The Humanisation of Socialism*, London: Alison and Busby.

Heller, A. (1974), *The Theory of Need in Marx*, London: Alison and Busby.

Henn, J. (1983) 'Feeding the Cities and Feeding the Farmers: What Role for Africa's Women Farmers?', *World Development*, **11**, (12), pp. 1043–55.

Heyzer, N. (1981) 'Towards a Framework of Analysis', *IDS Bulletin*, **12**, (3), pp. 3–7.

— (1986) *Working Women in South East Asia: Development, Subordination and Emancipation*, Milton Keynes: Open University Press.

Himmelstrand, K. (1990) 'Can an Aid Bureaucracy Empower Women' in Staudt, K. (1990).

Hoffman, K. and Kaplinsky, R. (1988) *Driving Force: The Global Restructuring of*

Technology, Labor and Investment in the Automobile and Components Industries, Boulder and London: Westview Press.

Humphrey, J. (1987) *Gender and Work in the Third World: Sexual Divisions in Brazilian Industry*, London: Tavistock.

IDS Bulletin, (1979) 'Continuing Subordination of Women', **10**, (3).

ILO, (1972) *Employment, Incomes and Equality: A Strategy for Increasing Production and Employment in Kenya*, Geneva: ILO.

— (1976) *Employment, Growth and Basic Needs: A One World Problem*, Geneva: ICO.

— (1988) 'Trade Unions and Women's Employment', *Women at Work*, No. 1, Geneva: ILO.

— (1988a) *The Bankura Story*, New Delhi: ILO.

INSTRAW (1984) Compiling Social Indicators on the Situation of Women, *Studies in Methods, Series F*, No. 33, New York: United Nations.

International Center for Research on Women (ICRW) (1980) 'Keeping Women Out: Structural Analysis of Women's Employment in Developing Countries', report prepared for the Office of Women in Development, Washington D.C.: USAID.

Jagger, A. (1983) *Feminist Politics and Human Nature*, Brighton: The Harvester Press Ltd.

Jazairy, I. (1987) 'How to Make Africa Self-Sufficient in Food', *Development*, (2/3), pp. 50–6.

Jelin, E. (1991) *Family, Household and Gender Relations in Latin America*, London: Kegan Paul International and UNESCO.

Joekes, S. (1985) 'Industrialisation, Trade and Female Employment in Developing Countries: Experience of the 1970s and After', *INSTRAW Research Studies* No. I-J, Santo Domingo: INSTRAW.

— (1987) *Women in the World Economy*, New York: INSTRAW/Oxford University Press.

Joekes, S. and Moayedi, R. (1987) 'Women and Export Manufacturing: A Review of the Issues and AID Policy', report prepared for the Office of Women in Development, Washington D.C.: USAID.

Jones, C. (1983) 'The Mobilisation of Women's Labour for Cash Crop Production', in *American Journal of Agricultural Economics*.

King, E. and Evenson, R. (1983) 'Time Allocation and Home Production in Phillipine Rural Households', in Buvinic, M. *et al.* (eds), *op. cit.*, pp. 35–61.

Kuznets, S. (1966) *Economic Growth and Structure*, London: Heinemann Educational Books.

Lal, D. (1983) *The Poverty of Development Economics*, London: Institute of Economic Affairs.

Leach, M. (1991) 'Locating Gendered Experience', in *IDS Bulletin*, **22**, (2/3).

Leon de Leal, M. (1984) 'Measuring Women's Work: Methodological and Conceptual Issues in Latin America', *IDS Bulletin*, **15**, (1), pp. 12–17.

Levi Strauss, C. (1969) *The Elementary Structures of Kinship*, Boston: Beacon Press.

Lewis, B. (1982) 'Women in Development Planning', in O'Barr, J. (ed.) *Third World Women in Politics*, Durham: Duke University Press.

Leys, C. (1975) *Underdevelopment in Kenya: The Political Economy of Neo-Colonialism*, London: Heinemann.

Lim, L. (1985) *Women Workers in Multinational Enterprises in Developing Countries*, Geneva: UNCTAD/ILO.

Little, I., Scitovsky, T. and Scott, M. (1970) *Industry and Trade in Some Developing Countries: A Comparative Study*, Oxford: Oxford University Press.

Longhurst, R. (1980) 'Rural Development Planning and the Sexual Division of Labour:

A Case Study of a Moslem Hausa Village in Northern Nigeria', *ILO Work Employ-ment Program Research Working Papers Series 10*, No. 10, Geneva: ILO.

Lorenz, K. (1967) *On Aggression*, London: Methuen.

Low, A. (1986) *Agricultural Development in Southern Africa: Farm-Household Theory and the Food Crisis*, London: James Currey.

Lyberaki, A. (1988) 'Small Firms and the Informal Sector in Greek Industry', unpublished Ph.D. thesis, University of Sussex.

MacEwan, Scott, A. (1986) 'Economic Development and Urban Women's Work: The Case of Lima, Peru', in Anker, R. and Hein, C., *Sex Inequalities in Urban Employment in the Third World*, pp. 313–69, London: Macmillan.

McCormack, J., Walsh, M. and Nelson, C. (1986) 'Women's Group Enterprises: A Study of the Structure of Opportunity on the Kenya Coast', World Education Inc., report prepared for AID/Bureau for Program and Policy Coordination, Human Resources Division, Massachusetts: Boston.

McGranahan., D.V. and Pizarro E. (eds) (1985), *Measurement and Analysis of Socio-Economic Development*, Geneva: UNRISD.

McSweeney, B.G. (1979) 'Correction and Analysis of Data on Rural Women's Time Use in Upper Volta', *Studies in Family Planning*, **10**, (11/12), pp. 379–82.

Macedo, R. (1987) 'Brazilian Children and the Economic Crisis: The Evidence from the State of Sao Paulo', in Cornia, A. *et al.*, *op cit.*, pp. 28–56.

Mamdani, M. (1972) 'The Myth of Population Control: Family, Caste, and Class in an Indian Village', New York: Monthly Review Press.

March, K. and Taqqu, R.L. (1986) *Women's Informal Associations in Developing Countries: Catalysts for Change?*, Boulder, Colorado: Westview.

Markus, M. (1976) 'Women and Work, Emancipation at a Dead End', in Hegedus, A. *et al.*, (eds) *op. cit.*

Maxwell, S. and Fernando, A. (1987) 'Cash Crops in Developing Countries', Brighton (mimeo): Institute of Development Studies, University of Sussex, revised version in *World Development*, (1990), **18**, (2).

Mezzara, V. (1989) 'Excess Labour Supply and the Urban Internal Sector', in Berger, H. and Buvinic, M. (eds) *Women's Ventures*, West Hartford: Kumarian Press.

Molyneux, M. (1985) 'Mobilization without Emancipation?', Women's Interests, State and Revolution in Nicaragua', *Feminist Studies* (Summer) 1985, **11**, pp. 227–54, also in Fagan, R. *et al.*, (eds) (1986) *Transition and Development: Problems of Third World Socialism*, pp. 280–302, New York: Monthly Review Press.

Morris, D. (1967) *The Naked Ape*, London: Cape.

Morris, M.D. (1979) *Measuring the Conditions of the World's Poor: The Physical Quality of Life Index*, New York: Pergamon.

Moser, C. (1978) 'Informal Sector of Petty Commodity Production: Dualism or Dependence in Urban Development?', *World Development*, **6**, (9/10), pp. 1041–64, also in Bromley, R. (ed.) (1979), *op. cit.*

— (1981) 'Surviving in the Suburbios', *IDS Bulletin*, **12**, (3), pp. 19–29.

— (1984) 'The Informal Sector Reworked: Viability and Vulnerability in Urban Development', *Regional Development Dialogue*, **5**, (2), pp. 135–78.

— (1989) 'Gender Planning in the Third World', in *World Development*, **17**, (11).

Moser, C. and Young, K. (1981) 'Women of the Working Poor', IDS Bulletin, **12**, (3), pp. 54–62.

Muntemba, S. (ed.) (1985) *Rural Development and Women: Lessons from the Field*, Geneva: World Employment Programme, ILO.

Mureithi, L. (1987) 'Crisis and Recovery in African Agriculture', *Development*, (2/3), pp. 44–9.

Mutharika, B.W. (1987) 'Special Assistance Needs for Africa', *Development*, (2/3), pp. 28–35.

Myrdal, G. (1968) *Asian Drama: An Enquiry into the Poverty of Nations*, London: Allen Lane/New York: Pantheon.

Nelson, N. (1979) 'How Women and Men Get By: The Sexual Division of Labour in a Nairobi Squatter Camp', in Bromley, R. and Gerry, C. (eds), *op. cit.*, pp. 283–302.

Oakley, A. (1972) *Sex, Gender and Society*, London: Maurice Temple Smith.

Pahl, J. (1983) 'The Allocation of Money and the Structuring of Inequality within Marriage', *Sociological Review*, **31**, pp. 237–62.

Palmer, I. (1985) *The Impact of Agrarian Reform on Women, Cases for Planners*, West Hartford, Connecticut: Kumarian Press.

— (1988) 'Gender Issues in Structural Adjustment of Sub-Saharan African Agriculture and Some Demographic Implications, WEP Research, Population and Labour Policies Programme, *Working Paper*, No. 166, Geneva: ILO.

— (1991) 'Gender and Population in the Adjustment of African Economies', *Women, Work and Development*, No. 19, Geneva: ILO.

Pareja, F. (1987, 1988) 'Problems That Concern Women' in Young, K. (ed.).

Payer, C. (1991) *Lent and Lost*, London: Zed Books.

Penniment, K. (1965) 'The Influence of Cultural and Socio-Economic Factors on Labour Force Participation Rates' in proceedings of the UN World Population Conference, Belgrade, New York: United Nations.

Pietila, H., and Vickers, J. (1990) *Making Women Matter*, London: Zed Press in association with INSTRAW.

Pinilla-Cisneros, S. (1987) 'Women in a Peruvian Experience in Support of the Informal Sector', paper presented at the International Seminar on Women in Micro- and Small-Scale Enterprise Development, Ottawa, October 1987.

Posthuma, A. (1987) 'The Internationalisation of Clerical Work: A Study of Offshore Office Services in the Caribbean', *SPRU Occasional Paper*, No. 24, Brighton: Science Policy Research Unit, University of Sussex.

Rathgeber, E. M. (1990) 'WID, WAD, GAD: Trends in Research and Practice', *Journal of Developing Areas*, **24**, No. 4, pp. 489–502.

Ridker, R. (1976) *Population and Development: The Search for Selective Interventions*, Baltimore: Johns Hopkins University Press.

Roberts, P. (1979) 'The Integration of Women into the Development Process: Some Conceptual Problems' in *IDS Bulletin*, Vol. **10**, 3.

— (1988) 'Rural Women's Access to Labour in West Africa', in Stichter, S. and Parpart, J. (eds) *Patriarchy and Class*, Boulder and London: Westview Press.

— (1989) 'The Sexual Politics of Labour in Western Nigeria and Hansa Niger', in Young, K. (ed.) *Serving Two Masters*, New Delhi: Allied Publishers Ltd.

— (1991) Anthropological Perspectives on the Household', *IDS Bulletin*, **22**, 1.

Rostow, W. (1960) *The Stages of Economic Growth: A Non-Communist Manifesto*, London: Cambridge University Press.

Roxborough, I. (1979) *Theories of Underdevelopment*, London: Macmillan.

Rubin, G. (1975) 'The Traffic in Women' in Reiter, R. R. (ed.) *Towards an Anthropology of Women*, New York: Monthly Review Press, pp. 157–210.

Sahn, D. (1985) 'A Conceptual Framework for Examining the Seasonal Aspects of Household Food Insecurity', paper presented to the IFPRI/FAO Workshop on Seasonal Causes of Household Food Insecurity, Maryland, revised version published as *Causes and Implications of Seasonal Variability in Household Food Security* (1987), Washington D.C.: International Food Policy and Research Institute (IFPRI).

Santo Thomas, P. (1991) 'Women in the Bureaucracy: The Philippine Case', paper at the National Women's Education Centre International Forum on Women in Development, Japan.

Schmitz, H. (1982) *Manufacturing in the Backyard: Case Studies on Accumulation and Employment in Small-Scale Brazilian Industry*, London: Frances Pinter.

— (1984) 'Industrialisation Strategies in Less Developed Countries: Some Lessons of Historical Experience', *Journal of Development Studies*, **21**, (1), pp. 1–21.

Scott, H. (1974) *Does Socialism Liberate Women?*, Boston: Beacon Press.

Seager, J. and Olson, A. (1986) *Women in the World: An International Atlas*, London: Pluto Press.

Seers, D. (1972) 'What are we Trying to Measure? in *Journal of Development Studies*, **8**, (3), 21–36.

Segal, L. (1987) *Is the Future Female? Troubled Thought on Contemporary Feminism*, London: Virago.

Sen, A. (1983) 'Economics in the Family', *Asian Development Review*, (1).

— (1985) *Women, Technology and Sexual Divisions*, New York and Santo Domingo: UNCTAD/INSTRAW and in revised form in 1987.

— (1987) 'Gender and Cooperative Conflicts', *WIDER Working Papers*, (18), Helsinki: World Institute for Development Economics Research.

Sen, G. and Grown, C. (1987) *Development, Crises and Alternative Visions*, New York: Monthly Review Press.

South Commission (1990) *The South Commission Report*, Geneva.

Southall, R. (ed.) (1988) *Trade Unions and the New Industrialisation in the Third World*, London: Zed Press.

Stacey, J. (1983) *Patriarchy and Socialist Revolution in China*, Berkeley: University of California Press.

Standing, G. (1989) 'Global Feminisation through Flexible Labour', *WEP Working Paper*, Geneva: ILO.

Staudt, K. (1985) *Agricultural Policy Implementation: A Case Study from Western Kenya, Cases for Planners*, West Hartford, Connecticut: Kumarian Press.

— (1990) (ed.) *Women, International Development and Politics*, Philadephia: Temple University Press, and *Gender Politics in Bureaucracy*, pp. 3–34.

Staudt, K. and Jaquette, J. (1988) 'Women's Programs, Bureaucratic Resistance and Feminist Organizations', in Boneparth, C. and Stoper, E., (eds), *Women, Power and Policy*, Second Edition, pp. 263–81, New York: Pergamon Press.

Stewart, F. (1987) 'Supporting Productive Employment among Vulnerable Groups', in Cornia, *et al.*, *op. cit.*, pp. 197–217.

Sunkel, O. (1969) 'National Development Policy and External Dependency in Latin America, *Journal of Development Studies*, **6**, (1), pp. 23–48.

— (1973) 'Transnational Capitalism and National Disintegration in Latin America', *Social and Economic Studies* (Jamaica), **22**, (1), pp. 132–71.

Timberlake, L. (1985) *Africa in Crisis: The Causes, The Cures of Environmental Bankruptcy*, London: Earthscan.

Tokman, V. (1978) 'An Exploration into the Nature of Informal-Formal Sector Relationships', *World Development*, **6**, (9/10), pp. 1065–75.

Tolson, A. (1977) *The Limits of Masculinity*, London: Tavistock.

Toye, J. (1987) *Dilemmas of Development*, Oxford: Basil Blackwell.

UNDP (1990) *Human Development Report, 1990*, Oxford: Oxford University Press.

— (1991) *Human Development Report, 1991*, Oxford: Oxford University Press.

— (1992) *Human Development Report, 1992*, Oxford: Oxford University Press.

United Nations (1965) Department of Economic and Social Affairs, 'Proceedings of the World Population Conference', Belgrade, E/CONF. 41 pp. 2–4 (4 vols), New York: United Nations.

— (1971) *Demographic Yearbook 1970*, New York: United Nations.

— (1975) Department of Economic and Social Affairs, 'Status of Women and Family Planning', Report of the Special Rapporteur Appointed by the Economic and Social Council under Resolution 1326 (XLIV).

— (1975a) 'Current Trends and Changes in the Status and Roles of Women and Men, and Major Obstacles to be Overcome in the Achievement of Equal Rights, Opportunities and Responsibilities', Report of the Secretary General, E/Conf. 66/3, New York: United Nations.

— (1975b) Meeting in Mexico; 'The story of the World Conference of the International Women's Year', New York: United Nations.

— (1976) 'World Plan of Action for the Implementation of the Objectives of the International Women's Year', Report of the World Conference of the International Women's Year. E/Conf. 66/34, New York: United Nations.

— (1979) *Patterns of Urban and Rural Population Growth*, 1950–2000, New York: United Nations

— (1980) World Conference of the United Nations Decade for Women: Equality, Development and Peace. Review and Evaluation of Progress Made and Obstacles Encountered at the National Level in Attaining the Objectives of the World Plan of Action, Copenhagen 14–20 July 1980, UN.A/Conf. 94/30, New York: United Nations.

— (1980a) Report of the World Conference of the UN Decade for Women: Equality, Development, Peace (Copenhagen), New York: United Nations.

— (1980b) World Program of Action for the Implementation of the Objectives of the UN Decade for Women. Report of the UN World Conference of the UN Decade for Women, A/Conf. 94/35, New York: United Nations.

— (1985) Forward Looking Strategies for the Advancement of Women. Report of the World Conference to Review and Appraise the Achievements of the UN Decade for Women: Equality, Development and Peace, A/Conf. 116/28/Rev. 1, New York: United Nations.

— (1986) and (1989) *World Survey on the Role of Women in Development*, New York: United Nations.

— (1988) *Demographic Yearbook 1986*, New York: United Nations.

UNAPCWD (1979) *Workshop Report on Feminist Ideology and Social Structure*, Bangkok: United Nations.

UNCTAD (1987) 'Revitalizing Development, Growth and International Trade: Assessment and Policy Options', Report by the UNCTAD Secretary to UNCTAD VII, TD/328/Rev.1/Add.1, New York: United Nations.

UNICEF (1989) *The State of the World's Children 1989*, Oxford: Oxford University Press.

Van der Wees, C. and Romijn, H. (1987) 'Enterpreneurship and Small-Scale Enterprise Development for Women in Developing Countries: An Agenda of Unanswered Questions', Geneva: Management Development Branch: ILO.

Vargas, V. (1990) *The Women's Movement in Peru: Streams, Spaces and Knots*, The Hague: ISS.

— (1990a) *The Feminist Movement in Latin America: Between Hope and Disenchantment*, The Hague: ISS.

Vickers, J. (1991) *Women and the World Economic Crisis*, London and New Jersey: Zed Books Ltd.

von Braun, J. and Kennedy, K. (1986) 'Commercialization of Subsistence Agriculture: Income and Nutritional Effects in Developing Countries', *IFPRI Working Papers on Commercialization of Agriculture and Nutrition*, No. 1, Washington D.C.: International Food Policy and Research Institute.

Wallace, T. and March, C. (eds) (1991) *Changing Perceptions*, Oxford: Oxfam.

Wamalwa, B. (1991) 'Limits of Women's Groups', in Wallace and March.

White, G. (1984) 'Developmental States and Socialist Industrialisation in the Third World', in *Journal of Development Studies*, **21**, (1).

Whitehead, A.

— (1979) 'Some Preliminary Notes on the Subordination of Women', *IDS Bulletin*, **10**, (3), pp. 10–13.

— (1984) 'I'm Hungry Mum. The Politics of Domestic Budgeting', in Young, K. *et al.*, *op. cit.* pp. 93–116.

— (1985) 'Effects of Technological Change on Rural Women: A Review of Analyses and Concepts', in Ahmed, I., *op. cit.*, pp. 27–64.

— (1990) 'Food Crisis and Gender Conflict in the African Countryside', in Bernstein, H. *et al.* (eds) *The Food Question: Profits vs. People?*, London: Earthscan Publications.

— (1990a) 'Gender-Aware Planning in Agricultural Production', *Module 7 of Gender and Third World Development*, IDS.

Williams, M. (1987) 'African Debt and Economic Recovery', *Development*, (2/3), pp. 6–10.

Wilson, G. (1991) 'Thoughts on the Cooperative Conflict Model of the Household in Relation to Economic Method' in *IDS Bulletin*, **22**, (1).

World Bank (1978) *World Development Report 1978*, Washington D.C.: World Bank.

— (1982) (IRBD) *World Development Report 1982*, Washington D.C.: World Bank.

— (1987) *World Development Report 1987*, Washington D.C.: World Bank.

— (1988) *World Development Report 1988*, Washington D.C.: World Bank.

— (1988) *World Debt Tables 1988-89*, Washington D.C.: World Bank.

Young, G. (1990) 'Hierarchy and Class in Women's Organisations', in Staudt, K. (ed.).

Young, K. (1976) 'The Social Setting of Migration', unpublished Ph.D. Thesis, London University, London.

— (1979) 'Editorial' and 'Conference Resolution Recommendations and Research Guidelines', *IDS Bulletin*, **10**, (3), pp. 1–4.

— (1987) 'Further Thoughts on Women's Needs' in *Planning for Women at the National, Regional and Local Levels*', UNESCO and republished in revised form in 1988.

— (1987a) 'Benefits and Barriers in the Policy Process', paper presented at the Second Meeting of Commonwealth Ministers in charge of Women's Affairs, Harare, available from Commonwealth Secretariat, London.

— (1988) 'Reflections on Meeting Women's Needs', in Young, K. (ed.) *Women and Economic Development: Local, Regional and National Planning Strategies*, pp. 1–30, Oxford: Berg Publishers/Paris: UNESCO.

— (ed.) (1979) 'The Continuing Subordination of Women in the Development Process', *IDS Bulletin*, **10**, (3), Brighton: Institute of Development Studies.

— (1989) (ed.) *Serving Two Masters*, New Delhi: Allied Publishers.

— (1990) 'Household Resource Management', *Module 6 of Gender and Third World Development*, Institute of Development Studies.

Young, K. and Moser, C. (1981) 'Women and the Informal Sector', *IDS Bulletin*, **12** (3).

Young, K., Wolkowitz, C. and McCullagh, R. (eds) (1984) *Of Marriage and the Market*, London: Routledge and Kegan Paul.

Further Reading

Aboagye, A. and Gozo, K. (1986) 'The Informal Sector: A Critical Appraisal of the Concept', in Nigam, S. (ed.) *The Challenge of Employment and Basic Needs in Africa*, pp. 261-69, Nairobi: Oxford University Press.

Adelman, I. and Morris, C. (1973) *Economic Growth and Social Equity in Developing Countries*, Stanford University, California: Stanford University Press.

Adelman, I. and Thorbecke, E. (eds) (1966) *The Theory and Design of Economic Development*, Baltimore: Johns Hopkins University Press.

Afshar, H. (ed.) (1985) *Women, Work and Industry in the Third World*, London: Tavistock Publications.

Agarwal, B. (1981) 'Agricultural Modernization and Third World Women: Pointers from the Literature and an Empirical Analysis', WEP Rural Employment Policy Research Programme, *Working Papers Series* 10, No. 21, Geneva: ILO.

Agarwala, A., and Singh, S. (eds) (1985) *The Economics of Underdevelopment*, Oxford: Oxford University Press.

Allison, C. (1985) 'Women, Land, Labour and Survival: Getting Some Basic Facts Straight', *IDS Bulletin*, **16**, (3), pp. 24-30.

Allison, C. and Green, R. (eds) (1985) 'Sub-Saharan Africa: Getting the Facts Straight', *IDS Bulletin*, **16** (3).

Amin, S. (1974) *Accumulation On a World Scale: A Critique of The Theory of Underdevelopment*, New York: Monthly Review Press.

Anderson, C. and Baud, I. (eds) (1987) *Women in Development Cooperation*, EADI.

Antrobus, P., in Wallace and March, (eds) (1991) *op. cit.*

Bandarage, A. (1984) 'Women in Development: Liberalism, Marxism and Marxist Feminism', *Development and Change*, **15**, (4), pp. 495-516.

Barber, W. (1967) *A History of Economic Thought*, London: Penguin Books.

Baster, N. (ed.) (1972) *Measuring Development: The Role and Adequacy of Development Indicators*, London: Frank Cass.

Beckerman, W. (1977) 'Some Reflections on Redistribution with Growth', *World Development*, **5** (8), pp. 665-76.

Beneria, L. and Sen, G. (1981) 'Accumulation, Reproduction and Women's Role in Economic Development: Boserup Revisited', *Signs: Journal of Women in Culture and Society*, **7**, (2), pp. 279-98.

Berger, M., Delancey, V. and Mellencamp, A. (1984) 'Bridging the Gender Gap in Agricultural Extension', International Center for Research on Women, Report prepared for Office of Women in Development, Washington D.C.: USAID.

Bergesen, H. (1982) *The Recalcitrant Rich: A Comparative Analysis of the Northern Responses to the Demands for a New International Economic Order*, London: Frances Pinter.

Bernstein, H. (ed.) (1973) *Underdevelopment and Development*, London: Penguin Books.

Black, C. (1976) *Comparative Modernization: A Reader*, New York: Free Press.

Booth, D. (1975) 'Andre Gunder Frank: An Introduction and Appreciation' in Oxaal, I. *et al.*, (1975), *op. cit.*, pp. 50-85.

Boulding, E., Nuss, S., Carson, D. and Greenstein, M. (1976) *Handbook of International Data on Women*, New York: Sage Publications.

Brewer, A. (1980) *Marxist Theories of Imperialism: A Critical Survey*, London: Routledge and Kegan Paul.

Bromley R. (1979) *The Urban Informal Sector: Critical Perspectives on Employment and Housing Policies*, Oxford: Pergamon Press.

Buvinic,, M. (1986) 'Projects for Women in the Third World: Exploring Their Misbehaviour', in *World Development*, **14**, (5).

Buvinic, M., Leslie, J. and Lycette, M. (1986) 'Weathering Economic Crises: The Crucial Role for Women in Health', International Center for Research on Women, Report prepared for Office of Women in Development, Washington D.C.: USAID.

Buvinic, M., Lycette, M. and McGreevey, W. (eds) (1983)*Women and Poverty in the Third World*, Baltimore: Johns Hopkins University Press.

Buvinic, M. and Youssef, N. (1978) 'Women-headed Households: The Ignored Factor in Development Planning', International Center for Research on Women, Report submitted to the Office of Women in Development, Washington D.C.: USAID.

Charlton, S. E. (1984) *Women in Third World Development*, Boulder, Colorado: Westview Press.

— *et al.*, (eds) (1989) *Women, The State and Development*, State of New York University Press.

Cheater, A. (1981) 'Women in Commercial Agricultural Production: Medium Scale Freehold in Zimbabwe', *Development and Change*, **12**, (3), pp. 349-77.

Cline, W. (1982) 'Can the East Asian Model of Development Be Generalised?' *World Development*, **10**, (2), pp. 81-90.

Cody, J., Hughes, H. and Wall, D. (eds) (1980) *Policies for Industrial Progress in Developing Countries*, Oxford: Oxford University Press.

Cohen, M. (1986) *Women and Urban Street Food Trade: Some Implications for Policy*, London: Development Planning Unit, University College.

Commander, S. (ed.) (1989) *Structural Adjustment and Agriculture: Theory and Practice in Africa and Latin America*, London: Overseas Development Institute.

Commonwealth Secretariat (1989) 'Engendering Adjustment for the 1990s', Report of a Commonwealth Secretariat Expert Group on Women and Structural Adjustment, London: Commonwealth Secretariat.

Connolly, P. (1985) 'The Politics of the Informal Sector: A Critique', in Redclift, N. and Mingione, E. (eds) B*eyond Employment: Household, Gender and Subsistence*, pp. 55-91, Oxford: Basil Blackwell.

Corea, G. (1980) *Need for Change: Towards the New International Economic Order,* A Selection from Major Speeches and Reports, Oxford: Pergamon Press.

Dixon-Mueller, R. (1985) 'Women's Work in Third World Agriculture: Concepts and Indicators', *Women, Work and Development Series*, No. 9, Geneva: ILO.

Dube, S. (1988) *Modernization and Development: The¯Search for Alternative Paradigms*, London: Zed Press/Tokyo: United Nations University Press.

Dulansey, M. and Austin, J. (1984) 'Small-Scale Enterprises and Women', in Overhold, C., Anderson, M., Claud, K. and Austin, J. (eds) *Gender Roles in Development Projects*, West Hartford, Connecticut: Kumarian Press.

Eicher, C. and Staatz, J. (1984) *Agricultural Development in the Third World*, Baltimore: Johns Hopkins University Press.

Eisold, E. (1984) 'Young Women Workers in Export Industries: The Case of the Semi-Conductor Industry in South East Asia', *ILO World Employment Program Research Working Papers Series*, **10**, No. 30, Geneva: ILO.

Ellis, P. (ed.) (1986) *Women in the Caribbean*, London: Zed Press.

Erb, G. and Kallab, V. (1975) *Beyond Dependency: The Developing World Speaks Out*, Washington D.C.: Overseas Development Council.

Folbre, N. (1986) 'Cleaning House: New Perspectives on Households and Economic Development', *Journal of Development Economics* (June), **22**, pp. 5-40.

Frank, A.G. (1967) 'Capitalism and Underdevelopment in Latin America: Historical Studies of Chile and Brazil', New York, Monthly Review Press.

Fraser, A. (1987) *The UN Decade for Women: Documents and Dialogue*, Boulder, Colorado: Westview Press.

George, S. (1988) *A Fate Worse than Debt*, London: Penguin.

Gerry, C. (1979) 'Petty Production and Capitalist Production in Dakar: The Crisis of the Self-Employed', in Bromley, R. (ed.), *op. cit.*

Gidwani, S. (1985) *Impact of Monetary and Financial Policies upon Women*, Santo Domingo: INSTRAW.

Gilbert, A. and Guglar, J. (1982) *Cities, Poverty and Development: Urbanization in the Third World*, Oxford: Oxford University Press.

Glaeser, B. (ed.) (1987) *The Green Revolution Revisited: Critique and Alternatives*, London: George Allen and Unwin.

Grant, J. (1986) *The State of the World's Children 1986*, Oxford: UNICEF/Oxford University Press.

Griffiths-Jones, S. (1983) 'The Changing International Environment and its Impact on Developing Countries', *IDS Discussion Paper*, No. 18, Brighton: Institute of Development Studies.

Gutkind, P. and Wallerstein, I. (1976) *The Political Economy of Contemporary Africa*, New York: Sage Publications.

Guyer, J. and Peters, P. (eds) (1987) 'Conceptualising the Household: Issues in Theory and Policy in Africa', *Development and Change*, **18**, (2).

Harris, O. (1984) 'Households as Natural Units', in Young, K., Wolkowitz, C. and McCullagh R. (eds) pp. 126-55.

Harriss, J. (ed.) (1982) *Rural Development: Theories of Peasant Economy and Agrarian Change*, London: Hutchinson.

Hart, J. (1983) *The New International Economic Disorder: Conflict and Cooperation in North-South Economic Relations 2974-1977*, London: Macmillan.

Hay, M. and Stichter, S. (1984) *African Women South of the Sahara*, London: Longman.

Held, D. and Pollitt, C. (eds) *New Forms of Democracy*, London: Sage Publications.

Helleiner, G. (1980) *International Economic Disorder: Essays in North-South Relations*, London: Macmillan.

Heyer, J., Roberts, P., and Williams, G. (eds) (1981) *Rural Development in Tropical Agriculture*, London: Macmillan.

Heyzer, N. (ed.) (1985) *Missing Women: Development Planning in Asia and the Pacific*, Kuala Lumpur: Asian and Pacific Development Centre.

ILO (1984) *Urbanisation, Informal Sector and Employment: A Progress Report on Research, Advisory Services and Technical Cooperation*, World Employment Programme, Geneva: ILO.

ILO/INSTRAW (1985) *Women in Economic Activity: A Global Statistical Survey (1950-2000)*, Geneva and Santo Domingo: ILO/INSTRAW.

INSTRAW (1985) *The Role of Women in International Economic Relations*, Summary of Series of Studies on the Role of Women in International Economic Relations, Santo Domingo: INSTRAW.

— (1986) ECLA/UN Statistical Office, *Women in the Informal Sector in Latin America: Methodological Aspects*, Santo Domingo: United Nations.

Jacquette, J. and Tinker, I. (1987) 'The UN Decade for Women: Its Impact and Legacy', *World Development* **15**, (3), pp. 419-28.

Johnston, B. and Kilby, T. (1975) *Agriculture and Structural Transformation*, New York: Oxford University Press.

Kandal, T. and Martin, M. (eds) (1989) *Studies of Development and Change in the Modern World*, New York: Oxford University Press.

Kandiyoti, D. (1985) 'Women in Rural Production Systems: Problems and Policies', Paris: UNESCO.

— (1988) 'Women and Rural Development: The Changing Agenda', *IDS Discussion Paper*, No. 244, Brighton: Institute of Development Studies.

Kaplinsky, R. (1984) 'The International Context for Industrialisation in the Coming Decade', *Journal of Development Studies*, **21**, (1), pp. 75-98.

— (1984) *Third World Industrialization in the 1980s: Open Economics in a Closing World*, London: Frank Cass.

Keynes, J.M. (1949) *The General Theory of Employment, Interest and Money*, London: Macmillan.

Killick, T. (1984) *The Quest for Economic Stabilisation: The IMF and the Third World*, London: Heinemann.

Kumari, J. (1986) *Feminism and Nationalism in the Third World*, London: Zed Press.

Kirkpatrick, C., Lee, N. and Nixson, F. (1984) *Industrial Structure and Policy in Less Developed Countries*, New York: George Allen and Unwin.

Lall, S. (1975) 'Is "Dependence" a Useful Concept in Analysing Underdevelopment?', *World Development*, **3** (11/12): pp. 799-810.

Leacock, E. and Safa, H. (eds) (1986) *Women's Work: Development and the Division of Labour by Gender*, South Hadley, Massachusetts: Bergin and Garvey.

Lele, U. (1986) 'Women and Structural Transformation', *Economic Development and Cultural Change*, **34**, (2), pp. 195-221.

Liedholm, C. and Mead, C. (1987) 'Small-Scale Industries in Developing Countries: Empirical Evidence and Policy Implications', *International Development Paper*, No. 9, East Lansing, Michigan: Michigan State University.

Long, N. (ed.) (1984) *Family and Work in Rural Societies: Perspectives on Non-Wage Labour*, London: Tavistock.

McNamara, R. (1973) Annual Address of the Board of Governors of The World Bank Group (Nairobi), Washington D.C.: World Bank.

Maxwell, S. (1984) 'Farming Systems Research: Hitting a Moving Target', *IDS Discussion Paper*, No. 119, Brighton: Institute of Development Studies. Also in *World Development* (1986), **14**, (1), pp. 65-77.

Mazumdar, D. (1976) 'The Urban Informal Sector', *World Development*, **4**, (8), pp. 655-79.

Mies, M. (1982) *The Lace Makers of Narsapur*, London: Zed Press.

Mitter, S. (1986) *Common Fate, Common Bond: Women in the Global Economy*, London: Pluto Press.

Moock, J. (ed.) (1987) *Understanding Africa's Rural Households and Farming Systems*, Boulder, Colorado: Westview Press.

Nash, J. and Fernandez-Kelly, M. (1983) *Women, Men and the International Division of Labour*, Albany, New York: State University of New York Press.

Nelson, N. (1981) *African Women in the Development Process*, London: Frank Cass.

New Internationalist (1985) *Women: A World Report*, London: Methuen.

O'Brien, P. (1975) 'A Critique of Latin American Theories of Underdevelopment' in Oxaal, I. *et al.*, (1975), *op. cit.*, pp. 7-27.

Ohg, A. (1987) *Spirits of Resistance and Capitalist Decline*, Albany, New York: State University of New York Press.

Overholt, C., Anderson, M., Cloud, K. and Austin, J. (1985) *Gender Roles in Development Projects*. West Hartford, Connecticut: Kumarian Press.

Oxaal, I., Barnett, T. and Booth, D. (1975) *Beyond the Sociology of Development: Economy and Society in Latin America and Africa*, London: Routledge and Kegan Paul.

Palmer, I. (1977) 'Rural Women and the Basic Needs Approach to Development', *International Labour Review*, **115**, (1), pp. 97-107.

— (1985) *Women's Roles and Gender Differences in Development, Cases for Planners*, West Hartford, Connecticut: Kumarian Press.

Phillips, A. (1977) 'The Concept of Development', *Review of African Political Economy*, No. 8 (January-April), pp. 720.

Pinstrup-Anderson, P. (1982) *Agricultural Research and Technology in Economic Development*, London: Longman.

Poats, S., Schmink, M. and Spring, A. (eds) (1988) *Gender Issues in Farming Systems Research and Extension*, Boulder and London: Westview Press.

Ranis, G. (1985) 'Can the East-Asian Model of Development be Generalised? A Comment', *World Development*, **13**, (4), pp. 453-545.

Redclift, N. and Mingione, E. (eds) (1985) *Beyond Employment Household, Gender and Subsistence*, Oxford: Basil Blackwell.

Reynolds, G. (ed.) (1975) *Agriculture in Development Theory*, New Haven, Connecticut: Yale University Press.

Roberts, H. (ed.) (1987) 'Politics in Command', *IDS Bulletin*, **18**, (4), Brighton: Institute of Development Studies, University of Sussex.

Rogers, B. (1980) *The Domestication of Women: Discrimination in Developing Societies*, London: Tavistock.

Rew, A. (ed.) (1978) 'Down To Basics: Reflections on the Basic Needs Debate', *IDS Bulletin*, **9**, (4), Brighton: Institute of Development Studies.

Safilios Rothschild, C. (1986) *Socio-Economic Indicators of Women's Status in Developing Countries 1970-1980*, New York: The Population Council.

Sauvant, K. (1981) *The Group of 77: Evolution, Structure, Organisation*, New York: Oceania Press.

Schmitz, H. (1982) 'Growth Constraints on Small-Scale Manufacturing in Developing Countries: A Critical Review', *World Development*, **10**, (6), pp. 429-50.

Scott, A. (1986) 'Urban Women in LDCs: Examining the Female Marginalisation Thesis', *Journal of Development Studies*, **22**, (4), pp. 649-80.

Seers, D. (1981) (ed.) *Dependency Theory: A Critical Reassessment*, London: Frances Pinter.

Sen, A. (ed.) (1973) *On Economic Inequality*, Oxford: Clarendon Press.

— (1983a) 'Development: Which Way Now?, *Economic Journal*, **93**, (December), pp. 745–62.

— (1984) *Resources, Values and Development*, Oxford: Basil Blackwell.

Sharma, U. (1986) *Women's Work, Class and the Urban Household: A Study of Shimla, North India*, London and New York: Tavistock.

Silvard, R. (1985) *Women . . . A World Survey*, Washington D.C.: World Priorities.

Singer, H. (1984) 'Industrialisation: Where do we Stand? Where are we Going?', *Industry and Development*, No. 12.

Somjee, G. (1989) *Narrowing the Gender Gap*, London: Macmillan Press.

Stern, B. (1985) *The Changing Role of Women in International Economic Relations*, Santo Domingo: INSTRAW.

Stewart, F. (1985) 'The Fragile Foundations of the Neo-Classical Approach to Development', *Journal of Development Studies*, **21**, (2).

— (1987) 'Alternative Macro Policies, Meso Policies and Vulnerable Groups', in Cornia, C. *et al.*, *op. cit.*, pp. 196-217.

Streeten, P. (1972) *The Frontiers of Development Studies*, London: Macmillan.

Tinker, I. and Bramsen, O. (1976) *Women and World Development*, Washington D.C.: Overseas Development Council.

— (1987) 'Street Foods: Testing Assumptions about Informal Sector Activity by Women and Men', *Current Sociology*, **35**, (3), pp. 51-73.

UNICEF (1984) Ghana 'The Situation Analysis of Children and Women in Ghana', Accra (mimeo): UNICEF.

— (1984) Kenya 'Situation Analysis of Children and Women in Kenya', Accra (mimeo): Nairobi.

180

— (1985) Tanzania 'Analysis of the Situation of Children and Women', Dar es Salaam (mimeo): Government of Tanzania and UNICEF.

— (1986) Burkina Faso 'The Situation Analysis of Children and Women in Burkina Faso', Ougadougou (mimeo): UNICEF.

— (1986) Zambia 'Situation Analysis of Children and Women in Zambia', Lusaka (mimeo): Government of Zambia and UNICEF.

United Nations Commission on the Status of Women (1967), 'The Participation of Women in Community Development', Report of the Secretary General, New York: United Nations.

— (1970) 'The Participation of Women in the Economic and Social Development of their Countries', Report of the Secretary General, E/CN.6/513/ Rev. 1, New York: United Nations.

UNCTAD (1984) *The Least Developed Countries*, New York: United Nations.

Vaughan, M. (1986) 'Household Units and Historical Process in Southern Malawi', *Review of African Political Economy*, **34**.

Wallerstein, I. (1974) *The Modern World System*, New York: Academic Press.

Weeks, J. (1975) 'Policies for Expanding Employment in the Informal Urban Sector of Developing Countries', *International Labour Review*, **111**, (1), pp. 1-13.

White, C. and Young, K. (eds) (1984) 'Research on Rural Women: Feminist Methodological Questions', *IDS Bulletin*, **15**, (1), Brighton: Institute of Development Studies.

White, G. (ed.) (1985) *Developmental States in East Asia*, Basingstoke: Macmillan in association with Institute of Development Studies.

Whitehead, A. (1981) A Conceptual Framework for the Analysis of the Effects of Technological Change of Rural Women', *Technology and Employment Programme Working Papers*, Geneva: World Employment Programme.

Williamson, J. (1983) *IMF Conditionality*, Washington D.C.: Institute for International Economics.

World Bank (1986) *Financing Growth with Adjustment in Sub-Saharan Africa 1986-1990*, Washington D.C.: World Bank.

Youssef, N. (1973) *Women and Work in Developing Societies*, Westport, Connecticut: Greenwood Press.

Youssef, N. and Hetler, C. (1984) 'Rural Households Headed by Women: A Priority Concern for Development', *WEP Rural Employment Policy Research Programme Working Papers Series*, **10**, No. 31, Geneva: ILO.

181

Index

family-based, and IS, 89–90, 120
head, 21, 59, 116–17
and income differentials, 52
inter- relations, 115–16
intra- relations, 106, 114, 117–19
nuclear, 58
polygamous, 58
resource distribution, 59–60, 95–7, 117, 126
tasks, analysis of, 56–7
women's responsibilities, 58
housework: as women's work, 111
Human Development Index, 16
human nature: theories on, 122–4, 137
human resource maintenance, 113
human resource production, 113
HYVs, high yielding varieties, 4, 6, 46

IBRD, World Bank, 34, 161
fund allocation to women, 63
illiteracy, 1, 23
ILO, International Labour Organisation, 7
Equal Remuneration Convention, 76
IMEs, Industrial Market Economies, 4, 15, 25, 26, 92
and debt, 33
and global recession, 31
maternal deaths in, 37
IMF, International Monetary Fund:
and debt, 34, 36
income: allocation, 59, 125
cash, need, for women, 156
differential, 52
generation, for women, 21–2
projects, 60, 63–4
inadequate, 89
levels, and women, 37
India, 70, 73, 116, 118
indicators: of development, 15
industrialisation, 12, 14, 32, 45, 66–7, 85
strategies for, 67–70
and women, 70–4
see also domestic industrialisation
industry: women's employment in, 22, 66–84
inequality, gender, 132, 135, 141, 144
informal sector, 7
women in, 22, 37–8, 66, 85–107
characteristics of, 93–100

data on, 113
information: need for, 157
networks, 105
infrastructure: cuts in, 35
and economic growth, 4, 32
inheritance rules, 119
INSTRAW, International Research and Training Institute for the Advancement of Women, 26
integration: of women, 24, 63
international networks: for women, 26–7, 29
see also women's organisations
invisibility: of women, 39, 109, 110, 130
IRD, Integrated Rural Development, 47, 50
irrigation schemes, large-scale, 48–9
IS, informal sector, 89–92, 95, 104
ISI, Import Substituting Industrialisation, 67–8, 69, 86
and EOI, 69–70

Kenya, 76
mission, 88–90
women's income-generating projects, 60

labour: access to, 61
deployment, 121–22
-intensive industry, and women, 73
sexual division of, 21, 45, 50, 55–9, 65, 77
and ideology, 71–2
short-term, throw away, women as, 23
surplus, 87
underutilisation, 89
unpaid, by women, 22, 37–8, 58, 128, 135
women's participation, 72–4
see also informal sector, women in
land: control, 60–1
fertility, decline in, 54
reform, 4, 52
Latin America: commercial debt, 32
GDP, 33
household composition, 115
household relations, 118
malnutrition in, 35
population growth, and labour surplus, 87

women in urban informal sector,
85–107
LDCs, Less Developed Countries, 2,
16, 25, 26, 33, 34, 48
debt burden, 32, 33–4
Mother Clubs, 37
population growth and labour
surplus, 87
legislation: male perspective of, 159
protective, for women, 80–1
liberal feminism, 129
life: quality of, 5, 16
listening to women: need for, 147–50
literacy levels: and debt, 35
see also illiteracy
living: standard of, 33
LLDCs, Least Developed Countries, 5,
10, 16
and debt, 53
per capita income decline, 53

Malaysia, 76, 80
male: authority, in household, 122
breadwinners, 103
domination, as policymakers, 151
perspective, on household, 124–5
superiority, 134–5
malnutrition, 35, 54
manufacturing: and economic growth,
2–3
small-scale, 95–8
see also industry
marginalisation: of women, 24
of women's issues, 133
marital position: and homeworking,
98, 103
market: liberalisation, and women,
38
organisation, and food crops, 49
maternal deaths, 36
men: dominance of women, 130
interdependence with women, 126
relations with women, 131, 135–6
resistance to change, 151
Mexico: ISI in, 86–7
Mexico City, 87–8, 91, 97
micro-enterprises, 95
migration: and household composition,
116
rural out–, 59, 88
and women's employment choices,
101

MNCs, multinational corporations, 9,
66
modernisation, theory of, 2
modern sector, 66
women in, 22, 45
Mwea irrigated rice project, Kenya,
50–1

needs: of women, and planning,
148–9, 160
see also under practical needs;
women, basic needs
neo-classical economics theory,
119–20
neo-liberals, 12, 13, 33–4, 36
networking, 42
NGOs, Non-Governmental Organisations, 25, 26, 42, 162–3
conferences, 26, 29, 41
and debt, 32
NHE, New Household Economics,
121
NICs, Newly Industrialised Countries,
5, 16, 92
NIEO, New International Economic
Order, 9, 10, 16–17
night work: restrictions on, 80
nutritional standards: decline in, 54
for women, 59

occupational segregation, 72
organisations: autonomous, 43
women's, 26–7, 29, 42–3, 127, 132,
144, 161, 162–4
outworkers, subcontracted, 91–2, 97
overtime: and women, 80, 91

Paraguay: work legislation, 80
people-centred approach: to
development planning, 19
Peru: malnutrition in, 35
traders in, 99
Philippines, 76, 80, 152
home production in, 112
strikes in, 76
planning process: and implementation
procedures, 148–9
women in, 64, 148–65 passim
policymakers: male domination, 151
pressure on, 159–62
role of, 150
political: equality, 127

representation, lack of for women, 160–1
situation, and development, 6
poor, the 21
  and decision-making, 8
  targeting, 7
population: control, 10, 23
  growth, 6, 10–13, 19, 54, 87
  and agricultural production, 4–6
poverty, 16, 35, 83
  alleviation, 44
  and trickle-down, 6
  and women, 7, 29, 39, 40, 127, 130–1, 144
practical needs, 154-5, 156
production: decentralisation, 92
  small-scale, 92-3
productive work: recognition of, 109, 110
  seasonal, 112–13
projects: large-scale, and environment, 46
  irrigation, 48–9, 50–2
  rural capital intensive, 46
public-sector services: women's dependence on, 38
PVOs, private voluntary organisations, 162

quota systems: in work, 80

recession, global, 31–2
resource: allocation, 12, 59–60
  use, 64
  women's lack of access to, 95–7, 101–2, 104–7, 119, 154
rural community development, 18, 32
  programmes, 63
  see also IRD
rural social organisation, 52
RWG, redistribution with growth, 6–7, 46, 86

SAP, structural adjustment policy packages: and cash crops, 47–8
  for debt, 34, 35
  and women, 36–7
savings: for small-scale entrepreneurs, 106
SDOL, sexual division of labour, 139–41
  see also under gender; labour

service industries: women in, 85, 98–100, 104
sex segregated production, 56
sex selective feeding, 59
sex sequential production, 56
shanty towns, 87
Singapore, 69, 74, 76
skills: and gender division of labour, 71–2, 76, 78
  upgrading, 105
smallholder: neglect of, 54
small-scale enterprises, 95–8, 104
social infrastructure: for women, 106
socialisation: and gendering, 137–8, 145
  in household, 123–4
socialist societies: women in, 153
South Korea, 69, 70, 73, 74, 76, 80
SOW, IDS Subordination of Women Collective, 136
Sri Lanka, 75, 76, 80, 88
SSA, sub-Saharan Africa, 10
  bilateral debt, 32
  household composition, 115
  household relations, 117–19
  maternal deaths, 37
  women in agriculture, 45–65
stabilisation policy packages: for debt, 33–4
state: intervention, and economy, 3, 12–13, 34
  role of, 8
  as support for women, 142, 144, 153
status: of women, 21
stereotypes: of women, 109, 110
strategic interests, 154–5, 156
subcontracting work, 91, 92
subsistence economy, 1, 4, 5, 49
SWAG, international senior women's group, 65

technical training, 105
technology: modernisation, 92
  for small-scale enterprises, 105
  and women's employment, 75
TNCs, transnational corporations, 22, 66–7, 68, 74, 77, 92
TP, transformatory potential, 155–7
trade: deficits, and global recession, 31
  inequalities of, 9–10
  south-south, 9